Dedicated to the-

'...quiet and gracious souls...'

Red Deer

FROM AN
OPEN WOODED
HILLTOP

Photography by

John Oakley

Written and compiled by

Allan Bamford
Erica Tomlinson
Glynis Oakley
John Oakley

Cover, design and layout by John Oakley
Copy editing by Katherine James
Proof reading by Thelma Briggs and Cathy Monkman

Printed in Great Britain by
Raithby, Lawrence & Co Ltd, De Montfort Press, 18 Slater Street, Leicester LE3 5AY

ACKNOWLEDGEMENTS

Firstly we would like to thank Alan Spencer for the use of his camera, without which many of the photographs in this book could not have been taken. The artists, Glyn Croman, Keith Johnson, Phil Kenning, Doug Lewis, Andy Shore and Alan Spencer for their excellent paintings, watercolours, sketches and illustrations. The Leicester Mercury and the Hinckley Times for supplying some of the images and all those who have kindly lent us their old photographs, postcards and paintings. We would also like to thank the people who helped to write this book, in particular Hugh Beavin, T.B. Heathcote, Roger Jackson, Keith McCarthy, John Nadin and Mrs Jill Webster. But also all those who gave us their time and allowed us to use their comments, observations, anecdotes and opinions and all the patient and understanding home owners who have kindly allowed photographs of their premises to be taken. It is to them therefore that we must express our most grateful thanks since without them this book could not have been produced.

Many individuals and organisations have also helped by contributing financially towards the production and printing costs. Special thanks are due for the Lottery Grant, received from Awards for All, and to the Leicestershire County Council; we are also very grateful to all of those who helped either by purchasing the special subscription edition or with direct financial contributions.

The bibliography, and all of the individuals and organisations that have directly contributed, in whatever way, are listed at the back of the book. However, so many other people have helped in many other ways that it is not possible to list them all. Special thanks are due to historian Hugh Beavin for his introductory section on local history, to John Rawson for his financial advice, to Joan Tomlinson for keeping track of pre-publication sales and to Paul Cattle who has given us invaluable help and guidance.

Finally we must express our very grateful thanks to the Venerable Archdeacon Neil Robinson. Having spent many years as Rector of St Peter's Church at Market Bosworth he is remembered and revered by many local residents, so we were very pleased when he agreed to write the Foreword.

We hope that you, the reader, will find as much pleasure from these few reflections on village life as we have enjoyed during the preparation of the book.

Allan Bamford, Glynis Oakley, John Oakley and Erica Tomlinson

Right: The moat, Bosworth Hall.

CONTENTS

CONTENTS 6

FOREWORD 8

INTRODUCTION 10

LOCAL HISTORY 14

ACKNOWLEDGEMENTS 4, 218

FINANCIAL CONTRIBUTORS 219

BIBLIOGRAPHY 219

INDEX 220

ARCHITECTURE:

Architecture-Introduction 17

The Saxons 20

The Normans 22

Cadeby Hall 25

The Gothic Period 26

The Early English Period 28

A Remarkable Window 30

The Decorated Period 32

St Margaret's Church 34

The Church of St Peter 36

The Perpendicular Period 41

Gothic Secular 43

The Tudor Period 44

The Elizabethan and Jacobean Period 46

Osbaston Hall 48

Odstone Hall 51

Shenton Hall 52

Buildings of the Classical Era 55

Bosworth Hall 56

The Queen Anne Country House 60

The Georgian Period 62

Gopsall Hall 66

The Victorian Period 70

Help Out Mill 71

The Water Tower 72

New Developments 76

COMMUNITY:

Community-Introduction 78

Doggy Bins & Bottle Banks 80

Twycross House School 82

Dr Robert Pull 84

Stan Fell's Post Office 86

Lady Penelope Dixie 87

New Aspect 88

Nurse Mary Cragg 90

The Practice 92

'Beat Bobby' 94

The Early Days 96

The Snow Leopard 100

The Mother Church 102

Lady Florence Dixie 104

The Benoni Evans family 106

The Man of Steam 109

The Grey Lady 111

The People 112

Bosworth Inns 118

The Fire Fighters 121

Churches, Ancient & Modern 122

Holy Bones 123

Back to the Future 124

Salvador 126

LOCAL INDUSTRY:

Local Industry-Introduction	128
Railway Ghosts	130
Digging up the Past	132
Fireproof	133
Turning Full Circle	135
Wulfs, Toads, Donkeys & Conkers	136
Virtual Reality	137
No. 9 Main Street	138
Boyton William Jellico	139
The Smithy	141
'Bean'	142
The Woodman	144
Mineral/Water	146
Leaner Times	148
'Clocky' Deacon	151

NATURE & ENVIRONMENT:

Nature & Environment-Introduction	152
Manor Farm, Barton	154
Bosworth in Bloom	157
'Old Beasty'	158
'Dingle Dell'	159
Greenfingers	160
Lady Agnes Drive	162
The Show	165
The Tree Surgeon	166
Thatch	168
The Secret Garden	172
The Vet	175
The Green Mantle	176
The Tree Garden	180
Foot & Mouth	184
Fungi	186
Ancient Roots	189
April Rise	190

LEISURE TIME:

Leisure Time-Introduction	192
The Pilot	194
Living History	197
Magic Lanterns	198
2-1 at Tacherting	200
The 'Bozzy Boys'	201
The Twitcher	202
The Water Park	203
The Grant of Arms	205
A Peaceful Translation	207
The Richard lll Society	208
The Thespians	210
The Music Makers	211
Hand Made	212
Brushstrokes & Needlework	215
The Wordsmiths	216

F O R E W O R D

BY
VENERABLE ARCHDEACON
NEIL ROBINSON

RECTOR OF MARKET BOSWORTH WITH SHENTON
1969 – 1983

I welcome this book and am pleased to be associated with its publication.

The 20th century was one of immense development and change. We moved from the age of the horse, oil lamps, gaslight and outdoor privies to a computer-driven world of extraordinary and widespread technological achievement. I sometimes marvel at the way in which the generation before us coped with the changes they witnessed.

And yet, as I considered this foreword, I quite surprised myself to realise how many were the changes in Market Bosworth alone even in my fourteen years there. But we took them aboard, accepted them, worked at them and used them to great advantage.

Pupils of the Dixie Grammar School moved to the new Leicestershire Plan Comprehensive at Desford; the Council Offices in Station Road were closed; the surgery moved from Dr Kelly's Beech House in Church Street to the new purpose-built premises; the infant school in Park Street was closed (encouraged by my threat as Chairman of Governors to the County Council to close it on health grounds when the outdoor toilets froze!); the bank moved across the marketplace into a new home; the second phase of the new primary school in Station Road was put in hand and completed – in spite of the three-day week – so that the infants could join the juniors on one site again; the Part 3 accommodation for the elderly at Westhaven was closed and replaced by a new building in its orchard, Orchard House; and Ambion Court was built and welcomed. Then a Community Centre was created along with the High School premises, and so there developed a whole raft of new activities associated with it and often organised by it, to which were added other new initiatives like *Aspect*, the Rotary Club, and the pre-school play group in St Peter's Hall – all augmenting the older established organisations like the Women's Institute and British Legion. There were other notable events too: Bosworth Park was developed and the Battlefield – which at one time was somewhat hazardous to get to – was opened by the Duke of Gloucester and tastefully developed. In the early days I organised a rota of car park attendants from the parish and took my turn each week, only to be horrified when a visiting senior layman from the diocese took me quietly aside and asked me, "Do you *need* to do this?" – thinking that I needed to augment my income with a part-time job! Several small housing developments appeared – among the larger ones was the estate in the field off Rectory Lane, between Sir Wolstan's home and the Rectory, Cedar Drive and Chestnut Close; and fields off Station Road where Harry

Weston and later John Coleman grazed their cattle were also developed – it was John who requested that Weston Drive be so named in memory of Harry.

All these and so many other of the century's changes are now themselves part of the heritage of today.

From an Open Wooded Hilltop is designed to set out that heritage for us, tell us about it, challenge us to learn from it, encourage us to seek out and make time for those immensely valuable features in Bosworth and its countryside, and hopefully appreciate more fully its richness and beauty.

We are so much the poorer if we fail to breathe in the splendour of creation and the created. Yet as this book will surely show us, Bosworth's greatest heritage is its people. But where does one start and finish when there are so many, even in my limited personal experience, who have enriched this place? For there is a wealth of 'quiet and gracious souls' who have made and are making such positive sense of life with its joys, sorrows and everyday routines and opportunities but who would not expect or wish to be named in print. The foundation of this and any society is made up of such folk who faithfully serve God and their families, neighbours, friends and community with love and dedication.

But, from the many, we recall just a few. I think of the local bank managers who had been brought up in the days of the bank ledger and who knew their clients as no computerised records do; of old Mr Proudman who was the Verger, and head gardener at the rectory, and who told us how he used to sheathe the hoofs of Susie, the pony, with leather shoes to pull the mower; of Jack Bailey, the World War One veteran who wanted, and got, a bugler to play the Last Post over his grave (and who told me on his 80th birthday, when he was unwell, that at least he was better on his feet than he was eighty years earlier!); of Dr Kelly who remembered the name of the first patient to whom he had administered new drugs such as penicillin; of the Matrons who wore the distinctive Matron's cap – so that no-one was left in any doubt as to who was running the show! I think of Teddy Boston who left his curacy at Bosworth for the distant realms of Cadeby and Sutton Cheney and whom so many of us remember with deep affection; of Canon Edryd Jones, my saintly predecessor, whose eyes lit up and whose arms stretched towards me as I visited him on his deathbed; of the ever cheerful father of the bride who arrived at church with his daughter, only to find that the forgetful future husband and son-in-law had left in haste to collect

the forgotten wedding ring from back home four miles away, leaving father and bride to fill the time by making several circuits of the town; and of Tom Drackley coming out of his home, 'Holy Bones', at the church gates with a drop of the hard stuff to fortify dad every time they made a fruitless return! I think of head teachers like William Gosling, Harry Frost, and Ted Jenkins who together with their teaching staffs brought a wealth of academic, pastoral and practical gifts to church and community and made exemplary contributions to the ethos of the whole area. I think of Percy Poole who every year wheeled his harvest offerings to church in a wheelbarrow full of home-grown produce; and of other local gardeners whose healthy rivalry and banter about the quality of

their produce was pure entertainment. And I think of the generation of superb youngsters – loyal, friendly, courteous, cheerful and an immense credit to their parents and schools.

There are so many people both in and behind the stories recounted in *From an Open Wooded Hilltop* who in their generation were, and are, the salt of the earth, giving Market Bosworth and its surrounding villages a unique quality – making this a very special place in which to live.

Laus Deo.

Above: St Peter, Market Bosworth.

INTRODUCTION

FEW ROMAN ROADS PASSED THROUGH THE

TRIANGULAR ENCLOSURE, BOUNDED NOW BY

DISTANT MOTORWAYS, IN WHICH MARKET

BOSWORTH SITS ASTRIDE ITS OPEN WOODED

HILLTOP, OVERLOOKING THE RICH AGRICULTURAL

LAND THAT ONCE MADE SELF-SUFFICIENCY

POSSIBLE FOR THE SURROUNDING VILLAGES.

A landscape of small green fields and hedges, spotted here and there with woods and spinneys where hump-backed bridges cross old canals, small rivers, a railway, but narrow country lanes that only lead to ancient churches, red-bricked farms, meandering villages – a jigsaw picture leading nowhere special.

A place by-passed for years by industry and travellers – but were these quiet centuries of isolation a blessing or a curse?

An earlier book, *The Bosworth and Gopsall Estates*, took a nostalgic look at the quiet life of village folk in this area at the start of the 20th century. But the close and perpetual companion of nostalgia is change – one cannot exist without the other, and rural life today is very different. The two manorial estates that once dominated the lives of the local population, exist no more, with only fragments left to tell the tale. The ruins of Gopsall Temple may be due for renovation, and the Dixie family crests can still be seen at Bosworth Hall, but as buildings crumbled and estates declined the lives of the people who served them had to change.

We decided, therefore, that this new book should both explore and illustrate the way we live now, and reflect the changes that have, and still do, affect those of us who live in this pleasant part of the English countryside.

Local people offered much support and interest, for which we are most grateful. Some even wrote items for the book, and these are acknowledged with the individual author's name. All other items, while based on information provided by many other people, were written by one of the three main authors, with each identified by their initials. Everyone who helped by talking about how things have changed is acknowledged towards the end of the book.

Not everything has changed, of course. Urbanisation and industrialisation have blighted and demolished much that was good, but the area is still blessed with a large number of interesting buildings. The medieval framework of the town of Market Bosworth still stands – the marketplace hemmed in, bedecked with flowers on stone and brick facades that nowadays bring in the tourist. And all around we see the handiwork of many builders – religious and secular, urban and rural – much of it worthy of attention.

So using photographs, artwork and narrative, our book starts with a detailed look at the *Architecture* of many of the more significant buildings that survive and grace today's landscape.

Self-sufficiency is now impossible, but maybe it's this old tradition of pulling and working together that makes for such a strong local community spirit. *Community*, therefore, is our second consideration. With comments, observations, anecdotes and opinions from and about those who serve the community, plus a mention of just a few rather special people past and present, we recognise the value of this dedicated group.

One hundred years ago, rural life was sedate, placid, timed by seasons on the farm, not by the clock. There was time to think, to stroll to church, for families to chat around the fire, to smoke a pipe whilst leaning on a fork. Life was slow and measured, predictable, unchanging. For most of us, regretfully, this leisured pace has gone, especially at work.

Far fewer now work locally. No-one now strides across the fields behind a plough, or hammers at the forge, there is no scything of corn or mining for coal. For most it's on a bus, or in the car and off to the office, factory or shop. Though many do commute, *Local Industry* does exist on our doorstep and some of those who work close-by have told us what they do, have shared their thoughts about today and even yesterday.

But the land is still there, although it's used in different ways – we're 'free to roam', farming's wounded and in decline, and soon hunting with dogs may be a thing of the past. Yet rural folk don't just lie down and die. Those who breathe fresh country air each day, whose livelihoods are tied to field and farm, to plants and trees, have also had their say – have told us how they work and play in *Nature and Environment*.

Finally, when work is done it's time to play, and many enjoy their *Leisure Time* in town and village. So we follow them, in school or village hall, on playing fields, at easels, keyboards, on stage, in study groups or flower clubs or choir – and enjoy, with them, their recreational and cultural pleasures.

It is hoped, therefore, that at the start of this new century these few reflections *From an Open Wooded Hilltop* may be a reminder not only of how yesterday is perceived but also of how rich and varied village life in rural Britain can be today.

Above: Black Horse and the Rotary Cottages. A pen and ink drawing by Cicely Pickering.

Right: A beech tree in the grounds of Bosworth Hall.

LOCAL HISTORY

By Hugh Beavin

SITTING ASTRIDE ITS OPEN HILLTOP AND

SURROUNDED BY A CLUSTER OF SMALL VILLAGES,

MARKET BOSWORTH IS A TOWN THAT HAS

WITNESSED BOTH GREAT EVENTS IN THE HISTORY

OF THE NATION, AND MUNDANE HAPPENINGS IN

THE EVERYDAY LIVES OF ORDINARY PEOPLE.

From an Open Wooded Hilltop aims to celebrate this place and these people, past and present, and this short historical perspective may help to set the scene on the modern stage where today's players live and tell their stories.

Entering a new millennium, it is of note that 'Bosworthian' records themselves span many millennia, writ large not only on parchment and paper, but in the very shape of the landscape upon which these later happenings were played out. Evidence from below the soil, laboriously but fruitfully tilled for so many years, gives a rich and varied impression of life many thousands of years ago. Both noble and humble buildings still stand witness, on one hand to wealth and vision, and on the other to the humdrum needs of ordinary folk. Supplementing these visual records are the works of painters and engravers, and more recently photographers, particularly well exemplified in this volume by the work of John Oakley. Written works of fact and fiction and a rich oral tradition are extensively represented here, and help to complete a tapestry of life in this western quarter of the old Sparkenhoe Hundred.

Bronze Age and earlier archaeological remains indicate that the Bosworth area was a preferred place of settlement from prehistoric times. The urns, ashes and axe-heads of these early people, followed by the pottery, tesserae and coins from Roman villa sites, recall the two millennia of inhabitants who settled on and around this low rounded hilltop. The Saxon, Bose, lives on in local history since his settlement was recorded as 'Boseworde' in the Domesday Book of 1086, as were Od's settlement of Odstone, the King's settlement of Congerstone, and the Norse settlement of Cadeby – Kati's village.

The Earls of Leicester were lords of the manor in the early medieval period, but in the 13th century the Beaumont family inherited the estate. However, it was the Harcourts who dominated the town as demesne tenants until the early Tudor period and in 1285 Bosworth obtained the first charter that provided for 'A weekly market on Wednesday'. Both name and market have existed in perpetuity.

Whilst ordinary Bosworth folk pursued their lives on the land and worshipped in St Peter's Church, the rich and famous came and went, including kings and dynasties. In 1485 the essence of medieval England was extinguished in sight of Bosworth and a new modern Tudor Age began. Towards the end of the reign of the first Queen Elizabeth, Sir Wolstan Dixie, Lord Mayor of London, became owner of the Bosworth estate and established a family dominance and link with the town that would continue for some 400 years. In the late Tudor and early Stuart period Bosworth became an important seat of learning. The Grammar School, re-founded by the Dixies, included amongst its scholars the Puritan theologian William Bradshaw, and Thomas Hooker, a founding father of American democracy.

The ghosts of many famous men linger in Bosworth marketplace. George Fox, born in nearby Fenny Drayton and founder of the Society of Friends, or Quakers, came to Bosworth in 1649 and noted in his diary: "The people of the town and market fell upon us and stoned us very sore and abused us". John Grundy, who was born in Market Bosworth in late Stuart times, taught at the Grammar School and later became one of England's first great civil engineers, draining much of the fens. Dr Samuel Johnson, the first great English lexicographer, would pass a brief but unhappy period as a schoolmaster at the Dixie Grammar School in 1733, recalling that he was uncertain "whether it was more disagreeable for him to teach or the boys to learn".

The end of the 17th century saw the building of one of Leicestershire's splendid stately homes, Bosworth Hall. The second baronet replaced his earlier country seat with the grand building that still exists today. The lives of the ordinary Bosworth residents underwent considerable change in the following century. Stocking frames became a feature of many homes, and the enclosing of the old medieval field systems eventually employed fewer folk in agriculture.

Life in Bosworth at the end of the 18th century was described by Joseph Moxon, Leicestershire High Constable and Steward to the Bosworth estates, in his diary. When he died, his newspaper obituary described him as 'a truly honest man', an epithet which has doubtless been appropriate for many of the inhabitants of the town throughout the centuries. The buildings surrounding the marketplace, which still survive today, symbolised the prosperity of the Bosworth community at this time.

In the 19th century the coming of canal and railway links to the town helped to aid in its expansion and involvement in the wider activities of Victorian Britain. Education was revived in Market Bosworth with the rebuilding of the Grammar School, and its new headmaster, Reverend Arthur Benoni Evans, supplied the text on the plaque of 1828 which still graces the entrance to the building:

'Education is a possession which cannot be taken away from mortal man'.

A colourful selection of baronets occupied Bosworth Hall, including one who had been a captain at Trafalgar, and Lady Florence Dixie who distinguished herself as an international traveller and author. In 1883 the Dixies finally left the Hall and Tollemache Scott took over the estate, which he 'enhanced' considerably at the end of the 19th century.

The 20th century saw Market Bosworth as the centre of a Rural District Council, a status it lost in 1974. Throughout the period the Bosworth Show was the largest one-day event of its kind in the Midlands. New housing, particularly in the latter part of the century, contrasted with the closure of the cattle market. A new industrial estate symbolised the energy and change in the local community, along with an upsurge in conservation and the growth in tourism.

The new Millennium will no doubt present more challenges to the wider Bosworth community, and the feelings and thoughts of many of those Bosworthians are expressed within this volume. I am sure they will be challenges that the people of the Bosworth District will meet effectively, as they have in the past. It is perhaps appropriate to end this introduction with the motto of the Dixies: *Quod Dixi Dixi* – 'What I have said I have said' – and to reflect on the words and thoughts of the people of Bosworth today.

ARCHITECTURE

IT IS SOMETIMES EASY TO TAKE FOR GRANTED THE

ARCHITECTURAL HERITAGE THAT WE HAVE PACKED

INTO THIS SMALL COUNTRY OF OURS.

In almost every village throughout the country there is an ancient
parish church; in England alone there are some 12,000. Often the
largest and most architecturally impressive building in the area,
towering above the surrounding rooftops, these structures have stood for
over half a millennium, relatively unspoilt by time, while the world
around has been savaged by war, fire, famine and death.

Crafted with skill and precision by an impoverished people, whose
homes have long since fallen, these ancient monuments provide us with
a tangible link to the past. Each has slowly amassed its own history, its
own treasures and its own unique, beguiling features; and yet we have
grown so accustomed to their presence that we forget just how
extraordinarily lucky we are.

Leicestershire has many fine parish churches, and the various phases of
ecclesiastical development are well represented. But, in particular, the
one hundred years between the middle of the 13th and 14th centuries,
spanning the Early English and Decorated styles, seems to be something
of a golden era for the area. This was a century of great prosperity for
the East Midlands and one which saw a general rebuilding of the parish
church. St Margaret, Stoke Golding is perhaps the most notable
example, with its magnificent arcade and window tracery, unmatched in
its beauty throughout the county.

Towards the end of the 15th century, with the Dissolution of the
Monasteries, church building all but stopped. The course of architecture,
which had for so long been dominated by the Church, was now
transferred into non-monastic hands, resulting in a massive increase in
secular building. At the same time a powerful movement had emerged
in Italy that was beginning to sweep, uncontrollably, across the
continent. This was known as the Renaissance and it brought with it a
new understanding in the arts, science, and learning. Outdated religious
doctrines and superstitions were abandoned as the general persuasion
shifted towards a more rational system of thought. The Reformation had
effectively cut Henry VIII's England off from the rest of Europe, but
threads of this new orthodoxy still managed to seep into the English
consciousness. This, coupled with the country's new-found wealth and

security, brought about a complete revolution in domestic architecture,
from the rambling medieval manor house, such as the Moat House at
Appleby Magna, to the refined classical beauty of the 18th-century
Georgian town house – like the Dower House at Market Bosworth.

While this first chapter attempts to classify certain architectural periods
and to place some of the area's more significant buildings within them,
it is important to note that the development of different methods of
construction and design do not fall into clear divisions.

New styles generally emerged in and around the capital, through the
designs of a few pioneering architects, and gradually filtered up through
the country. Fashions tended to bleed into one another, especially in
rural areas like ours, where transport and communication links were
poor. Old techniques and patterns continued to be used for many years
unchanged. In such communities, builders had to make do with the
materials at hand, which gave rise to much regional variation. Such
building has become known as 'Vernacular' architecture, and most
buildings in the smaller towns and villages in this area would be

Above: St Peter, Market Bosworth. Although the Domesday Book documents the existence of a church on this site in 1086, the present church owes much
of its appearance to the 14th and 15th centuries.

Left: Coton Priory, the earliest part of which dates to around 1550–60.

Anne Revival of the Water Tower and East Lodge. This movement sparked furious debate, with many people regarding the medium as regressive.

The 20th century saw the birth of suburbia. Towns and cities fingered their way through the green belt. Infinitely better than their Victorian predecessors, the post-war suburban house did indeed possess considerable charm, even though, on the whole, they were poorly built.

Towards the end of the 20th century, a preoccupation with minimising costs had the effect of retarding development, and in the process all aesthetics were forgotten. With new, exotic materials available, houses no longer 'melted' into their surroundings; ugly, unpolished structures were thrown across the countryside with no regard to their appearance. The British landscape has been infested with poorly designed and often appallingly built estates that do nothing to enhance their environment and even less to further good design. Ironically, the many practical advances in construction and engineering seem to have done little to enhance the aesthetic quality of the average home.

classified as such. This would all change, however, with the Victorians.

The invention of the steam engine and the development of the railway network changed the face of the nation and transformed the lives of millions. Hundreds of fragmented communities were now suddenly part of a new industrialised society.

The mass production of bricks, the arrival of cast iron and sheet glass, along with an integrated transport system and an improvement in the quality of the roads, enabled development to increase at a frightening rate. Factories started to appear all over the country, necessitating the frenetic construction of rows of indistinguishable, cheap houses which quickly degenerated into the slums of the Victorian era. Even Bosworth suffered to some extent, although here most if not all such dwellings have long since disappeared.

And then, out of a need to escape the grim reality of 19th-century life, a powerful movement was born with the aim of reviving past traditions and styles. There is much evidence of this in Bosworth, for example the Gothic Revival style of the old school on Park Street, and the Queen

Recently, however, much like the Victorian Revival movement, there has been a resurgence of older styles, in particular that of the Georgian period. Such housing can be seen all over the country as developers exploit the new fashion for traditional designs. Market Mews (the development that replaced the cattle market), and the houses adjacent to the Park, both offer good examples of this new trend.

Urban architecture, on the other hand, is moving in the opposite direction. To make best use of limited space, developers are having to build upwards instead of outwards, so instead of single detached units, apartment buildings are springing up. Revolutionary advances in building techniques now give the architect options in design. Entire structures can be faced with glass, flooding interiors with light, while large open rooms, with a minimum of partitions, give residents the freedom to customise their own living space. But how this translates into the average person's home is not yet apparent and it remains to be seen whether modern urban architecture can actually revise people's expectations of how their homes should be. With the rising popularity of revivalist designs, the course of our architecture seems to be stuck between the two opposing forces of tradition and progression.

Above: The Dower House was originally built in 1760–80 by the Noel-Wentworth family from Kirkby Mallory, who had owned the site since the 16th century, and was remodelled at a later date with the addition of a third storey. The huge Georgian doorway on the south elevation, with its ornate fanlight, was taken from another building in the late 19th century. The cellars, which pre-date the house by some 200 years, would have undoubtedly been part of the 16th-century George Inn, when, according to a survey taken in 1592, the freehold belonged to a Mr William Noell. There are records of an inn in Market Bosworth dating as far back as 1320 but whether this was the George Inn is unknown.

Above: East Lodge on the outskirts of Market Bosworth, was built by Charles Tollemache Scott in 1885 as an architectural show piece. It stands next to the 17th-century stone gate-piers which once formed the grand east entrance to the Bosworth Hall Estate. The Lodge was designed in the Queen Anne style, a particular favourite of Scott's, and each drainpipe bears his initials and date: CTS 1885.

The Tollemache Scott coat-of-arms sits above the main entrance in between the leaded-light window and front doorway. All four sides of the house have protruding bays above which stand the Dutch gables.

THE SAXONS

600 – 1066

AFTER THE DEPARTURE OF THE ROMANS IN AD 409, BRITAIN PLUNGED INTO THE DARK AGES. ROADS, BUILDINGS, TOWNS — IN FACT ALL CIVILISATION AND CULTURE — WERE LOST TO THE WAVES OF INVADERS WHO PILLAGED THE COUNTRY. BRITAIN RETURNED TO THE PRIMITIVE NOMADIC LIFE THAT HAD EXISTED BEFORE THE ROMANS SETTLED HERE.

For the next 600 years or so, Britain's shores were subjected to various onslaughts. But it was the Saxons who maintained the tightest grip.

Ecclesiastical and defensive architecture were at the forefront of their civilisation and the mention in the Domesday Book of a deacon and priest at Bosworth signifies the existence of a church in pre-Norman times.

The important buildings would have been fashioned from stone but most domestic dwellings would be little more than a mud hut, expected to last no more than a generation. The Saxons were not accomplished masons and were more comfortable using wood.

Very little evidence of this period remains in the county's churches, as most would have been rebuilt, in stone, by the Normans or destroyed with the successive rampages of Scandinavian invasion.

None of the buildings in the immediate area date back this far although it is perhaps worth mentioning that behind Hall Farm, Stoke Golding there is a small Anglo-Saxon burial ground.

It was from this period that the cruck form of construction developed, a tradition that would remain until the 18th century, which is a clear testament to its simple and effective design. A cruck house basically consists of pairs of curved tree trunks sunk into the ground (later crucks were placed on a plinth of rough masonry to stop the wood rotting) and tied together at the top to form a pointed arch. Several pairs of these trunks were placed opposite each other, roughly 16 feet apart. Grand houses would have as many as five crucks with timber beams inserted in between and the gaps infilled with wattle and daub. The roofs were covered with thatch.

As seasoned oak was hard to work with, builders used unseasoned green wood which often warped as it dried out, causing the buildings to twist and tilt, sometimes at alarming angles. The timber was nearly always cut in the local forests and the crucks constructed on the same site; it wasn't unusual for a house to be moved to its final location in sections or, if it was small enough, fully completed.

Church Cottage, Cadeby is of cruck construction with brick infilling. The cruck, which is not complete but jointed, can be seen from the road rising from a stone plinth; the timbers have been dendro-dated to a felling date of 1472–73. Cruck constructions in Market Bosworth are to be found at: Rainbow Cottage, Peppercorn Cottage in The Square and at No. 30 Park Street, opposite the old school.

Saxon churches were on the whole quite primitive in design. Plain, unsophisticated structures with small gloomy windows, these buildings remained unchanged for centuries until a far more skilful and accomplished method of construction emerged with the country's next and most formidable invader – the Normans.

Above: A typical Saxon window. Pencil drawing by Doug Lewis.

Right: The jointed cruck of Church Cottage, Cadeby with a timber-framed cottage in the distance.

THE NORMANS

1066 — 1180

THE NORMAN INVASION OF 1066 BROUGHT WITH IT THE NEXT WAVE OF ARCHITECTURAL DEVELOPMENT. DUKE WILLIAM OF NORMANDY IMMEDIATELY SET TO AN AMBITIOUS BUILDING PROGRAMME WHICH SAW HUNDREDS OF CASTLES AND STRONGHOLDS PUT UP TO RESIST REBELLION AND THE BUILDING OF MANY CHRISTIAN CATHEDRALS AND CHURCHES.

Norman, or Romanesque, architecture is characterised by its massive stone walls and semicircular arches, similar to those used by the Romans. The Normans made their walls very thick to counter the sideways thrust of the arches but this in turn meant that windows had to be small and so interiors were dark. Norman churches are unmistakably small and squat, with square towers, like that of St Peter, Higham on the Hill (c.1130), where the Norman round-headed arches of the blind arcading are clearly visible. The huge arch on the western face of the tower suggests that the building is incomplete and that the tower was intended to have been the central section of a cruciform plan. Norman towers are rare in Leicestershire, although another can be seen at St Nicholas in Leicester, behind the Jewry Wall.

Doorways and windows were also round-headed, the former often surrounded by a series of concentric arches that receded into the wall above. Each separate ring would be decorated with a series of recurring motifs, such as chevrons or zigzags, squares, circles and other patterns carved in the stone. The stonework surrounding the south doorway at Fenny Drayton church is late Norman, displaying a frieze of recurring triangular patterns. There is also a small Norman window in the northeast wall of the chancel while a plain, round, Norman font can be seen at St Peter, Swepstone.

The other principal work of the Normans was the castle, built by the lords to assert their power and authority over the local people. There are reputedly some twenty or more castle sites in Leicestershire, most of which date to the 12th century, erected during the civil wars of Stephen's reign.

Raised up on a mound of earth called a motte, the castle would have had an outer bailey surrounded by a curtain wall and defended by a ditch. A 12th-century castle site, with a flat-topped mount, surrounded by a fragment of vallum (rampart) and remains of ditches, can be seen north of the church at Shackerstone.

Early Norman castles were generally made of wood so that they could be erected as quickly as possible to prevent Saxon rebellion, but these wooden structures were often replaced by a stone keep at a later date. The Norman cellar below Cadeby Hall would, at one time, have been part of a keep.

After the peace treaty of 1153 most of these castles and keeps became redundant and as the country settled into a more peaceful state the way was made clear for a new and more highly developed style of architecture to evolve.

Above: The late Norman doorway of St Michael, Fenny Drayton decorated with a frieze of triangular motifs.

Right: The Norman tower of St Peter, Higham on the Hill, c.1130. From the huge blocked arch on the west face of the tower it is evident that it was intended to form the central section of a cruciform plan. The semi-circular Romanesque arches of the blind arcading are also characteristically Norman. The nave was rebuilt by Henry Couchman in 1791 and the south aisle and porch were added in 1870 by R. Jennings of Atherstone.

C A D E B Y   H A L L

SCREENED ON ONE SIDE BY A TALL STONE WALL AND ON THE OTHER BY AN AVENUE OF LIME TREES, THERE IS NO CLEAR VIEW OF CADEBY HALL FROM THE ROAD. BURIED DEEP WITHIN THE ANCIENT VILLAGE OF CADEBY, THIS DARK, GOTHIC, HALF-TIMBERED HOUSE HAS A CERTAIN MAGICAL, ETHEREAL CHARM.

Although the site has been occupied since medieval times, the front elevation of the present Hall only dates back to the Victorian Revival period (mid-19th century). However, remnants of an earlier Jacobean hall, part of which burnt down in 1830, still make up a significant portion at the back.

Perhaps the most exciting feature of the house, though, is the cellar accessed through a trap door, hidden under a rug in the study. A stepladder drops down onto the first of three giant stone steps which emerge from a brick wall (a later addition) and curve down onto the cellar floor. These steps, along with a massive stone block partition, are the subterranean remains of a Norman keep, which is mentioned in the Domesday Book of 1086, when Hugh de Grentemaisnell, Baron of Hinckley, was in residence.

Norman keeps were constructed for defensive purposes, often raised up on a mound of earth called a motte, and surrounded by a moat. In this case no evidence of these features has emerged, but the landscape has doubtless altered over the last 900 years. While the cellar was made from stone, the keep above ground was probably constructed with timber, which would explain why nothing of it remains.

From the main road the house is approached through an avenue of lime trees and to the left of the drive is a small lake called the 'Duckery'. The village tale suggests that suspected witches were 'ducked' here to see if they would sink or swim.

The present owners, Mr & Mrs Warner, bought the hall in a dilapidated state and were determined to recapture its former splendour. They have begun the process of restoring the grounds to parkland, and have planted over 700 trees. Mr Warner regularly visited the Hall as a small child and as a result of fond memories and his genuine love of the place, he takes a keen interest in enhancing the Hall's natural environment.

In 1998, when a second lake was being dug out, a wall was discovered constructed from horse bones carefully placed together in a symmetrical fashion, stretching from the house towards Bosworth and eventually disappearing into Cadeby Lane. The exciting possibility of their connection to the Battle of Bosworth was regretfully ruled out when they were carbon-dated to the 1700s. Interestingly, the use of animal bones in this way has been noted in a number of post-medieval contexts, particularly in the Midlands. This practice ceased in the late 18th century.

On much the same theme there is a small 19th-century graveyard for dogs, situated on the other side of the house.

Inside the building there is evidence of how the Hall has evolved over the years, with various floor levels upstairs showing subsequent extensions and alterations. Traditional colours of the Victorian period maintain the original theme throughout the house, and the overall feel is of tradition, with the comfort and convenience of the 21st century.

Above: The 12th-century castle site at Shackerstone, with flat topped motte and remains of ditches.

Left: Cadeby Hall harbours a Norman cellar.

THE GOTHIC PERIOD

1201 – 1500

AT THE BEGINNING OF THE 13TH CENTURY A NEW FORM OF ARCHITECTURE, KNOWN AS THE

GOTHIC, SPRANG UP ACROSS BRITAIN, INITIALLY THROUGH THE BUILDING ACTIVITIES OF THE

CISTERCIAN MONKS FROM FRANCE.

Dominated by the Normans for centuries, the vast majority of architecture was now controlled by the monastic orders and there was a gradual shift from the defensive to the religious style. Nearly all construction during this period was ecclesiastical. Cathedrals, churches, monasteries and abbeys were erected to symbolise the religious beliefs of an uneducated nation, and it was the job of the sculptors, woodcarvers and stonemasons to bring biblical stories to life in their ornate carvings.

The essence of the Gothic style and its main structural element was the pointed arch, which was superior to the Norman round arch because it was stronger and allowed greater height.

The ordinary people, however, lived a very simple existence in the shadow of the church's vast power and wealth. Most houses would have been single-storey, timber constructions, with wattle and daub infilling and roofed with thatch.

There are three phases of the Gothic period:

* The Early English Period   1201–1290
* The Decorated Period   1291–1400
* The Perpendicular Period 1401–1500

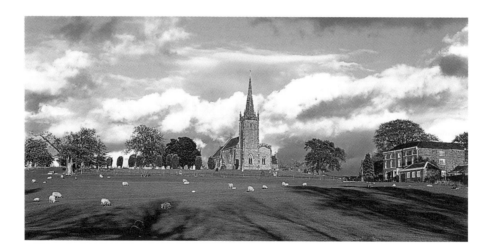

Above: St Mary Magdalene, Peckleton. Most of this church dates back to the 14th century–apart from the north windows and some of the windows in the south aisle, which are Perpendicular. The tower is also Decorated with a recessed, crocketed spire. The oldest feature of the church, however, is the Norman piscina in the chancel, which is treated with large dog-tooth decoration. To the right of the church is Peckleton Hall, which is late Georgian.

Right: St Peter, Swepstone. Although the tower was rebuilt in 1842, the nave and aisles date back to the early 14th century. Inside, the plain, circular font is most probably Norman, which suggests the presence of an earlier Norman church. There are two effigies inside the church. One is an alabaster monument to William Humphrey who died in 1591, and the other is a lady wearing a wimple, set on an embattled tomb chest with shields and balusters between.

THE EARLY ENGLISH PERIOD

1201 – 1290

THE EARLY ENGLISH PERIOD IS THE INITIAL PHASE OF GOTHIC ARCHITECTURE AND, ALTHOUGH THE DISTINCTION IS NOT CLEAR, IT MARKS THE FIRST STEP AWAY FROM NORMAN ARCHITECTURE. IT WAS A PERIOD THROUGH WHICH THE CHURCH AMASSED HUGE WEALTH, ENABLING A RAPID INCREASE IN ECCLESIASTICAL BUILDING.

The early English masons built their cathedrals as tall and as magnificent as they dared, to symbolise man's struggle to reach Heaven, while the smaller parish church was made as simple and austere as possible, to embody the renunciation of the flesh.

The defining feature that distinguishes this period from Norman architecture is the change from the round to the pointed arch – a feature brought over from France by the monks of the Cistercian Order. While the Normans used huge, thick walls to counter the sideways thrust of the arch, the English masons found that they need only strengthen the points where the arch met the wall, using a buttress. In between the buttresses the walls could be much thinner, allowing the incorporation of larger windows to let in more light.

There is little trace of this period left in the churches of the area, and only fragments remain throughout the county, incorporated into later structures.

The tall, narrow lancet window, pictured below, was a typical feature of the period and an example can be seen inside St Margaret's Church, Stoke Golding in the wall that separates the chancel from the south aisle. The chancel at All Saints, Nailstone is also 13th century and has two blocked lancet windows. At St James, Sutton Cheney the arches, circular piers and circular abaci of the arcade are all Early English work. And finally St James, Dadlington is a small 13th-century church with 13th-century sedilia and piscina in the chancel.

However, the most striking artefact that we have from this period – which according to Pevsner, that great advocate of British architecture, 'is worth a pilgrimage of many miles' – is the stained-glass east window in St James, Twycross. Imported from various sources in France, it is said to be of the finest-quality glass in the whole of Europe, dating back to 1243–48. The central light is much older (c. 1145), and originally came from the Royal Abbey of Saint-Denis near Paris, reputedly the first Gothic church ever built.

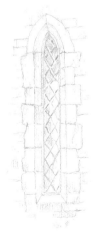

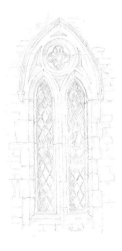

Left: An Early English lancet window. Pencil drawing by Doug Lewis.

Right: Plate tracery. The Early English masons found that by using buttresses the walls between could be thinner and windows larger. Soon lancet windows were grouped together and hoods were placed above to prevent rain dripping in. In between the hoodmoulding and the window, decorative holes were then punched through the stone. Pencil drawing by Doug Lewis.

Far Right: St Michael, Fenny Drayton. The oldest part of the church is the late Norman south doorway (picture, page 22) and the Norman window in the chancel. The tower and its recessed spire are both late 13th century.

A REMARKABLE WINDOW

STAINED-GLASS WINDOWS HAVE DECORATED RELIGIOUS BUILDINGS SINCE MEDIEVAL TIMES. IN AN AGE WHEN THE POPULATION AS A WHOLE WAS ILLITERATE, THESE WINDOWS BECAME KNOWN, WITH THEIR BIBLICAL SCENES, AS 'POOR MAN'S BIBLES'.

A wonderful example of this art, originally designed for French churches, is installed in the east window of the 13th-century church of St James the Greater, Twycross.

During the French Revolution (1789–95), mobs roamed the streets sacking and looting churches and smashing windows, so the churchwardens of the Sainte-Chapelle, Paris and the Royal Abbey of Saint-Denis, near Paris, among others, removed the glass for safety and made it into panels. These were brought to England by Sir Wathen Waller (although some say that they were smuggled across the Channel by a French chef), and presented to King George III. The glass passed down through the monarchy to William IV, who in turn presented it to his great friend, Earl Howe of Gopsall Hall. At the time, Earl Howe was renovating Twycross Church and had the glass panels installed in the east window by Thomas Willement, a famous glazier, in 1840.

The deep reds and blues glow with a jewel-like radiance that dominates the small, humble church. The glass, reputed to be the finest quality in Europe, dates back to c.1243–48 but the central panel, 'The Presentation of Christ in the Temple', which originally came from the Lady Chapel of Abbot Suger's Saint-Denis near Paris (the earliest Gothic church ever built), is dated c.1145.

For safe-keeping during World War Two the glass was removed, crated and stored in the cellars at the home of a local resident, Mr Harry Phillips. A local glazing firm put in a temporary window and then after the war replaced the panels, but in the 1980s the Parochial Church Council discovered that the inch-thick glass was being eaten by algae. To avoid any further damage it was again removed for cleaning and renovation by the York Minster Glaziers Trust. They advised that the green diamonds that abut the inner stone mullion were artistically incorrect, so the glass was tinted on the outside to make the diamonds appear mauve.

Meanwhile the French authorities, negotiating for the return of the glass, offered to replace it with a window to be created by famous French artists to Twycross's specifications. Although this had some local support, the French window remains, in all its glory, adorning the east end of the church.

Perhaps for the preservation of this beautiful glass window an extra prayer might be added to the inscription on one of the church bells: 'God save Church Wardens 1621'.

Laura Croman

Right: The stained-glass of the east window, St James, Twycross. Removed from the Saint-Chapelle in Paris during the French Revolution (1789–95), it is said to be some of the finest-quality glass available in the whole of Europe and dates back to 1243–48. The central light, 'The Presentation of Christ in the Temple', is much older (c.1145), and originally came from the Lady Chapel of Abbot Suger's Saint-Denis Abbey near Paris, which was the earliest Gothic church ever built.

THE DECORATED PERIOD

1290 – 1400

14TH-CENTURY ECCLESIASTICAL ARCHITECTURE IS MUCH MORE ELABORATE THAN THAT OF THE PRECEDING PERIOD — AS ITS NAME SUGGESTS.

Carving became much more intricate and ornamental, particularly in window tracery where the masons used their great skill to produce complicated, flowing curves.

This was a golden age of ecclesiastical building for the county, and much was of first-class quality. The basic size and form of most of our parish churches would have been determined early in the 14th century.

As glass became more readily available, windows could be larger, allowing much more light to flood interiors. The characteristic feature of the period was the ogee, a double or S-shaped curve that appears chiefly in arches and in window tracery. The finest example of decorated window tracery in the area and, according to many, in the whole of Leicestershire, can be seen at St Margaret's Church, Stoke Golding.

The windows of the south aisle – added to the building c.1290–1300 – and the chancel east window, are excellent examples of geometrical tracery (tracery which consists primarily of circles or foiled circles and is typical of the early Decorated period). A transition from this period to the later High Decorated, when window design became more elaborate and complex, can be seen in the windows of the north nave, rebuilt c.1340. This type of tracery is known as flowing, curvilinear tracery.

The arcade, also c.1300, is equally admirable with its moulded arches, clustered piers and finely sculptured capitals – a "lavishness" Pevsner states, "worthy of a cathedral".

A number of other churches in the area display Decorated work:

St Peter, Market Bosworth – the nave and the base of its tower (see the west doorway) were constructed c.1325.

All Saints, Ratcliffe Culey is unique in that it is wholly Decorated, with no subsequent additions. Here all the windows, except those in the southeast of the nave, are reticulated. This type of tracery is typical of the early 14th century and consists entirely of circles made at the top and bottom into ogee shapes. The stained-glass in the east window is by Kempe, 1900.

The nave at St Peter, Swepstone and both its aisles are 14th century. The windows in the south aisle display intersecting tracery which is typical of c.1300. Another example of intersecting tracery may be found in the east window of St Botolph's Church, Sibson, and this, along with the chancel, is also c.1300.

Finally, St James, Twycross has a Decorated nave and chancel with an arcade of four bays, where the piers have no capitals and continue into the arches without a break. This is again a common feature of Decorated design.

There was little building activity in the second half of the 14th century owing to the Black Death.

Alan Spencer. 2002

Above: St Margaret, Stoke Golding. A pencil drawing by Alan Spencer.

Right: The arcade, c.1290. Lavishly moulded arches have finely sculptured capitals of foliage. One of the capitals has a row of heads underneath the foliage – a bishop, a knight, some ladies and a young boy with a crooked mouth.

ST MARGARET'S CHURCH

THE EARLIEST DATE THAT CAN BE GIVEN TO ST MARGARET OF ANTIOCH'S CHURCH AT STOKE GOLDING IS 1220, WHEN IT CONSISTED OF A NAVE AND CHANCEL ONLY.

In about 1290 a south aisle was set out, which ran the whole length of the original construction and was divided into seven bays. On the inside of the south wall is a 14th-century tomb recess, possibly of the founder of the church and thought to have been Sir Robert Champaigne. The tomb has a chamfered arch and is set to the east of the fourth bay from the west end.

The font is richly sculptured and on one of its panels is a figure of St Margaret the Virgin, with the conquered dragon beneath her feet, into whose mouth she has thrust the end of her staff, while a praying figure kneels before her. On another panel is a crowned figure of St Catherine, holding a spiked wheel in her right hand and a sword in her left. Another panel contains a bishop, possibly St Nicholas, while the other four consist of tracery and shields.

The top of the spire was destroyed by an earthquake in 1580 and again in 1788. The spire was in such danger that it was feared it would fall and crush the church. It was repaired again in 1860 and in 1925. During World War Two it was removed temporarily and stored on concrete platforms to enable a safe take-off and approach for the aircraft using Lindley aerodrome.

Some heavy restoration work was done in 1633 when buttresses were placed on the north wall, where the foundations were found to be insufficient, possibly as a result of the 1580 earthquake.

On the south wall next to the porch, is an old dial dated 1620, from which the gnomon, the pin of the dial whose shadow shows the hour, has long been broken off. This was known as a 'mass clock'.

It is probably the windows of St Margaret's Church though, with their geometric and flowing tracery, that have brought people from far and wide to admire the craftsmanship of the stone-masons of old. As quoted by the poet, Sir John Betjeman: "This is a church that is worth cycling twelve miles against the wind to visit".

Jill Webster

Above: The floodlit north and east side of St Margaret, Stoke Golding. Just visible is the flowing, curvilinear tracery of the north windows which date back to 1320–40, when the north side of the church was remodelled.

Above: The geometrical tracery of a south aisle window, consisting of three lights crowned by three quatrefoiled circles. Pencil drawing by Doug Lewis.

THE CHURCH OF ST PETER

THERE IS AMPLE EVIDENCE OF A RELIGIOUS

PRESENCE WITHIN THE SMALL, OPEN WOODED

HILLTOP SETTLEMENT WE NOW KNOW AS MARKET

BOSWORTH, DATING BACK TO WELL BEFORE THE

TIME OF THE NORMANS.

The Great Survey of 1086 records the fact that the settlement of 'Boseworde' was ministered by both a priest and a deacon – one of only two locations in Leicestershire to be so served in early Norman times. The church was so well established in Bosworth at this time, that this record would certainly seem to support the theory of its existence in pre-Norman times.

From a visual perspective, the Church of St Peter seems to belong more to the former manor house, with its ancient trees and spacious grounds, than it does to the town. From very early times it has been influenced by the various owners of the Hall, which often conflicted with its objective of maintaining an independent status as the mother-church of a large number of parishes. However, during its long history the church has played a significant part in the development of the town.

Although the Domesday Book confirms that a church stood on the present site in 1086, the earliest records of any note relating to its construction state that rebuilding started in 1325 with the nave, the north aisle and the base of the tower. From the point of view of size and structure, the major part of the reconstruction work was completed by 1485 and had King Richard III been able to find the time to lift his eyes from his trials and tribulations on the battlefield at Ambion Hill, he would have taken in a picture of the church very similar to the one we see today.

The church tower has four pinnacles around the base of its spire, which was built in the mid-15th century. A weathercock crowns the spire at a height of over 40 metres above the base of the tower – it can be seen for

miles in every direction. The circular clock face, fitted in 1953, replaced an 18th-century clock whose diamond-shaped face, bearing the date 1755, can still be seen on the west face of the tower above three empty niches and the west door. It is thought that these niches probably housed statues before the time of Cromwell. Recent work in 1982, following storm damage which resulted in the fall of two pinnacles and the discovery of a structural deficiency in a third, included the rebuilding of the top of the spire and the pinnacles.

Inside the church there is scant physical evidence of its medieval connections. There are no effigies or relics relating to the Middle Ages; no altar-tombs, slabs or brasses. It is thought that the south aisle was added in the late 14th century by order of Sir Thomas Harcourt and the Lady Maud, who held the manor until 1417. A major programme of restructuring was set in motion in the mid-15th century which incorporated the redesign of the nave, the addition of the clerestory and the extension of the chancel with its beautiful set of half-windows, tall shelved piscina and impressive sedilia, which provided seats for the priest and servers. It is believed that this work, which also included another fine piscina situated in the south aisle, was carried out by Sir Robert Harcourt, the then Sheriff of Leicestershire and Warwickshire.

On entering the south aisle of the church, a screen by the south door conveys to passers-by the names of the rectors of Market Bosworth for the period from 1222 to 1588. As one continues to the nave, and turns to face west, the font comes prominently into view. The base of the font is very old, possibly dating from the early 13th century. Its hexagonal top, bearing shields with the names of Clare, Verdon and Harcourt in faint letters, dates from about 1355. The tower, which is accessed through a newly installed oak screen behind the font, houses eight bells. Two of the bells are dated 1624 and two 1630 and a fifth bell can recall the return of Charles II in 1660. The three remaining bells were added in the 20th century as recorded on the World War Two memorial plaque located to the left of the archway.

In the north aisle is the old Dixie family entrance, above which hangs the Dixie coat-of-arms. If, from this position, one carefully examines the base of the nearest pillar, several grooves can be seen; it is said that they were created by medieval bowmen sharpening their arrows. It is in

Right: St Peter, Market Bosworth. The chancel and the panel tracery of the east window are Perpendicular, with stained glass by Kempe, 1900. The crenellated north aisle and west tower date to c.1325. The recessed spire was added during the following century.

Overleaf: The west tower and spire.

this tranquil area of the church that, with the help of a grant from the Dixie Educational Foundation, a children's corner was established in 1985 to enable youngsters at an early age to become aware of, and participate in, the work and teachings of the church. Recently moved from this area of the church is the medieval parish chest which now sits at the chancel end. Made of oak, bound and studded with iron, it was used for centuries to keep safe the parish registers and the church plate, some of which dates back to 1567.

On re-entering the nave and approaching the pulpit one can observe, on the wall above it, a bricked-up door. This once led, via the rood-stair housed in its own separate turret, to the rood-loft, which ran across the chancel arch where the rood-screen, bearing a cross and two angels, now stands. Above the screen are two tablets containing the Ten Commandments, which replaced older tablets illustrated in drawings of 1847. As one turns again to face the font a glance overhead reveals the clerestory, which was added in the 15th century to give height and light to the nave. The last window to the right has a square top contrasting somewhat with the pointed arches of the others. Before the clerestory was built, the church roof was thatched with steep sides. The marks of

the old roof timbers can be seen on the tower wall, running upwards towards the apex of the roof from below window level.

As one turns into the chancel and moves towards the altar, one passes the weeping lady on the left. In front of her is the marble tombstone of her brother John Dixie, Rector from 1695 until his death in 1719. The door next to her leads into the modern vestry constructed on the site of a much older one. St Peter, with church and keys, is to the right of the east window; St Paul, with sword in hand, is to the left.

Today the east window, showing Christ on the road to Emmaus, is dedicated to the memory of Canon Bowers, a former rector. This window carries a wheatsheaf in the detail within its lower left-hand section, this being the mark and signature of its designer Kempe. The window above the altar tells the story of The Good Samaritan; that to the right is dedicated to the memory of Florence Holden and is also designed by Kempe.

On the left as one leaves the chancel one can turn, through the first pew in front of the lectern, to look through the 'squint' (its proper name being *hagioscope*, which means 'holy seeing place'). It is so named because it allowed people outside the nave to see what was happening at the altar at communion time. Since the chancel was extended and the altar moved it is no longer possible to see the altar through the squint and a look through it today yields a line of vision that falls to the left of the altar.

On leaving the church by the south porch, one passes through the glazed oak doors, which were installed in 1985 to the memory of William Gosling, a former headmaster of the Dixie Grammar School and a churchwarden of St Peter's for twenty-three years. Finally, pausing for a moment's reflection in the churchyard itself, one's eyes come to rest on the detail inscribed upon the many headstones, each of which pays tribute to loved ones from a former age who made their individual contribution to the life and times of the community in which they lived and served.

Keith McCarthy

Above: The lead roof of St Peter's nave seen from the tower with Bosworth Hall in the background.

THE PERPENDICULAR PERIOD

1401 — 1500

THIS PERIOD OF ECCLESIASTICAL ARCHITECTURE BECOMES MUCH MORE RESTRAINED AS THE FASHION TURNS FROM THE FLAMBOYANT AND COMPLEX TO MORE SIMPLE, GEOMETRIC DESIGNS.

The Perpendicular period, unlike the other two phases of the Gothic, which were closely connected to the continent, is wholly unique to England.

There was great emphasis on vertical and horizontal lines, especially in the windows. Through their increased knowledge of construction the masons were now able to make the walls less thick and to have huge windows that spanned greater distances. Their technical abilities in masonry have yet to be surpassed.

The arch became lower and flatter and the tracery made more simple. The window's increased size meant that it had to be divided into smaller rectangular shapes with glazing bars to hold the individual glass panes in place. Each pane could then be of a different colour or form part of a picture, and this period provides us with the best examples of stained-glass. This is known as panel tracery.

The 15th century was not responsible for any radical rebuilding in Leicestershire, as by now the basic shape and form of the parish church had been determined. In fact there are no churches, in the immediate area, built entirely in this style. This was a period when many existing structures were enlarged and improved.

Typical 15th-century alterations consisted of adding a clerestory to the nave, widening an existing aisle or adding a new one, and heightening or rebuilding the tower. All such alterations can be seen at St Peter, Market Bosworth. The panel tracery of the east window in the chancel is typical of Perpendicular design. The ashlar-faced west tower of All Saints, Sheepy Magna is Perpendicular. Originally a giant arch framed the west doorway but this is now partly filled in and at the bottom is a tomb recess with a badly worn effigy.

GOTHIC SECULAR

AS CONDITIONS BECAME SAFER FOR PEOPLE TO MOVE AWAY FROM FORTIFIED SITES, THE SMALLER ENGLISH HOUSE BEGAN TO DEVELOP.

The gentry now had time to establish more permanent estates and manor houses, though it was still deemed necessary to fortify with moats and gatehouses. With the invention of the cannon, outdated medieval forms of defence were rendered useless.

From the early 13th century up until the middle of the 14th century, many of the more important dwellings would have had a moat. In Leicestershire, with its thick, heavy clays and a network of streams, they were in abundance. Most are now dry ditches but they can still be detected.

Good examples can be found north of the church at Ratcliffe Culey – the oval mound and its deep ditch have been dated to the early 13th century; and at the Moat House at Appleby Magna, which provides us with the best-preserved medieval moated homestead in the county. Here the original stone gatehouse of the 15th-century medieval hall remains mainly unaltered – behind it, and attached to it, is a 16th-century timber-framed house which replaced the original medieval manor.

The manor house that pre-dated Bosworth Hall had a three-sided moat, two-thirds of which have possibly been incorporated into the present moat.

The roads laid out by the Romans had by this time fallen into disrepair, leaving large parts of the country isolated. This meant that builders had to make do with resources they had at hand, giving rise to localised styles of architecture – now termed 'the Vernacular'.

As wood was the most readily – and in many cases the only – available material, the vast majority of medieval houses were made of it. Timber houses generally fall into two forms of construction – cruck and box-frame.

The first cruck houses were open to the roof where there would be a small opening from which the smoke from a central fireplace could escape. This is now termed the 'openhall' house and was in existence up until the introduction of the chimneystack in the 16th and 17th centuries. The hall remained for centuries the most important room in the house; a place where everyone would eat, sleep and entertain. The early medieval hall

was very similar in form to that of the parish church and it is likely that domestic architecture of the period developed from the ecclesiastical.

Church Cottage, Cadeby is of cruck construction. The cruck beams, individually known as blades, which are visible from the road, were recently dendro-dated to 1472–73. Originally the building would have been infilled with wattle and daub and roofed with thatch.

Box-frame construction came after the cruck and was superior in that it allowed for two full storeys as opposed to one and a half. Unlike cruck houses the length of the timber did not determine the size of the house. Because timber was expensive, only the wealthy could afford to use it prodigiously. Such houses would have many parallel upright beams, or studs, the richer the occupant the closer these were together. The 16th-century timber-framed house at Appleby displays such work.

Another feature adopted to reflect the status of the owner was the jetty, where the upper storey oversails the lower. A jetty can be seen in the right-hand property of the two former farm workers' cottages at Wellsborough, now known as Manor Cottages, which date back to the late 15th, early 16th century.

The death of King Richard III on Bosworth Battlefield brought an end to both the Wars of the Roses and to the feudal system, and a transition from medieval to Classical architecture began. This transition was divided up into two main parts: 'Tudor' which was mainly Gothic in detail, and 'Elizabethan and Jacobean' which was influenced by the Renaissance movement in Italy.

Left: The Old House, Wood Lane, Cadeby – parts of which date back to the 16th century.

Right: The Cock Inn, Sibson – a 16th-century timber-framed construction, although sections inside are believed to date back further. Because oak is such a hard wood it would have to be cut green, as the sap dried out the timber would warp and twist – in this case to quite a severe degree.

THE TUDOR PERIOD

1485 — 1560

THE TUDOR PERIOD IS CHARACTERISED BY THE FACT THAT NEARLY ALL BUILDING WAS SECULAR. IT WAS A PERIOD OF RELIGIOUS UNREST AS THE NATION BECAME INCREASINGLY DISILLUSIONED WITH A MISGOVERNED CHURCH.

The economic and political power, which had belonged to the monastic orders for so long, was now in the hands of the king. With the Dissolution of the Monasteries, brought about by Henry VIII, churches, abbeys and other ecclesiastical buildings were swept away and replaced by manor houses.

On the other hand society was no longer preoccupied with defending itself. Houses could now be built more for comfort and convenience than fortification, although many dwellings still had moats, gatehouses (such as Appleby Magna's Moat House), mock fortifications and turrets almost as fashion accessories.

Tudor architecture is characterised by the fact that houses became smaller but more intimate with a focus on detail. Windows and doors were smaller but more complex and finely decorated. Gradually the arches of the Gothic gave way to the flattened Tudor arch.

With the widespread adoption of coal for heating and cooking, enclosed fireplaces and chimneys were needed to take the increased amount of

smoke out of the building. Chimney-stacks were often elaborately decorated in all shapes and sizes: octagons, hexagons, circles and twists.

Although Coton Priory's exterior owes its appearance to a 19th-century renovation, parts of the original building date back to the 1550s, such as the stone plinth on which the present structure sits. The building was constructed in three sections, starting from the left. Here some of the bricks are extremely thin, and are perhaps original. Hidden inside, behind a cupboard, is an arched, stone window.

The Moat House at Appleby Magna also dates to the period. Situated east of the church, this medieval moated homestead is the finest and best preserved in the county. Of the 15th-century manor house only the gatehouse remains. Here the windows are ecclesiastical in style – arched and cusped, they clearly differ in design from the rectangular windows of the house behind, which was built in the following century, replacing the original manor house. The close-stud framing indicates the status of the building, since oak had become an incredibly expensive building material.

It was at this time that the use of bricks started to increase. From the 15th century, bricks were used to replace the wattle and daub infilling between timbers and became the preferred material for constructing chimneys. For many the cost of building the entire house in brick would have been too great, so often just the chimney was built of brick, to reduce the risk of fire.

Fleets of merchant ships headed for Europe with wool and came back laden with bricks, a great many of which came from Flanders. At first the Dutch bricklayers were brought over with these loads in order to teach the English masons their skills. The crow-stepped gable is a direct descendant of Dutch architecture (the porch of Warwick House adopts this design). With fireplaces and chimneys built on the side of the house instead of in the middle, the old hall could now be separated into two storeys, and houses started to take the shape of the dwellings we see today.

By the middle of the 17th century the demand for bricks was greatly increasing and as a result many towns had to have their own brickworks, including Bosworth. This often led to regional variations in colour due to the different types of clay used.

It is believed that the paddock in front of Manor Cottages, Wellsborough was a rich source of clay for a nearby brickworks. This may explain the small cut-away area which forms a steep bank down to the road.

Above: The Moat House, Appleby Magna. The 15th-century stone gatehouse is all that remains of the original medieval manor, which was replaced in the following century by the timber-framed building seen behind.

Right: Parts of Coton Priory date back to the 1550s, such as the stone plinth and stone window hidden behind a cupboard in an interior wall, although much of the present building owes its external appearance to a 19th-century renovation.

This area of Leicestershire is covered by boulder clay and below this Lower Lias clays or deep red Triassic marls, which yield rich, red bricks, such as those of Bosworth Hall. The earliest bricks were irregular and misshapen as the kilns could not produce the necessary even temperatures. It is usually possible to date a brick with some accuracy and, in general terms, the thinner and more misshapen it is, the older it is. As the bricks became more standardised in shape it was possible to lay them in a bond. From the Tudor period the English bond was the most common method used, consisting of alternate headers and stretchers; an example of which can be seen at No. 28 The Square. This was replaced by the Flemish bond in the late 17th and 18th centuries, which can be seen in many of the other buildings in the Square, and by the stretcher bond in the 20th century. Each successive bond was more economical in that it used fewer headers and more stretchers.

THE ELIZABETHAN AND JACOBEAN PERIOD

1560 – 1620

ELIZABETHAN ENGLAND ENJOYED A PROSPERITY NEVER SEEN BEFORE. SECULAR BUILDING CONTINUED TO BE PREDOMINANT, REPLACING THE ECCLESIASTICAL DOMINANCE OF THE MIDDLE AGES.

Between 1570 and 1625 the country witnessed a period of energetic building activity, later known as the Great Rebuilding, not of cathedrals and churches but of country mansions and the smaller yeomen's cottages. Because of the Dissolution of the Monasteries, the current trends taking place in Europe, in particular the Renaissance, were not fully adopted. Only through the travelling aristocracy could this new movement be assimilated. New ideas gradually filtered through, usually by way of Holland – from where Britain imported bricks – but they were interpreted in a way unique to Britain.

The classical architecture of the Renaissance gradually became the new mode, not so much structurally as ornamentally. Houses started to follow a more symmetrical plan, often assuming an 'E' shape as opposed to the

T' and 'H' shapes of the Tudor period. Windows were now completely rectangular and larger than ever before and the long gallery became a very important feature.

The best remaining example of Elizabethan architecture that we have in the area is Sutton Cheney Hall, built in 1601, although only one wing of the original H-shaped building remains. The spirit of the hall is still Gothic with its imposing gables, and apart from the rectangular, stone-mullioned windows there has been no attempt to introduce classical details such as cornices or pilasters.

Shenton Hall, built in 1629 for William Wollaston, is Jacobean. The original building, which can be seen from the road amid substantial Victorian extensions, was in fact symmetrical and although still built in the Gothic style, shows how the influence of the Italian Renaissance was beginning to spread beyond mere ornament, such as the two pilasters on either side of the east doorway, to a more symmetrical plan.

A house made from bricks was a lavishness reserved only for the wealthy. The more humble house would continue to be made with timber, infilled with wattle and daub and roofed with thatch.

Several properties in Bosworth date from this period, though these early features are often hidden within or behind subsequent frontages such as the properties in the Wheatsheaf Courtyard, once part of the Wheatsheaf Inn, and Peppercorn Cottage, renovated by Charles Tollemache Scott in the 19th century, which is a cruck construction, with one of the cruck beams clearly visible inside. The half-timbered thatched cottage in Sutton Lane also dates back to the 16th century.

A row of Elizabethan cottages with Victorian facades stretched down Barton Lane from the Red Lion until the 1960s, when they were replaced by the present town houses. One of these cottages still remains and is now incorporated into the Red Lion Inn. These cottages would have been box-framed like the Rotary Cottages in The Square, with wattle and daub infilling. Much of the pottery discovered on rebuilding dated from the period between 1450 and 1550.

The 19th-century facade of the Grey House on Church Street hides a timbered farmhouse which also dates back to this period, and opposite, the Dower House still harbours the cellars of the former Elizabethan George Inn.

Above and Right: Sutton Cheney Hall, built in 1601. A stone block with this date and the initials WR (William Roberts) can be seen above a back door. (An effigy of William Roberts can be seen in St James' Church, Sutton Cheney). Only one wing of the original H-plan building remains, complete with stone quoins, continuous string courses and mullioned and transomed stone windows. Attached to this, on the left, is a later gabled addition.

OSBASTON HALL

A WHISPER OF DAYS GONE BY ETCHED IN THE GLASS OF THE NURSERY WINDOW:

THOMAS CRISTY, AUGUST 29TH 1750.

AS A SERVANT OR PERHAPS A GUEST OF THE FAMILY, MR CRISTY LIVED 250 YEARS AGO

AND LOOKED THROUGH THE SAME WINDOW THAT STILL FACES OUT ONTO THE COBBLED

COURTYARD BELOW.

A manor house stood on the site of Osbaston Hall at the time of the Domesday Book in 1086, when Ralph de Mortimer was in residence. The original manor would undoubtedly have been constructed from oak timber and extended over the years in red brick. Sir Thomas Pope Blount restored the Hall in 1620 and subsequently sold it to the Wrightson Mundy family at the close of the 17th century. Although the house has been subjected to much alteration over the centuries, to all outward appearances it is their Queen Anne building that we see today. Rainwater heads on the south entrance front show Mundy's initials and the dates 1743 and 1750.

However, the Wrightson Mundy's Hall hides within its brick walls an older timber-framed structure. There is evidence of this in the east range where several of the windows are either partially or fully blocked by the older and lower structure behind. Further evidence can be found inside, with the 17th-century staircase in the west range which abuts a square-panelled timber-framed wall and the 17th-century wood panelling in the old music room on the second floor. There is also a crown-post roof in the attic above the main entrance hall, which dates the house back even further, as this type of roof construction became redundant early in the 16th century and earlier still in important houses such as this, where current fashions were adopted much more readily.

In 1827 the Cope family became the Hall's residents and remained there for three generations. The last in line, Sir Thomas Cope, was a traditional English gentleman who would amble along the lanes in his horse-drawn carriage. He died in 1966 and was buried with his wife in St Peter's churchyard, Market Bosworth. The Hall was in such a poor state of repair around the time of his death that it is believed he died holding an umbrella over his head.

During World War One, Sir Thomas Cope met his wife Charlotte, Comtesse d'Abbans, whom many believed was French although she was actually of Irish descent. She gained her French title from her first husband. Their marriage became very stormy over the years at Osbaston, which inevitably led to them living in separate parts of the house. One particularly snowy winter evening, Lady Cope went out onto the roof to clear away some of the snow. Whether Sir Thomas knew she was out there is debatable, but he proceeded to close and fasten the hatch,

shutting Lady Cope out. This exposure led to the loss of one of her fingers to frostbite. Another time when Sir Thomas asked where the family silver was, she showed it to him melted down in a pot on the kitchen range.

Lady Charlotte Cope was widely regarded as an artistic eccentric. She wrote many poems in her diary, this particular piece expressing her despair:

> I long to shut the door on life
>
> I long to shut the door on life
> It's grown too hard to bear such weary strife
> Men's hearts grown cold and souls quite dead.
> And ghouls walk around instead, cruelty and strife
> abound.
>
> And deep in the cold damp ground the bodies of the
> best lie dead.
> Their souls to heaven have fled, and mine so longs to
> take flight.
> But this weary body holds it still quite tight.
> I feel it beating to get free, but God is not ready yet
> for me.

In 1967 Sir Jonathan Guinness bought the Hall at auction against a second bidder who had plans to demolish the building for the bricks. The extensive restoration work needed to recapture the original splendour of the hall lasted six years, by which time the house was once more a fine country residence. Owning a second property in London, the Guinness's spent very little time in the hamlet and after twenty years they sold the Hall, grounds and outlying properties to the de Lisles, an ancient, aristocratic family from the Loughborough area. Quietly screened behind a coppice of willow, the Hall has once again become a warm and friendly family home.

Left: Externally, Osbaston Hall is almost entirely 18th century. Rainwater heads on the south entrance front show the dates 1743 and 1750. The two storey east range (shown in the picture) was built a little earlier, around the beginning of the 18th century, in the Queen Anne style. Incorporated into the building is an earlier structure, indicated by the crown-post roof in the attic.

ODSTONE HALL

YOU COULD BE FORGIVEN FOR NOT NOTICING

ODSTONE HALL AS YOU JOURNEY FROM BARTON

IN THE BEANS TOWARDS THE TINY HAMLET OF

ODSTONE, SINCE ONLY TEMPORARILY DOES IT

FLICKER INTO SIGHT THROUGH THE SCREEN OF

TREES THAT OBSCURES IT FROM VIEW.

Probably the best vantage point from which to appreciate the main features of this impressive mansion is from the high ground near Barton looking out across the valley.

The 17th-century Hall, originally built in the H-plan Elizabethan style, lies to the southwest of the village. In the 18th century it underwent substantial remodelling when the present Georgian front was grafted onto the older structure. The Elizabethan origins of the house are evident in the timbers on the upper floors and in the brickwork of its gabled rear wings; further confirmation of the period is present in the main staircase and a 17th-century stone fireplace. Also of note is an elaborate chimney-piece of coloured alabaster, said to have been transported from Kenilworth Castle.

In the 18th century the house was given a fine five-bay front featuring a pedimented central bay with a hipped roof, supported by a modillion cornice.* On each side of the front door stands a Doric column with a broken pediment sitting above, shadowing the Venetian fanlight. The house is strongly built and very well fortified, some of its walls being almost 2 metres thick.

In truth the Hall is likely to have gained fame more as a result of those who occupied it than because of its architecture. In 1649 the then owner, John Bradshaw, was President and Judge of the High Court which condemned Charles I to death (other signatories to the Death Warrant were William Purefoy, whose family tombs are to be found at Fenny Drayton, and Peter Temple of Temple Hall, Wellsborough). Ironically

just eleven years later, after the restoration of Charles II, Odstone Hall, or Odestone as it was otherwise called, passed into the possession of the Astleys, a family of staunch Royalists. It remained the home of the Astley family until the early part of the 19th century, when Sir John Astley sold the estate to Lord Howe of Gopsall Hall. With a change of ownership the house was renamed Edestone.

Under its present owners, Shaun and Joanne Woodward, the Hall has recently been restored, both internally and externally, with a degree of sensitivity and excellence.

Today the village of Odstone consists of no more than twenty households clustered around the meeting point of two minor roads. It is thought that the settlement was once much larger than it is today and extended a greater distance westwards – the great plague of 1348–49 forced villagers to flee their homes and re-locate to the present site. In later years, fire destroyed many of the thatched dwellings. The remains of old buildings can still be detected in the adjacent fields. In 1846 the population numbered 180 living in 40 houses. Many homesteads incorporated small shops and workshops in which, amongst other tradesmen, a shoemaker and a blacksmith were in residence.

Keith McCarthy

Above: From this angle it is possible to see Odstone Hall's 18th-century Georgian facade, grafted onto the Elizabethan structure behind.

Right: The five-bay south front, with pedimented central bay and hipped roof, has recently been restored by the present owners, Mr & Mrs Woodward. The grand stone-balustrades, in the foreground, are a new addition.

*Small ornamented brackets placed at regular intervals.

SHENTON HALL

IN 1485 THE INHABITANTS OF SHENTON MAY WELL HAVE TURNED OUT IN FORCE TO WITNESS, AT FIRST HAND, THE CONCLUDING SCENES OF THE WARS OF THE ROSES, WHICH ENSURED THEM A PERMANENT PLACE IN THE NATION'S HISTORY, AS HENRY SEIZED RICHARD'S CROWN.

The village, which was not enclosed until 1646, at that time skirted the site of the final battle, and its people would probably not have needed to leave their homes to witness the events that unfolded; it was the construction of the canal and railway in the 19th century that deprived the populace of a direct view of the very spot where Richard is said to have drawn his last breath.

The name of the village is derived from *Scentone* which means 'Farmstead on the River Sence' (the word *scenc* is old English for 'drinking cup' and *tun* means 'settlement'). The population remains to this day very small and may number even fewer than it did at the time of the battle. The buildings of note include Shenton Hall, St John's Church and the Old School, the last being set up by the Dixie Educational Foundation in 1843 but now converted into a private home.

THE HALL

Shenton Hall is a Gothic-style brick mansion which was built in 1629 by William Wollaston, Lord of the Manor. The original house was typical of the period and was built of dark red bricks with stone dressings. At that time an inscription scorched on a beam over the inside of the front door read: "This house was built by me William Wollaston Esquir, Lorde of Shenton, AD 1629". A gatehouse was built at the same time and in the same style as the main building, and only this and the northwest front of the house remain substantially unaltered from their original design. The southeast side of the building was considerably extended around 1800 with projected pedimental wings being added. In 1769 the Lord of the Manor gave three bushels of wheat to the king in return for permission to build the splendid square, brick dovecote, one of only three of this shape in the country.

The northwest front of the house consists of three storeys plus a basement and a gabled attic, with four projecting bays of equal height. The outer two are semicircular and three-storeyed, the inner two, serving the central hall and great Chamber between the bays add much to the symmetry of the building and the windows have completely circular mullions and transoms.

Further extensive modifications were made in 1862 when the space between the new wings was filled and a billiard room and replacement service court added. A tower was constructed on the angle, which gave the building what Pevsner describes as "a romantic, distinctly Victorian silhouette when viewed from the southwest". At this time also the whole southeast front of the Hall was remodelled, with flattish bays being added and the main entrance to the house moved to the northeast end. It is probable that during this period of major construction the extensive stables were added.

Entrance to the Hall is now gained by way of the Victorian two-storey northeast porch built in the 17th-century style, which leads into a

Above: The northwest front, to the left of the picture, was built in 1629 by William Wollaston.

corridor running the whole length of the interior of the original building. The former hall was divided into a lobby and a kitchen; the kitchen now houses a moulded beam with scorched inscription which may well be the same one described above.

The main internal features of the house include moulded beams, some imported pieces of old panelling, and a late 17th-century dogleg staircase with extensively detailed balusters. In the 19th-century drawing room on the southeast front there is a good example of a Jacobean-style overmantel and moulded ceiling in its original colours. The adjacent sitting room features a fine chimney-piece dating from 1649 and carved with hunting and biblical scenes; in fact this is only half of what was once a massive chimney-piece which is thought to have originally stood in Gopsall Hall. The basement under the hall displays possible evidence of an earlier house, showing a section of large ashlar blocks and an apparently early 16th-century door surround.

The gatehouse is, like the house, of dark red brick and stone dressings and consists of two storeys plus an attic, with gables on each face featuring mullioned windows. The semicircular gate arch, having a section of entablature above bearing the date 1629, is constructed in line with the northwest front of the mansion.

The Hall remained in the ownership and occupation of the Wollaston family from its time of construction until 1943, when it was taken over

by the War Office to house German and Italian prisoners of war. It was de-requisitioned in 1947 and has had several owners since.

St John's Church

The current building is relatively new. By 1859 the old church had fallen into such a state of disrepair that it had to be demolished. The Reverend Wollaston, with the help of his brother, friends and parishioners, raised the sum of £3,000 to fund the cost of rebuilding, which was supervised by W.H. Knight of Cheltenham and completed by 1861. The rugged stone for the outer walls of the new building came from Sydnop in Derbyshire, the stone from the old church being used for the internal walls. The church is constructed in the cruciform style with a west tower. The stained-glass east and west windows were designed by Chance of Birmingham in 1861. Inside the church, as a monument to William Wollaston who died in 1666, are featured two busts standing freely under segmental arches, topped with steep, broken, semicircular pediments with thick garlands. The fittings are all contemporary, the pews and many other items being fashioned by carpenters from the local Shenton estate. It was to prove very poignant that the end of the occupation of Shenton Hall by the village squire should be marked with the laying to rest, on 6th June 1930, of the body of Mr Fred Eustace Arbuthnot Wollaston, in the burial ground of the same church that his forebears had struggled to restore 70 years before.

Keith McCarthy

Above left: The north-west front of Shenton Hall seen from the church tower.

Above right: St John's Church, built in 1861.

BUILDINGS OF THE CLASSICAL ERA

1620 – 1800

UP UNTIL THE 17TH CENTURY MOST BUILDINGS WERE CONSTRUCTED UNDER THE AUSPICES OF AN ORGANISATION SUCH AS THE CHURCH, BUT THIS WAS A PERIOD IN WHICH INDIVIDUAL ARCHITECTS ASSUMED A MORE IMPORTANT ROLE. THE FIRST, AND PERHAPS MOST SIGNIFICANT, OF THESE WAS INIGO JONES.

A new movement had been developing in Italy for some time, seeing a rebirth of styles gleaned from Ancient Greek and Roman architecture; it was known as the Renaissance. Up until this point little attention had been paid to symmetry and proportion. With no overall set plan from which the builder could work, buildings were composed asymmetrically and yet, in their own way, still managed to achieve balance and proportion. It was through the masons, carpenters, plumbers and plasterers that the quintessential style of English architecture was born.

This was all in stark contrast to Classical architecture, however, where the architect took a more important role. Harmonic proportions were essential elements of his design, from which the builders could not deviate. It was through the studies of Andrea Palladio, an Italian architect of the time, that the first comprehensive synopsis of Classical architecture was established.

Palladio produced a series of books which laid out the rules of Classical proportion and symmetry. Standard modules, from which the grandest house or the ordinary terraced dwelling could be assembled, were now available and it was through the English architect Inigo Jones, who studied Palladio's work, that this new concept quite suddenly parachuted, fully formed, into England.

However, the country was not yet prepared for such a revolution in its architecture. Indigestible in its pure form, the cool Classical style met with British sumptuousness to produce the idiosyncratic 17th-century English country manor house. Beech House, Snarestone (c.1679) typifies this perfectly. Built traditionally with brick, the steeply pitched roof and large windows – features that go hand in hand with a dull, wet climate – sit uncomfortably with the military uniform of Classicism, yet this house oozes eclectic beauty. The back of the building is in stark contrast to the front, sprawled with gables and windows: it is completely Jacobean in style.

Beech House provides a wonderful example of how the English masons were making their first tentative steps towards Classicism. It seems rather odd that it was from the Italians that we derived the very essence of Britishness that changed our towns and cities for ever.

Bosworth Hall, built at roughly the same time, shows even greater Italian influence – with its symmetrical plan and use of Classical features, such as the Corinthian pilasters, pediments and stone dressings.

Left: The south front of Bosworth Hall, built c.1680 in the Neo-Classical style.

Right: Beech House, Snarestone, built c.1679, in the Queen Anne style.

BOSWORTH HALL

While there is no indication of what the manor would have looked like at this period, its size and position would have been determined by the moat, two-thirds of which were possibly incorporated into the present moat, but an exact location of the manor house has never been pinpointed. The ancient fishpond, situated on the slope of the hill north of the Hall, would have undoubtedly belonged to the Manor.

In a survey of Bosworth made in 1588, there is mention of a 'new bilded ... faire mansion house' and a later survey records that it was a moated homestead of some considerable size, constructed from timber, with many outbuildings.

In 1589 the hall was sold to the first Sir Wolstan Dixie, knight, and it was probably for his son, Sir Beaumont, that the present hall was built.

The Hall itself is a simple but significant example of a late Stuart country mansion. It is constructed of red brick with stone string courses between the first and second storeys, a combination that shows off the stone carving and columns to good effect. The roof is of small grey Swithland slates.

FRAMED BY LOFTY TREES AND A SMOOTH SWARD OF LAWN, THE RICH RED BRICKS OF BOSWORTH HALL STRETCH ELEGANTLY BETWEEN THE ANCIENT STEEPLE OF ST PETER'S CHURCH AND CHARLES TOLLEMACHE SCOTT'S QUEEN ANNE WATER TOWER.

Dating from about 1680 to 1700, the hall was built in the Neo-Classical style by an unknown architect, probably for Sir Beaumont Dixie, the 2nd Baronet, as the home for the Dixie family. There is evidence, however, that the site has been occupied since Saxon times when in 1048 Fernot, a knight, was lord of the manor.

In 1193 the hall passed into the hands of the Harcourts, one of the most notorious and prestigious families of medieval England and in whose ownership the hall would remain for some 400 years. (The Harcourt arms, along with those of the Verdons, can be seen on the 14th-century font in the church.)

Originally the Hall consisted of two L-shaped wings with eleven bays on the south side and nine bays on the west. The west elevation, which forms the main entrance to the building, is divided into three bays with the centre one, containing the main doorway, having four full-height fluted stone Corinthian columns. Over the doorway is a small stone pediment reaching to the window overhead. Above the centre bay, in the main pediment, is a stone cartouche of the arms of Sir Beaumont Dixie.

The south elevation faces the park and is also divided into three bays, the two outer ones being larger than the centre one which is slightly projected. The middle windows have stone columns on either side. Of the upper-storey windows the centre one has a pediment matching that over the main doorway but with the addition of a carved basket of flowers. The pediments of the two outer windows have carved stone swags of fruit and pendants of cloth. The main pediment above contains another large stone cartouche containing the arms of Sir Beaumont's parents, Sir Wolstan Dixie, the 1st Baronet, and his wife, Barbara Beaumont.

Above: The stone cartouche of the arms of Sir Wolstan Dixie, the 1st Baronet, and his wife, Barbara Beaumont above a second floor window on the south elevation.

Right: The west elevation of Bosworth Hall built c. 1680. The court d'honneur gate in the foreground bears the initials of Charles Tollemache Scott, 'TS'.

Originally the approach to the main entrance was a gradual slope. The wrought-iron gates and stone steps were added in 1887 by Sir Charles Tollemache Scott, who carried out many internal alterations and much restoration work after purchasing the mansion from Sir Alexander Beaumont Dixie (Beau), the 11th Baronet, in 1885.

The interior of the house is in late 17th-century style but, due to the alterations made by Scott, has many late 19th-century features. The front door is of oak and has a decorative fanlight set into the stone porch leading into the entrance hall which is oak panelled, with a beautifully pargetted ceiling, virtually unchanged from the day it was constructed. The stone fireplace has the motto *STET FORTVNA DOMVS* (May good fortune be upon this house) carved above it.

The south front of the house was the 'show' front and overlooked the Terrace Walk, the lawns and the L-shaped moat with the deer park in the distance. The ground floor comprised a dining room, a library, with a morning room on either side, and a billiard room at the far end.

The major part of the west front is taken up by the entrance hall which leads, through a double oak doorway, to the inner hall, with its richly

decorated plaster ceiling and whose walls once displayed a collection of arms and armour. From here the main staircase leads to the first floor where the wide oak staircase, built to accommodate the extravagant fashions of the time, has finely turned banisters richly carved with large baskets of fruit and flowers. Originally it was probably formed around a square well but, following restoration, it now consists of a single flight.

The first floor houses the original suite of state rooms and the private suite of apartments. The former consists of the long drawing room, ante-bedroom and dressing room. The long drawing room, which is immediately above the dining room, has a polished oak floor with panelled walls set beneath an ornate plaster ceiling. Its green marble fireplace has an overmantel carved in the manner of Grinling Gibbons.

Also situated on the first floor, immediately above the entrance hall, are three rooms which were given their names in the 19th century: The Oak Room, The Brown Room and The Green Room. The Oak Room is entirely panelled in oak in the Jacobean style; The Brown Room is decorated in a similar style to the state rooms; and The Green Room has a domed ceiling. The second (top) floor of the mansion, which was mainly the accommodation for the servants, contains little of note.

In 1932, private ownership of Bosworth Hall came to an end when it was purchased, at auction, by Leicestershire County Council for conversion into a 177-bed hospital for the chronically sick. The alterations made during the conversion to a hospital were minimal and did not detract from the craftsmanship and beauty of the house. The hospital closed in 1988 and the building has, to a certain extent, re-fulfilled its original function by becoming a country house hotel. It is of some comfort to know that visitors the world over now have the opportunity to enjoy, albeit as paying guests, the atmosphere, history and splendour of a fine mansion that was once only afforded to a privileged few.

Keith McCarthy

Above: The south front of Bosworth Hall.

Right: The avenue of lime trees that lead from the Hall to the Wilderness.

THE QUEEN ANNE COUNTRY HOUSE

TURN OF THE 18TH CENTURY

THE QUEEN ANNE TOWN HOUSE DEVELOPED UNDER THE INFLUENCE OF SIR CHRISTOPHER WREN, WHO REBUILT MANY OF LONDON'S CHURCHES AFTER THE GREAT FIRE. THIS WAS THE HOUSE THAT MET THE CRITERIA OF THE CLASSICAL FORM WITHOUT BEING ON THE SCALE OF A PALACE.

Steeply pitched roofs, gable ends, large windows and chimney-stacks, all of which owe their design to the cold, dull, wet climate of Britain, did not fit the pure Classical style and had to be changed to fit in with the new style.

The design of the Queen Anne house would invariably be a plain rectangular shape, always symmetrical, and built of brick or stone. The angles had quoins made of brick or stone to complement the rest of the house.

Gable ends were replaced by slightly pitched, hipped roofs while the windows were given a stone or brick surround. It was at this point that the sash window was introduced – a feature that was to become so popular with the Georgians.

Queen Anne doorways were almost always given a canopy though there were many variations. A popular device was to make them deep and curved to give the appearance of a shell.

Several houses in the area were built at this time, such as Osbaston Hall, Cadeby Manor House and Twycross House School (1703) but possibly the best example is Twycross Manor Farm (c.1712) which sits opposite the church on the edge of the village. The building is completely rectangular and symmetrical in form, with a slightly pitched hipped roof. Built in red brick with stone quoins and a horizontal string course, the front elevation has all the qualities of the idiom.

It is important to note that the average person's house at this time differed little from those of medieval times – basic, timber-framed constructions with thatched roofs. However, this would all change in the 18th century with the advent of the Georgian period.

Above: Pen and ink drawing of Twycross Manor Farm by Doug Lewis. A double-pile house of c.1712 with quoins and a hipped roof. The windows have stone surrounds and the doorway is decorated with a segmental pediment.

Right, above and below: The Manor House, Cadeby dates back to the 1700s and was built in the Queen Anne style, with warm red bricks, rectangular form and hipped roof, but like many older dwellings, traces of an earlier building can be found inside. The lofty elegant windows we see today are the result of significant alterations which took place under James Tollemache Scott, brother of Charles, to reflect those of Bosworth Hall. The front porch, added at the same time, is said to have been taken from a house in Lincolnshire.

THE GEORGIAN PERIOD

1720 – 1800

THROUGHOUT THE 18TH CENTURY, ENGLAND WAS THE WORLD'S LEADING TRADING NATION. IT WAS CHANGING FROM AN AGRICULTURALLY BASED COMMUNITY TO THE MOST URBANISED CULTURE IN EUROPE AND AMERICA.

Across the country, towns and cities were expanding rapidly and, instead of isolated buildings, squares and terracing became the fashion. Bosworth was no exception – in fact most of the buildings seen in The Square today are Georgian in design. However, these are only facades grafted onto much older medieval structures. This renovation was overseen by the Dixies in the latter part of the 18th century.

The haphazard Tudor interiors still remain, hidden behind uniform Georgian frontages. Dating back to the 16th century, properties of this time were largely built of timber and mud (wattle and daub) with thatched roofs. To make the best use of limited space, the gable end would face the street, with the rest of the building extending along the back. The plan of the new buildings nearly always followed the lines of those they superseded.

The size of a town's square often reflected the wealth of the community and, like most market towns, Bosworth prospered from its rich agricultural surroundings. The Square has for some 800 years been the nucleus around which the rest of the town grew.

At the beginning of the 18th century, with the publication of several architectural pattern books, the designs of the famous architects, in particular Andrea Palladio, were now available to builders all around the country and because of this, a standard design started to emerge. The Georgian preoccupation with geometry and proportion reached a stage where any deviation from this was considered substandard. Many older buildings, such as those in The Square, were remodelled to comply and harmonise with the Palladian template. Such alterations can be seen all around Bosworth and district – perhaps most significantly around The Square, but also at Odstone Hall, for example.

Throughout history the one element of a building most susceptible to change has been the window, which is not surprising as it is the window through which the owner can see and be seen. The window was by far the most important feature of the Georgian house – it gave a feeling of balance and proportion to the whole building. The ubiquitous white sash met all the criteria; even when open the symmetry of the building was not broken. Architects of the time would generally follow the same rule when it came to dealing with the window: short windows on the ground floor, to give the building a sense of solidity; tall, elegant windows for the first floor; slightly shorter windows for the next storey; and finally, square windows at the top – as if to create a full stop.

Another aspect of Georgian window design was the shop front. Large elegant windows were applied to entice the prospective customer: bowed, barrel-shaped, arched or plain, all with delicate wooden glazing bars and all in perfect balance with the rest of the building – unlike the shop fronts of today which seem to leave gaping voids in often very old and beautiful buildings.

It was in the Georgian period that the timber tradition, which had prevailed from the Middle Ages, gradually came to an end. Bricks were infinitely preferable to wood. Not only had timber become scarce but the planners were well aware that a wooden city was a serious fire hazard.

Left: Barlestone Manor House, built in the 18th century.

Right: Manor House, Snarestone is a fine example of 18th-century Georgian architecture.

Overleaf: A watercolour of Bosworth Square by Doug Lewis. During the final phases of the enclosure movement (1750s) and the construction of the Ashby Canal (1794–1805) the town, in particular The Square, underwent a gradual process of Georgian renovation. Many of the existing Elizabethan timber-framed buildings were given 18th-century frontages, such as No.3 Main Street built c.1780. The warped beams and low ceilings of the older structure are clearly visible once inside. Next door, at No.7 is a signed and dated brick '1789 EW'. The three-storey buildings on the other side of the road (No. 2 and No. 4 Main St) were built c.1790, while Nos. 5–7 The Square (the building society and antiques shop) are earlier, around the third quarter of the 18th century. Softleys, on the corner of The Square and Station Road, was built in 1794, but Richmond House to its left came a little later, c.1810. The brick chapel, hidden behind these buildings, also belongs to the period, c.1794.

G O P S A L L   H A L L

IT SEEMS ALMOST INCOMPREHENSIBLE THAT BEHIND THE SLEEPY VILLAGE OF CONGERSTONE, ACROSS

THE FIELDS FROM CASTLE FARM, THERE ONCE STOOD A PALACE. WITH ITS SHARP STONE EDGES

CUTTING THROUGH THE SPRAWL OF TREES AND HUGE CORINTHIAN COLUMNS RISING OUT OF THE

RAMBLING COUNTRYSIDE, GOPSALL HALL WAS A TRULY ARRESTING BUILDING, DOMINATING THE

LANDSCAPE FOR MILES AROUND, YET NOTHING OF IT NOW REMAINS.

The estate of Gopsall was huge – 33,000 acres in all, spread over eleven counties. It absorbed many of the surrounding villages, and formed the social and economic nucleus for a very large community. Its meticulously groomed parkland carved out the simple countryside between Congerstone and Twycross, rolling out and refining what had been, for many years, agricultural land.

Three carriage drives, lined with trees, swept through the park onto the gentle rise where the Hall and its formal gardens were seated. The most impressive of these was an avenue of oak and elm trees, hundreds of yards wide and two miles long, which marched in a straight line from the Hall to Shackerstone. (A more recent plantation of trees follows the same route today.)

Beautiful specimens of beech, cedar, oak, lime and many other species were scattered all over the park. Grand temples, pavilions, follies, statues and fountains were conspicuously placed in a wooded copse or at the end of a rolling grass vista to achieve the full picturesque effect. Fine herds of deer could often be seen grazing between the clumps of dark woodland.

Extending out from the west elevation of the building was a small village of outhouses, stables, coach houses, store-rooms, glasshouses and vineries, gun rooms, blacksmiths' shops and potting sheds, along with thirty small cottages to house the staff and under-gardeners. Some remain but most have long since gone.

To the casual observer the imprint of this sumptuous landscape will be all but invisible; only to the inquisitive are hidden relics of the Hall's glorious past revealed.

Gopsall Hall was built in 1747, replacing an earlier Jacobean structure. The earliest records of the Manor of Gopsall, or Goppeshull, date back to 11th-century Norman England when it was held, along with the village of Twycross, by Earl Henry de Ferrers, who had come over with William the Conqueror in 1066. Several buildings have occupied the site since but there is little or no trace of their existence. Now farmland, the area is used only for grazing and cannot be ploughed due to the many bricks buried in the soil.

The estate was bought in May 1685 by Humphrey Jennens, a wealthy industrialist from Birmingham who had made his fortune from selling ironmongery. But it was his grandson, Charles Jennens, who had the Hall built some 60 years later.

Above: Shackerstone Walk – an avenue of oak and elm trees that led from the hall to the village of Shackerstone.

Right: The south front of Gopsall Hall (1747) with its portico of six Corinthian columns and pediment bearing a sculpture of a ship in a storm.

Charles Jennens was an artistic man. Many of his friends were artists, musicians and poets who between them established a brotherhood named the 'Gopsall Circle'. It was during this time that he met George Frederick Handel, who frequently visited the Hall. It has been suggested that part of the 'Messiah' was written here, although in fact Handel composed his masterpiece, based loosely on a libretto composed by Jennens in 1741, several years before the new Hall was constructed.

The Hall was built at a time when Georgian England had become preoccupied with the Renaissance and the principles of Classical architecture laid out by Palladio. The austere ashlar stonework and strict symmetrical plan met all the criteria of Palladian architecture, as did the huge portico of six Corinthian columns which dominated the south front. Above the portico was a pediment, carved out of white stone, bearing a sculpture of a ship in a storm, which formed the principal feature on the facade added at a later date by Lord Howe. The two wings, at either side of the building, formed the chapel and library respectively.

The whole house was richly and elaborately designed with a profusion of chandeliers, commemorative busts and elegant fireplaces. The chapel was described as being the most beautiful in England with its vast stuccoed ceiling chased with intricate patterns of flowers. The panelling, seats and altar were carved from Lebanese cedar, as was the swooping eagle pulpit. Boscobel oak was used for the communion table. The lofty ceiling of the library rose up from the moulded curving cornice and the room was arranged with reading chairs and occasional tables set around the marble fireplace. With its collection of rare books, Gopsall's library was considered, at that time, the best in the Midlands.

Gopsall Hall was inherited by the Howes at the beginning of the 19th century. During their occupancy they displayed a large and notable collection of original art. Paintings by Rembrandt and Canaletto adorned the walls of the picture gallery alongside portraits of the family and friends. A large painting of Handel hung in the dining room, and above the fireplace in the chapel, an image by Van Dyck of the Crucifixion.

At the beginning of the 20th century the Hall was owned by the 4th Earl Howe, and in 1902 the family was honoured by the presence of King Edward VII, Queen Alexandra and their daughter, Princess Victoria. Prior to this visit, extensive alterations were undertaken which involved the total re-decoration of the house and the restoration of Shackerstone Station for their arrival. It is hard to imagine the 10,000 strong welcoming committee lining the route from Congerstone to the Hall, such a huge event it was in that era of peaceful and mostly uneventful village life. A solid silver bath was especially commissioned by Earl Howe for the King's suite.

The gamekeepers at Gopsall reared many pheasant and partridge for the shooting seasons which proved very popular with the gentry and visiting royalty. This all came to an end after World War One when the Earl sold the estate to Lord Waring of Waring and Gillow, who rarely stayed at the Hall.

The 4th Earl was a kind and generous benefactor. He built many small but dignified cottages for his workers, some of which still stand in outlying villages, such as Twycross and Sibson. These charming dwellings are characterised by their eyebrow windows.

During World War Two the Hall was requisitioned by the army and used as a training centre, under the ownership of the Crown. This period marked a rapid decline in the condition of the building, with many of the magnificent trees being felled as part of the war effort. The damage caused by the military, and a lack of funds, marked the end of an era and the Hall sadly fell victim to demolition, disappearing from the landscape in 1951.

The splintered bones of a Greek temple are still visible in the woods. The large pillars have now crumbled and are lying lost in the undergrowth. This building is sometimes confused with another more substantial temple, which Jennens had built to commemorate his friend, Edward Holdsworth, who died in 1746. The dome of that temple which collapsed in 1835, carried a Statue of Religion carved by Louis Francois Roubiliac, recognised at that time as the finest sculptor in England. Inside stood a cenotaph, inscribed in Latin, which now stands alongside the Statue in the Belgrave Museum, Leicester.

For just over 200 years Gopsall Hall graced this small portion of Leicestershire. It was one of the most striking yet endearing buildings that our county had to offer and now it has gone. Apart from the remains of the small temple and a few outhouses, there is nothing to show of the overwhelming magnificence that once was.

It seems appropriate to sum up in the words of Bill Bryson, from his book *Notes from a Small Island*:

"The British have more heritage than is good for them. In a country where there is so astonishingly much of everything it is easy to look on it as a kind of inexhaustible resource."

Above: Earl Howe.

Right: The Greek temple built by Charles Jennens to commemorate his friend Edward Holdsworth, who died in 1746. The Statue of Religion on top of the dome was carved by Louis Francois Roubiliac, recognised at the time as being the finest sculptor in England. Watercolour by Phil Kenning.

THE VICTORIAN PERIOD

1801 — 1901

DOMESTIC ARCHITECTURE OF THE 19TH CENTURY

CAN BE CLASSIFIED CRUDELY INTO TWO FORMS:

REGENCY AND REVIVAL.

REGENCY

Regency architecture follows on from the Georgian period, spanning the first thirty years of the 19th century. Most buildings were of brick and covered with painted plaster or stucco, giving an air of the Mediterranean. Houses of the Regency era are very elegant, with lavish designs adorning frontages whilst maintaining the symmetry and proportion of Georgian architecture.

The use of stucco was an idea imported from Italy, and it was used to imitate stone. Carvings, columns and cornices could all be reproduced

with stucco at a fraction of the cost of stone. The Grey House on the corner of Church Street was given a false stucco front in about 1830 hiding the 16th-century timbered farmhouse that still constitutes a considerable part of the house. The Dixie Arms also received a stucco front around 1824. The inner core of the building, constructed at a different level and angle, could well be part of the former 16th-century Bull's Head Inn.

The bow window was also a very fashionable feature at this time and could be seen in several shops around Bosworth in the 18th century and one can still be seen on the front of No.18, The Square.

GOTHIC REVIVAL

The Gothic Revival developed from a romantic hunger to escape the dirt and squalor brought by the Industrial Revolution. Many people felt a great unease as machines displaced the workforce, so they attempted to bring back medieval craft techniques.

It was a powerful movement that brought with it violent dispute. To the Victorian traditionalists it seemed a static, even regressive philosophy, and it wasn't long before two camps evolved: the classical versus the medieval.

Throughout the last half of the 19th century and the first twenty years of the 20th, a small compromise was met in that most ecclesiastical or scholastic buildings took the Gothic style (the old schoolhouses of Park Street, Market Bosworth and Main Street, Carlton, are fine examples, as is the old rectory at Sutton Cheney). Many other buildings were built in a Greco-Classical style, such as town halls and business premises – for example the old bank chambers in The Square, Market Bosworth. Although the Gothic Revival saw designs drawn from the Tudor, Elizabethan and Jacobean periods, the Queen Anne style was the preferred choice of the speculative builders. It was this style that Charles Tollemache Scott adopted for most of his buildings. The Water Tower, East Lodge and Home Farm are all in the Queen Anne Revival style.

Above: The Water Tower built by Charles Tollemache Scott in the 1880s, in the Queen Anne style.

HELP OUT MILL

THE MILL OWES ITS EXISTENCE TO THE RIVER

SENCE WHICH RISES NEAR BARDON HALL ABOUT

14 MILES AWAY.

There has been a mill on this site since 1313, possibly much earlier, and the importance of this little river can be gauged by the fact that at one time it powered eleven mills along its length before joining the Anker near Atherstone.

The River Sence was also a useful trout stream and in the early part of the 20th century, Mr Robinson, the river keeper who lived at Keeper's Cottage in Gibbet Lane, Bilstone maintained the river in good order and guarded the fish from poachers.

In recent times the history of Help Out Mill is linked to the Timms family who lived here from 1734 to 1971. Elijah Timms, the last of the line, was an eccentric bachelor who died in 1971, and many of the family are buried in Swepstone churchyard. In the 1950s the Swepstone parishioners levelled the gravestones in a large part of the churchyard to facilitate mowing the grass but Elijah resolutely refused to have his ancestral stone moved and it now stands in lonely splendour near the church gate. The mill provided flour and provender to many establishments in the neighbourhood and Elijah Timms would drive around in his horse and trap collecting cheques and delivering invoices – he was a first class business man. In later years he bought an ancient motor car which he drove at a sedate 20 m.p.h. but in the 1960s he had a 'rush of blood' to the head and bought a brand new car. However, he then decided that the new car was too good to drive on the road so he kept it in the garage and continued driving the old one. On his death the whole estate was sold and the 'new' car, now fairly old in years, was sold with minimal mileage and in mint condition.

In spite of his eccentricity everyone liked him – he would stop and talk to anyone and he was a mine of information on local history. Although

something of a miser, he lavished money on his beloved mill and in 1923 he spent large sums of money installing new machinery to bring the mill up to date. During the sale week in 1972, potential buyers flocked to the mill to see what was on offer and all remarked on the magnificent condition of the mill and machinery while most other items were neglected.

Adjoining the mill is a fine Georgian-style house dating back to 1734, which has pleasing views over a lovely river bridge and a large open field. In the grounds surrounding Help Out Mill are many ancient trees, which one would expect to find on a property held by one family for more than 240 years.

In the 1870s Shackerstone Station was a railway junction, and a branch line ran to Loughborough passing close behind the mill. A siding was built to serve the mill, thus enabling flour and provender to be sent anywhere in the country.

T. B. Heathcote

Above: The Help Out Mill, parts of which date to 1811, adjoins a fine Georgian house of 1734.

THE WATER TOWER

THE WATER TOWER ON THE EDGE OF MARKET BOSWORTH IS A PROMINENT LANDMARK AND A STRUCTURE OF ARCHITECTURAL BEAUTY.

Directly behind it marches an avenue of lime trees leading from Bosworth Hall to the Wilderness garden and in front is the sweeping expanse of the Country Park.

In 1885 Charles Tollemache Scott and his wife Lady Agnes bought the Bosworth Hall Estate. Improvements commenced forthwith on the property, its grounds, and in the town in which it stood. Scott was keen to restructure the park and to renovate and restore many of the existing buildings, with ideas to build a few new ones.

The imposing three-storeyed Italianate belvedere tower seems somewhat elegant for a structure primarily required to pump water to the hall, but Scott, after inheriting the crumbling remains of the Dixie dynasty, was determined to make his mark.

Lying directly in the shadow of the tower are the remains of the old kitchen garden, situated a modest distance from the house. The garden would have been divided into four central quarters by gravel paths and enclosed by broad borders, but stepping through the arched entrance today, one sees only a stretch of barren and forgotten ground. In its heyday in the late 19th century, it would have been a hive of industry. A large variety of vegetables would have been grown in the plots to feed the owner's family and his servants, while bedding plants, exotic flowers and fruits of all descriptions flourished in the heated greenhouses behind. The north-facing wall was liberally adorned with fruit bushes, rambling blackberries, redcurrants and gooseberries, while across the front wall of the orangery, a magnificant grapevine spread its gnarly fingers.

Bosworth Hall served as an infirmary from 1932 up to 1987 when it was sold to a hotelier eager to renovate the building and convert it into a prestigious hotel. This marked the end of the kitchen garden and it fell into disuse and neglect. There were plans for redevelopment on the site and, sadly, the old greenhouses and central orangery were torn down. Although the project never came to fruition it left the garden redundant and the main entrance arch strangely detached. This once splendid building continues to slip into a possibly irretrievable state of disrepair, with the bricks flaking in the winter winds and hapless shrubs tearing at the foundations.

Above: The grand stone-arch which once formed the entrance to the glass-houses – pencil drawing by Alan Spencer.

Right: The Water Tower was built by Charles Tollemache Scott in the 1880s, in the Queen Anne style. The statue in the tower is possibly of Rhea, Greek goddess of countless fruits and produce known to man. The canopy above is in the shape of a shell suggesting a water theme. Queen Anne buildings were invariably decorated with sunflowers, an example of which can be seen, carved in stone, on the east facing wall.

Overleaf: Sutton Cheney Rectory

New Developments

THE INCREASING DEMAND FOR NEW HOUSING

CONTINUES TO SPREAD ITS SEARCHING ROOTS INTO

THE HEART OF RURAL VILLAGES.

When in keeping with the surrounding buildings, new developments can benefit a village, such as The Grange along Barton Road in Market Bosworth. This elegant building set in its own space is perfectly suited to the site. Unfortunately this is not always the case.

There is a regrettable tendency for many houses to be crammed into a site more suited for one. With developers intent on making as much money as they can, buildings are thrown together as quickly and cheaply as possible and little attention is given to quality of design. The charm and indiosyncratic beauty that has, throughout history, distinguished our domestic architecture from any other country in the world has all but disappeared from the average house, which seems to be inferior in almost every way to its predecessors. But experts maintain that the traditional, solid-brick house of the Georgian/Victorian period is now obsolete. In terms of energy efficiency these structures are considered wasteful by environmentalists and have no place in the modern world. But in fact this couldn't be further from the truth.

The life expectancy of many modern estate houses is a mere 40-60 years, despite the fact that they are built using immense amounts of fossil fuels. Plastic windows, doors and guttering, features that go hand in hand with modern development, are not expected to last more than 10-20 years, yet wooden windows and doors and cast-iron guttering will last well over a life-time, providing that they are well maintained. Bricks that used to be produced in a local brickworks and delivered to the site by low-energy horse power are now shipped across the country in petrol-guzzling lorries. The soft lime mortar that they were bedded into allowed them to be re-used time and again. This is certainly not the case with modern bricks bedded into hard cement mortar which, incidentally, uses far more energy to produce than lime mortar. Even the modern foam insulation materials we use to conserve heat are made from oil, while plasterboard is imported from Europe, expending yet more energy. There are houses in this area that were built over four centuries ago and even earlier in the case of Church Cottage, Cadeby (1472) which will last generations to come, but many of the houses constructed in the 1960s and 70s will probably be demolished within another 50 years. So it seems, in the long term, we are in fact wasting more energy than we are saving.

However, it is not all doom and gloom. While many houses are still built in the same characterless, box-like way there is a growing fashion for adopting older styles of architecture, not just in motif, such as a mock-Tudor gable or a few out-of- place Greek columns for instance, but to the extent that houses are being constructed with re-claimed bricks and roofed with thatch to look indistiguishable from the real thing. In fact there have been recent plans for the development of several thatched dwellings in Market Bosworth.

Architects are beginning to draw designs from many different periods of architecture, in much the same way as the Gothic revivalists did in the 19th century. But it is the Georgian style of architecture, with its neat, symmetrical grandiosity, that has proved so popular with designers and consumers alike. And contrary to what the experts would have us believe, the solid brick-built house still seems to have its place.

The houses on Sycamore Way leading off Cedar Drive in Market Bosworth typify the recent trend for revivalist designs. These pleasant neo-Georgian town houses, similar in style to those on Market Mews, the development that replaced the cattle market, work well with the local vernacular, such as the Georgian houses in the Square and the Dower House, and fit in well with the surroundings. A similar development can be seen at Sibson, but here the huge houses dwarf the humble village dwellings and contrast sharply with Earl Howe's 'eye-brow window' cottages.

But while some are finding solace in the past others are searching for new ideas of what their homes should look like. There is a rising popularity for minamilistic designs, with function and practability the main consideration around which exterior design concepts are hung. Interestingly, in much the same way as the medieval, multipurpose 'openhall' house, architects are incorporating fewer internal partitions into the structure allowing the owner freedom to customise his/her own living space. Another major factor in modern design is the consideration of light. Garden House, Back Lane, screened from view in the old Club House garden was built very much with these concepts in mind and proves that modern, forward-looking, architecture can be successful. The building works well because it doesn't impose itself arrogantly on the surroundings and care has been taken to marry it to the contours of the site. Perhaps its best feature is the large, open-plan lounge on the first floor. With east, south and west facing windows the room is flooded with light all day long, creating a feeling of warmth and spaciousness, with fine views over the surrounding countryside.

In this new millennium we are forced to accept change and our once peaceful villages have to move with the times. Market Bosworth itself is in line for some major development: a marina is soon to spring up alongside the canal at the end of Station Road, a development of 80 houses on the site of Palgrave Brown has been put forward, while plans to turn Godsons Hill, and many of the surrounding fields, into a golf course are always lurking in the background. The inevitable increase in traffic that will come as a result will undoubtedly lead to the construction of a bypass to eleviate a problem that has cursed so many quaint little towns across the country. The seeming need for the countryside to be urbanised is perhaps getting out of hand and so we have to ask ourselves – where is the line to be drawn?

south

Above: South elevation of Garden House, Back Lane, Market Bosworth. Architect – Alan Spencer.

Right: During spring a winding trail of crocuses leads up to the houses on Sycamore Way from Cedar Drive.

COMMUNITY

ONE THEORY SUGGESTS THAT A BIG BANG BEGAN THE UNIVERSE. EXPANDING CLOUDS OF GAS AND DUST CLUSTERED TOGETHER AND EVOLVED INTO COMMUNITIES — GALAXIES, STARS, PLANETS AND MOONS.

The force of gravity holds everything in place, each dependent on the other for existence and survival, yet still evolving, never completely stable and unchanging.

In a similar way human life on Earth expanded around the globe, clustering together to evolve into communities – nation states, cities, towns and villages. The force of civilisation too holds everything in place, each dependent on the other for existence and survival, yet still evolving, never completely stable and unchanging.

Civilisation requires trust and co-operation: an acceptance that 'civic' matters can be placed in the hands of a minority who are willing to act for the good of the community, whilst the majority pursue those activities necessary to produce wealth and security for family and community. History shows that this formula has been successful, not least in developing and maintaining the communal spirit that gives Bosworth and its cluster of surrounding villages their strong appeal today.

Although local government is now merged with Hinckley, from 1894 the Market Bosworth area operated as a self-governing Rural District. Early in the 20th century the community boasted its own Council Offices, Fire Service, Police Station, Magistrates' Court, 'ash cart' and 'posy-wagon' (to collect those unlovely unwantables its residents continually produced both day and night), Parish and Parochial Councils, schools, churches, post offices and shops in most villages, policemen on bicycles, doctors visiting the sick day and night, pubs, clubs and societies. Fortunately not all are gone, but much has changed at the beginning of this new century. So what remains and what has gone?

Lord Raymond Hylton once defined, in the House of Lords, the 'seven Ps' required for the perfect village: public house, primary school, post office, parson, public transport, phone box and petrol station. None of our local villages can still claim all seven of these attributes, but despite this community spirit still thrives, and this chapter explores The Community.

The Chairperson of Sheepy Magna talks about her role today, while holders of the 25-year long-service medal in the Fire Service and two local police constables discuss their past and future. From opposite ends of the Christian religious spectrum the Anglican United Benefice and the Elohim Church explain how they work alongside both Roman Catholic and the non-conforming churches.

The scope of communication now seems limitless and while the old ways still thrive – from gossip to parish noticeboards to New Aspect to local newspapers – new and complex ways advance. New Aspect occupies an important place in spreading community news and views and the postmaster of Newton Burgoland talks about the ever-changing electronic face of the Post Office.

Education and health are vital keystones in the structure of all successful communities and whilst many village schools have gone, some still remain, so the stories of the primary schools are related alongside those of the Bosworth Community College, the Dixie Grammar School and Twycross House independent school.

The Infirmary closed long ago and where local councillors once deliberated, private nurses now care for the elderly and ailing. Most would have been pleased to see the end of the workhouse – Westhaven Bosworth Union House, 'The Spike' – and its conversion into private houses and a residential home for the elderly. However, civic pride was hurt when Orchard House was later axed and sold into private hands. A retired District Nurse recalls some of her local memories; and NHS services that once required a visit to an A & E department are now available from the expanded and developed local surgeries.

The administration – civil servants, councillors, local government, bureaucrats, called by whatever name, supportive or insulting, this oft unsung, unloved but stabilising force – does hold everything in place, does provide the civic backbone for this community.

But mention is made too of just a few of the other people – the extraordinary 'ordinary' ones – who, past or present, flesh out community, make this place special, interesting, memorable, desirable: a place where many choose to live.

Right: Ben Toft, Avril Hatton, Louis Massarella, Mr Poulson, Norman Oldacre, Graham Pearson, Ciss Glyde, Eleanor Hodgson, Roger Jackson, Calley Wilkinson, Denise Gravell, John Nadin, Brian Hunt, Margaret Clark, Rosemary Rickard, Walter Rickard, Bruce Coleman, Father Terry Fellows, Jürgen Schwiening, Frank Calderwood, Eugene Salvador, Erica Tomlinson, Ruth Schwiening, John Thorp, James Churchill, Stan Fell, John Rawson, Peter Folwell, Joe David, Napoleonic soldier, Rosamunde Thompson, Brian Oakley, Judy Hendicott, Alan Spencer, Tom Powell, Pam Nadin, Eleanor Hodgson.

D O G G Y   B I N S   &   B O T T L E   B A N K S

TAXES ON WINDOWS, HAIR POWDER, ARMORIAL

BEARINGS, EVEN AN UNWORKABLE TAX ON CLOCKS,

AND FINALLY... INCOME TAX!

"Not content with squeezing us dry in 1799, it is now actually proposed to place a tax on incomes! It is a vile, Jacobin, trumped-up jack-in-office piece of impertinence. Is a true Briton to have no privacy? Are the fruits of his labour and toil to be picked over, farthing by farthing, by the pimply minions of bureaucracy?" *

Many might agree with this 1799 description of the Government when John Knyveton, surgeon in the King's Fleet, railed against William Pitt's new tax on income. But money was needed to fund the ongoing war with Napoleon, and how else could a Government pay for defence and other public services, if not by taxes?

But surely our local government today cannot be so reviled?

Certainly Peggy Hall, a proud Lancashire lass, and Chairperson of Sheepy Parish Council for more than 30 years – "because no-one else wants to sit in this seat..." – doesn't fit this angry description. She's more like everyone's ideal school teacher, which for many years she was – perhaps valuable experience when controlling unruly Parish Council discussions on planning issues at Wellsborough, doggy bins in Sutton Cheney, or bottle banks at Upton?

'Parish Council' no longer means the church parish, of course, but, as Peggy explains, church affairs do matter:

"We need a new burial ground because the old one at the church is now full. I checked back in the records and in 1976 it seems that the Queen very graciously gave the churchyard to the Parish Council – so we now have to maintain it! Perhaps the Queen would like to come along with her spade sometime...?

"The Parish Council have helped to improve local traffic problems and to stop the River Sence from flooding. The children loved the floods, of course; wellies full of water, they'd wait around for a car to get stuck and then offer to push it out for two shillings. After someone drove off without paying you had to pay before the push – even our own daughter caught us: 'Two bob or get your own feet wet!'"

Peggy and her husband, Os, remember the first Field Day the Parish Council organised for the village:

"There was a Scout Band, a Silver Band, football and sack races and we hired a fair, but we had to run it – Os was turning the handle on the kiddies' roundabout from eight in the morning till eight at night! For one of the Field Days the chap living in the vicarage made this huge dinosaur – pulled around on a low loader – and a local lad used to crawl up and hang out of the teeth!

"The Field Days didn't last but we did have some cricket matches – the farmer didn't allow us to mow the outfield after a certain time, so the ball used to get lost, and we had a chap stationed on the bridge to fish out the balls that went in the river.

"But none of that has survived – lives are changing, and the local characters are gone. Two postmen, Charlie Bates and Lenny Ling, were domino kings: they'd sit in the pub and if you got mixed up with them you soon got fleeced – they'd have all your money. I think they knew every chip on the edge of those dominoes! The village has more than doubled in size – lots of new houses, and a new restaurant where the mill office was. They used to keep steam lorries there and Os remembers these puffing up the hill to Orton, billowing smoke and frightening the cows.

"There are still some small businesses around – the printer and glass engraver, a carpenter and a builder. For 2000 we all helped to make a millennium rose garden and a new weathervane for the church tower – with a sheep's head for Sheepy, and MM for the millennium. When the sun shines and the vane turns in the wind it flashes like a morse lamp onto our sitting-room wall – just to remind us we're next to the church."

Right: The tithe barn, Sheepy Magna. Over 140 foot long, this timber-framed construction is thought to have stood on the site since the early 16th century. The whole structure, underneath the tiled, half-hipped roof consists of 6 bays constructed of axe-hewn oak. A tithe was the tenth part of the annual parish profit derived from a given piece of land. This was an ancient custom established to support the church and the tithe barn was where the grain, representing the portion payable by the parish, was stored. The ethereal calm amongst the mass of oak timbers is almost spiritual, with the awe-inspiring presence of a cathedral.

* From: *A Truly Honest Man* by Peter Foss and Timothy Parry

TWYCROSS HOUSE SCHOOL

"FROM THE BEGINNING WE SAW OUR FARMHOUSE KITCHEN AS A CENTRAL PLACE IN THE SCHOOL, SINCE EVERYONE EATS THERE. WE ATTACH IMPORTANCE TO THE PROVISION OF A HEALTHY, PALATABLE, OLD-FASHIONED COOKED LUNCH FOR ALL OF THE PUPILS. LUNCHTIME HAS BECOME ONE OF THE MOST IMPORTANT PERIODS OF THE DAY."

Opened by Mrs Kirkpatrick in 1977 as a small independent school with just six pupils, Twycross House School has been allowed to grow – "in easy stages, year by year, piecemeal, a bit like Topsy" – and now has over 300 pupils.

Starting at 5 years old at The Hollies pre-prep school, children then cross the road to Twycross House when they are 8 years of age, and most spend the rest of their schooldays there, leaving finally at 18 for university.

As Mr Kirkpatrick says: "Because they have been in the same environment and with the same friends and staff for possibly ten years, they become secure and confident and there is beneficial behaviour. Bullying? Well, verbal bullying can happen in any community but staff are very sensitive and vigilant about that. Drugs? We have had just one occasion in 1992, when three 'speed' tablets were brought into school by a pupil – sadly, the inevitable consequence of that had to be expulsion."

The Kirkpatricks fell in love with the old 1703 Queen Anne country residence and decided to start a school there because they wanted to work together, educating children in a close environment. They had no fixed philosophy for the school, but did believe in creating an environment in which education, as they understood the word, could take place properly. Their aim was to maintain the highest possible standards of teaching in a caring environment pervaded by underlying Christian principles. Small numbers keep relationships close, with everyone intimately involved in all aspects of school life.

"We have lived in the middle of the house from the beginning, which helps to make it rather like a home. We try to make it like a family house – the Old Hall lends itself to this, especially in winter, when at the first hint of snow a log fire is lit. Unfortunately, in 1995, we had an accidental fire at the top of the house, caused by a builder's blow-lamp, and lost both libraries and a teacher's study – but the school opened as usual the following morning."

The Kirkpatricks try to meet individual preferences with small class sizes, and a high teacher to pupil ratio helps to make this possible. For example, full A Level courses are provided in minority subjects, such as Greek, regardless of numbers. Latin and Greek were introduced to the school by the one-time captain of the Birmingham Bullets basketball team, Steve Assinder, who is now Headmaster at The Hollies, and churchwarden at Twycross Church.

"We believe that teachers contribute most if they have the scope to do things in their own way. Of course, forty teachers do not agree about everything, but we hope that we all, more or less, pull in the same direction. We do expect consistency and rigour in regard to academic standards, in the care and concern

Above: Twycross House School, formerly the dower house to Gopsall Park. This front elevation was built in 1703, in the Queen Anne style, with red and blue chequered brickwork.

for the children and the mutual respect and reciprocal courtesy between pupil and teacher, but otherwise we believe children benefit from contact with a rich variety of human kinds and minds."

All manner of sporting and cultural activities take place on the playing fields, in the sports hall and swimming pool. The girls have an outstanding record of winning the Nuneaton Schools League in hockey and netball in most age groups over the past few years, and the boys have had a similar success in cricket. Recently, using the drama and music rooms for rehearsals, a cast of almost one hundred produced and performed a Gilbert and Sullivan operetta in the Old Stables.

Intellectual freedom and social benefits are part of such a privileged education, so should these Twycross House children be envied by other schoolchildren in the area? Perhaps, although all of today's children, wherever they are educated, do enjoy activities, privileges and lifestyles that would have been unimaginable and completely unattainable in the early part of the 20th century.

The needs of all children, then and now, have not changed – care and concern, mutual respect and reciprocal courtesy – and Education, Education, Education.

Above: An old copper beech tree in the grounds of Twycross House School.

DR ROBERT PULL

IN A QUIET CORNER OF ST PETER'S CHURCHYARD, MARKET BOSWORTH, PARTLY HIDDEN BY A YEW TREE AND OVERGROWN WITH GRASS, LIES THE GRAVESTONE OF DR ROBERT PULL WHO LIVED IN THE TOWN DURING THE EARLY PART OF THE 18TH CENTURY.

He was a well-respected member of the community and was documented by John Throsby, a well-known local historian of that era, who stated that "no man stood higher in the opinion of the open-mouthed multitude swallowing pills of a quack than Pull".

On a pleasant spring afternoon amid the throng of crowds attending Market Bosworth's May Fair, Dr Pull collapsed suddenly whilst standing beside the butcher's stall. His wife, assuming that he was dead, insisted on him being interred that same night.

By the light of the waning moon a villager took a short cut through the churchyard, past the looming tower, back to his home. He claimed to have heard strange rasping noises coming from the direction of the new grave. For fear of his mysterious story being disbelieved, he did not report it until the following day.

When the coffin was opened the next morning, they found that the body of Dr Pull had moved on to its front with "much blood about the vein in his arm". In those days it was routine to open a vein on the occurrence of sudden death, perhaps to confirm that the person was actually dead. It would appear that Dr Pull's was one of the first recorded incidents of a person being buried alive.

Above: The gravestone of Dr Robert Pull.

Right: A view of the graveyard from St Peter's tower.

STAN FELL'S POST OFFICE

"GD MRNG .. HOW RU?"

"HI .. NCE 2CU .. IM VRY WLL THKS — HOW RU?"

LANGUAGE EVOLVED FROM SIMPLE WORDS SPOKEN FACE TO FACE THROUGH MORE EXPRESSIVE WRITTEN FORMS THAT ALLOWED COMMUNICATION FROM PLACE TO PLACE, FROM GENERATION TO GENERATION AND RIGHT UP TO TODAY'S TEXT MESSAGING ON MOBILE TELEPHONES.

Conversation no longer needs eyeball contact, and the telephone, video, camera, satellites and the Internet make instantaneous communication possible, anywhere in the world, on the moon and even in deep space.

At the beginning of the 20th century the options available for people to stay in touch with one another – the telephone, telegram and letter post – were very limited and all relied on the Post Office. Sophisticated low-cost electronics have dramatically broadened these options for both business and personal communications but most are still dependent in some way on the old Post Office systems. As one of the oldest and most important public services, the Post Office, is, itself, considerably changed, as Stan Fell, postmaster at Newton Burgoland, explains:

"People used to think of the Post Office as old-fashioned, out of date, but with our new electronic facilities this is no longer the case. BT took over the telephones but the new 'Your Guide' system recently tested in Leicestershire's post offices shows just how modern we now are. We thought the Horizon system marvellous – this computerised all Post Office business transactions, saving lots of time and paperwork – but during the trial period the 'Your Guide' system was brilliant and I hope they introduce it across the country in a year or two.

"Just after it was installed, two of our customers thought this new 'toy' would not be able to help them. One needed to find extra hotel accommodation for relatives who wanted to join them on an already booked holiday, and the second needed student digs close to the University of London for her son. I helped them to use the touch screen, entering postcodes and then street names, and in about five minutes each they both went away with printed lists and telephone numbers.

Both called later to say they had been successful, and all courtesy of the Post Office – no charge whatsoever!"

Babbage, the 19th-century inventor, could not have guessed how the principles of his mechanical computer would be applied and used in later years, with IT devices everywhere: complex and powerful computers developing the genome sequence, simple devices at Leicestershire bus stops advising travellers on how many minutes before the next bus arrives, and the tiny post office at Newton Burgoland offering free access to an enormous computer network.

At one time the village post office was also the local telephone exchange – an apt name since along with the village church, shop and pub, the post office was where the local gossip could be exchanged. It was a place where, whilst sending a telegram or renewing the dog licence, you could find out who was doing what to whom, or about the bargain found at the Scouts' jumble sale, and why the cricket team stood no chance next weekend – all invaluable village communication. Unfortunately, as those intimate telephone exchanges disappeared, so too did many of the other invaluable epicentres of village life: the post offices, shops and sometimes even the pub, so Newton Burgoland is indeed fortunate.

Stan Fell's family have run their shop for more than seventy-five years and in the year 2001 celebrated their twenty-five years of post office service for Newton Burgoland and the local 'stone villages' – Swepstone, Shackerstone, Snarestone and Odstone. Although, like the shop, the village is small with only about 450 people, Stan feels that "it's a really good place to live, a true village".

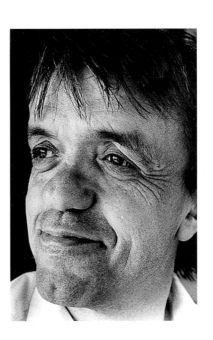

Above: Stan Fell – Newton Burgoland's postmaster.

LADY PENELOPE DIXIE

ON MONDAY 3RD JANUARY 2000, LADY PENELOPE DIXIE DIED PEACEFULLY IN THE COMFORT OF HER MARKET BOSWORTH HOME. MARRIED TO THE 13TH BARONET SIR WOLSTAN DIXIE, WHOSE FAMILY HAD LIVED AT BOSWORTH HALL FOR OVER 300 YEARS, SHE WAS THE LAST IN A LONG LINE AND TOOK TO HER GRAVE ONE OF LEICESTERSHIRE'S MOST ANCIENT FAMILY TITLES.

In 1589 the Bosworth estate was sold to the first Sir Wolstan Dixie, who was Lord Mayor of London in 1585, but it was for his son, the 2nd Baronet Sir Beaumont Dixie, that the present hall was built.

The Hall was sold to the Tollemache Scott family in 1885, so Lady Penelope sadly failed to join the long line of illustrious Dixie women to live at the old house. This was due to the demise of the family wealth during the tenancy of the 11th Baronet, Beaumont Dixie, whose long-suffering wife, Lady Florence Dixie, stated:

"My husband has ventured a large sum, and the last remnant of a once splendid fortune must at once go to pay off this debt."

The family returned to Market Bosworth in 1958 when Sir Wolstan Dixie, and his wife Penelope moved into a house on the edge of Bosworth Park. After the death of the 13th Baronet in 1975, Lady Penelope moved on and the building became 'The Inn on the Park' which was demolished in the mid-1990s and replaced by a housing development.

Lady Dixie enjoyed the town in which she lived and was involved in both community activities and charitable associations. When the Dixie Grammar School was re-founded in 1987 she became its first patron. The Wolstan Preparatory School, named after her husband, has now moved to Temple Hall in Wellsborough.

The family still owns the rights to the Wednesday market and during her lifetime Lady Penelope was often seen wandering between the stalls while her husband sold Bosworth tea towels. She conversed with both shoppers and market traders and dutifully collected her dues. Since Penelope's death, her daughter Caroline has taken on this responsibility. Much in the spirit of her great-grandmother Florence, Penelope Dixie's eldest daughter Eleanor sent a petition to the Queen, after her father's death, requesting the opportunity to put an end to the tradition of the male heir solely owning the right to carry on the family title.

On the day of Penelope Dixie's funeral, a minute's silence was held in the marketplace to respectfully remember the last Lady Dixie of Market Bosworth:

"A chapter ends, yet the name lives on."

Above: Bosworth Hall.

NEW ASPECT

"A NEW MAGAZINE FOR MARKET BOSWORTH AND SURROUNDING DISTRICT: PRODUCED BY A FEW PEOPLE WHO FEEL THERE IS A NEED FOR SOME MEDIUM WHEREBY WE CAN KEEP EACH OTHER INFORMED OF MATTERS OF INTEREST AND IMPORTANCE."

This was how Philip Jenkins opened the editorial of Volume 1, Number 1 – the very first issue of Aspect – in September 1973. He continued by outlining three things that would be needed for it to be successful and to be maintained:

1. Providing material for inclusion.
2. Joining a team of volunteers to compile and distribute the magazines.
3. By buying the magazine at a cost of 5p per issue, preferably by paying 60p in advance for 12 issues.

The rest is history – only the price has changed, now ten times more at 50p, but still worth every penny. Whereas some things do not change – they just advance with development – in the course of more than twenty-seven years there has only been one real halt to the production-line of *Aspect,* following the retirement of John Gladman as Editor in July 1990. Market Bosworth survived, or rather did not survive without complaint, for six months without its community lifeline, until, in February 1991, it was relaunched as *New Aspect.*

New technology had undoubtedly improved and changed the process of production. A successful National Lottery bid was used to purchase hardware that has helped to improve the quality, and colour photocopying for the front cover allows the magazine to be completely produced in-house. However, some things remain the same: it has been calculated that on average a total distance of 12 miles is still walked by the collators on the *New Aspect* treadmill. Walking round and round the table, picking up page by page, they assemble each issue.

There are too many memories and significant happenings to include in this short appreciation, but suffice to say that the 'scoop' of the twenty-seven years was certainly the agreement of the Archbishop of Canterbury to write the editorial 'Points of View' for the December 1999/January 2000 Millennium issue.

If this was the high spot then, perhaps, the lowest – since the Editorial Board had to have their wrists slapped – was the feature, with photograph on the front cover and a suitably excited article inside, on the Bosworth Park alligator.

The responses to this story were completely unexpected, with night visitors to the lake carrying torches and sticks, a special trip from London of an important natural historian who later tried to reclaim his rail fare from *Aspect* and even a mention in some of the national newspapers! Unfortunately no-one had spotted, until it was all too late, that this was an April Fools' issue of *New Aspect!*

And so, as each month rolls by, whilst it may not quite be the sound of printing presses rolling to produce thousands of copies, for each successive issue the dedicated stalwarts cajole, sift, edit, type, produce, assemble and distribute 750 copies, and continue to wear out their shoe leather on our behalf. Thanks to the team, and thanks for *New Aspect.*

Right: Previous front covers of *New Aspect.*

NURSE MARY CRAGG

IN JUNE 2000, 92-YEAR-OLD ELEANOR MARY CRAGG WAS VOTED 'VILLAGE HERO' FOR THE MARKET BOSWORTH AREA, AND IN OCTOBER 2001 SHE WAS HONOURED BY THE MAYOR OF HINCKLEY & BOSWORTH WITH AN ACHIEVEMENT AWARD — "IN RECOGNITION FOR HER CONTRIBUTION TO SOCIETY".

Chatting with Mary during her weekly visit to the local garage, her apple-red cheeks glowed as she smiled and reminisced about the past. In 1948, with the National Health Service still in its infancy, she was the first NHS nurse appointed to serve the Market Bosworth area. Although she retired more than 32 years ago, she still enjoys recounting some of her experiences.

"When I was 19 I lived at Bosworth Hall, more or less as a companion to 11-year-old Daphne Delius. Her governess Mademoiselle Briffaut, who is now 101 years old and still my friend, moved to France as Directress of a girl's boarding school in Amiens. I went with her as Supervisor, but nine years later war was declared, just two days after I had come home for a holiday, and I couldn't go back. I loved France. I didn't unpack my luggage for a long time afterwards, hoping that I might return, but it was not possible. At home people would ask where I was from because I spoke English with a French accent."

Mary loved babies and always wanted to be her own boss, so at the age of 30 she decided to become a general and midwifery nurse. While training at Leicester Infirmary she lodged for a time, along with three other trainees, at a bachelor's vicarage.

"When asked about the accommodation, one of the others replied that it was fine, the vicar was a good man who had filled her with new life – to which Matron immediately replied 'Not literally, I hope!'

"Because I twice failed my driving test I had to start my nursing career cycling round the Fen Lanes on an old bicycle – not pleasant even in those days. One dripping foggy night I had to cross the old deserted Higham airfield and got completely lost. There were no roads or hedges to guide me, and it was only by following the sound of some knocking on a distant door that I thankfully got to a house where a kind lady took me in and gave me some tea."

There were squatters in the old airfield buildings at that time and Nurse Cragg and Dr Baldwin held clinics there: "Some had made really cosy homes, but others were very basic – women would give birth on a mattress on the floor and there was never a cot for the baby. Sometimes a woman would say 'I was Mrs so-and-so last time but now I've changed' and we would have to remind her to think carefully since the birth would be legally noted in whatever name she gave."

Mary helped deliver hundreds of babies in the eight villages that she covered. They are all now grown up, and one is even a grandmother, but not all births were as one might expect: "When arriving at one house I was shown to the mother, holding her newborn baby and sitting on the toilet, where it had been born. Another time, one very frosty night, I was told that the mother was in the garden, and there she was lying on the ground, with her new born baby – and the husband had made no attempt to keep her warm."

Having retired in 1969, Nurse Cragg has spent lots of time helping other people, including knitting bedsocks for the W.I. At least one of her Higham neighbours has cause to thank Mary: "She's a grand old lady – I don't know what we would have done without her. We're many years younger than Mary, and invalids, but she used to do our shopping every week."

Playing Scrabble against herself – "to keep my mind going" – until recently Mary enjoyed driving – "my wheels gave me my independence". Her 20-year-old 'Q' registered Mini was finished in British Racing Green – perhaps the colour explaining why she used to enjoy driving it so fast?

This remarkable, attractive 92-year-old lady never married, and she comments, with a mischievous twinkle in her eyes, that one of her friends thinks this may be why she was able to enjoy such an active life – "You've never had a man to knock you about!" Mary might agree but suspects that her daily glass of sherry also helps!

Right: Nurse Mary Cragg.

THE PRACTICE

A PURGING MIXTURE	*2s. 6d.*
A DRAUGHT	*1s.*
A GLYSTER	*2s.*
AN OINTMENT	*6d.*
A DECOLATION	*3s.*
A JULEP	*2s.*
A BOLUS	*6d.*
A BOX OF PILLS	*1s. 6d.* *

PERHAPS IT WOULD BE UNWISE TO SPECULATE ABOUT THE INGREDIENTS, CONSISTENCY, TASTE AND COLOUR OF THESE OLD MEDICINES PRESCRIBED IN 1815 BY FORMER LOCAL PHYSICIAN, JOHN POWER.

Grandson of Robert Power, whose family farmed at Manor Farm, Barlestone for many generations, John Power was also adviser to Joseph Moxon's Public Bath House, built at the end of Back Lane in 1799 for the "...relief of the poor of Bosworth". He therefore undoubtedly contributed, as have all subsequent physicians and doctors in the Bosworth area, to the overall health of the community.

Long after John Power's time, a back room at Beech House, Church Street – now the home of the Schwiening Language School – was used as the surgery by Dr Gordon Kelly, assisted by the receptionist Rosamund Thompson.

Established there in the 1930s the medical practice remained in what would now seem to be very old-fashioned quarters, until a new surgery was built in Back Lane in 1969 – standing for a short time between an abattoir and the public toilet! Long's abattoir has long since gone, as has their butcher's shop in the marketplace, but the public toilet remains, now fortified with its high black railings.

Dr Richard Brittain arrived in Market Bosworth just before the Beech House surgery closed and he was soon able to transfer to the new Back Lane surgery.

"Initially, and for some time, this was run by one doctor and a single receptionist. However, as the local population increased, and as primary care changed towards a more proactive style of medicine, it soon became too small. Therefore, in 1990–91 we decided we needed more facilities to allow in-house treatment procedures, so the present surgery was built around the old one.

"We normally have two doctors consulting, supported by a regular staff of receptionist, secretary and two nurses. However, we regularly have other practitioners here – health visitors, physiotherapists, a dietician, midwife and consultant gynaecologist – so the surgery gets quite busy at times."

"When we moved to Back Lane there was a huge population expansion in Newbold Verdon and Desford so it was decided to extend the medical practice. We relocated all administration to Newbold, opened a surgery in Arnold's Crescent and later built a new one on the site of the old George & Dragon public house. Quite soon there were three doctors consulting but this increased again in 1999, supported by a regular team of receptionist, secretary and nurses."

Doctor Brittain has now retired but the Infirmary was still in place at Bosworth Hall when he arrived in Bosworth, and some of the retired nurses still remember, with pleasure, the new doctor dancing with every nurse in the room at the first dance he attended. The Infirmary has long gone but despite the many changes in the area, Market Bosworth surgery remains essentially a rural practice.

John Power would be amazed, and Dr Kelly would probably be quite envious, to see how things have progressed, and just how extensive are the medical treatments available to patients at these two surgeries today.

---

* From *A Truly Honest Man* by Peter Foss and Timothy Parry

Right: Church Street, leading to Dr Kelly's old surgery at Beech House.

'BEAT BOBBY'

THE WAY THAT CRIMINALS ARE PUNISHED HAS CHANGED DRAMATICALLY. THE REMAINS OF THE FRIGHTENING OLD GIBBET POST CAN STILL BE SEEN NEAR BILSTONE, BUT THE STOCKS AND THE 'LOCK-UP' HAVE LONG SINCE BEEN BRUSHED INTO HISTORY'S DUSTY CORNERS.

The local barber apparently spent so much time in the lock-up at Snarestone village centre that a local wag once printed an ad in the newspaper that this was the only place to get your hair cut!

Even the two cold cells at Warwick House no longer reverberate to the drunken Friday night snores of an inebriated farm hand, nor does the scritch-scratch of the sergeant's pen break the oppressive silence of the Old Police House in the Market Place at Bosworth.

Retired police constable Phil Tebbatt lived at this police house when he first came to Bosworth and he recalls how much the policeman's lot changed during his twenty-seven years as a local bobby.

"People might not know how much of a rural policeman's time was taken up with tasks associated with farming. For example, we had to supervise all sheep dipping – watch and record the whole messy business twice a year, on all local farms. We also did far more during the 1967 outbreak of foot and mouth – not just guarding the farms but supervising the digging of pits and procuring the wood for pyres."

Twice a year all farm records had to be checked – including gun licences. Each year, a police officer had to walk all round the farmer's land and then draw a map showing that it was still safe to shoot there. However, time was also spent on more traditional police duties.

"Our equipment was a bit basic: a whistle, truncheon, handcuffs, the heavy old communications radio – dangerous because the aerial shot up and could poke you in the eye – and of course a bicycle. Being close to the motorways we needed some mobility but it was no good thinking about chasing someone in a car on your bicycle, so the 'Panda' car was introduced. I had two funny incidents in them: at the first ever Carnival Pram Race an out-of-control pram 'speared' the car: and on another occasion two horses which had bolted and pulled down part of a wrought-iron staircase ended up with their hooves on the roof and the stairs through the side of the car!"

Phil was the first local bobby to ask a driver to 'blow into the bag' of the breathalyser. Introduced only two days before, news quickly spread that he was about to try it out, so all his colleagues arrived. The car driver was not aware of any of this – so drunk he could hardly sit up. He failed to see Phil, his sergeant, the traffic police and even a dog handler who all crowded around a headlamp to see if the bag had changed colour.

The breathalyser is still part of the policeman's kit, but the whistle has gone, along with the bicycle. The baton replaced the truncheon; handcuffs are easier to use, and the radio is lighter and more efficent. The uniform is also very different – a jumper and lighter boots. PC 535 Graham Anderson, based at Market Bosworth, comments on rural policing in today's world:

"I always wanted to be a traditional 'beat bobby' working in and with the community, but time only permits a few of the village things nowadays. Civilians have taken over most of the farming duties but as crime increases and our numbers go down we are always short of time and always needed elsewhere. My area is quite large and includes relatively wealthy commuter villages. Today's villains often travel in from neighbouring counties so we like the public to keep their eyes open to help reduce daytime burglaries."

Graham knows that public expectations of the police are still high but also knows that their perception of the number of police on duty at any one time is often way out. The workload is now much heavier, and the problems faced are very different – but there is still the odd moment of light relief:

"I can't think of anything that at some time or other someone hasn't called and asked about – they must think we are a branch of the Citizens' Advice Bureau – we have to laugh sometimes. We also occasionally play a practical joke on a new probationer – we once got one, on night duty, to investigate the report of a suspicious character in the Coalville Cemetery, where we lay in wait for him! And a long time ago we sent a woman probationer to a sheep dip dressed in the silver aluminium suit that was used at that time for scene-of-crime officers – the farmer thought she was mad!"

Phil Tebbatt commented that once the pubs had emptied we could "lock the gates of Bosworth – everyone's gone to bed", but Graham's experience is different: "Now there's something happening 24 hours a day – it never stops".

Above: Snarestone's one time lock-up and the regular residence of Harry Meakin, the local 'Hairdresser and Perfumer'.

THE EARLY DAYS

HANGING ON THE WALL OF THE BLACK HORSE IN THE SQUARE OF MARKET BOSWORTH ARE THREE FADED BLACK-AND-WHITE PHOTOGRAPHS.

The children of St Peter's Church school sit attentively behind their desks facing the camera whilst the teacher stands at the back of the classroom keeping a watchful eye over her pupils. These precious windows to the past reflect a time never to be seen again.

The old primary school at the top of Park Street was bought as a private residence some twenty years ago and was redesigned to accommodate two comfortable living spaces. The earliest part was built in 1848 and ceased to function as a school on the opening of a new building on Station Road in the early 1970s. For over 120 years the walls rang with the laughter of generations of children. Through all weathers they would have trudged along the footpaths and across the fields to Park Street without the luxury of a school bus or the cosy advantage of the four-wheel drive. Miss Tapp was the Headmistress in the 1930s and is remembered as a kind and considerate teacher. For the children who had walked to school on a cold wintry day she would make hot chocolate and let them hang their coats on the guard around the coke-burning stove.

Adjacent to the school building was a water-pump, sensibly kept chained as during the summer the small playground would have been crowded with high-spirited children, glad for the chance of freedom away from their desks. In those seemingly pleasant days it was a safer world for children and with the permission of the teacher they could cross the road for a midday treat. In one of the once thatched cottages on the other side of Park Street was a cobbler, Mr Cooper, whose wife Mary ran a small tuck shop selling sweets such as liquorice laces, sherbet dabs, one penny lucky bags and seaside pebbles. This was long before the days of cars lining the street and motorbikes screaming up the road towards the park. Today the old school on Park Street has fallen silent and stands quietly behind the wrought-iron gate, the distant echoes existing now only in the imagination and in the memories of the older generation.

Built around the same time as St Peter's, the old schools of Carlton and Cadeby still stand, positioned on the outskirts of the villages. The size of these buildings emphasises the change in our social environment. Fifty to a hundred years ago, fewer children attended school and many certainly left at an earlier age, so the buildings were not required to be on the huge scale they are today. Along with St Peter's these buildings are no longer viable for their original use and they too have also been converted to houses.

The village of Congerstone is an exception. Although the school is not as old as the buildings in Bosworth, Carlton and Cadeby, it has maintained its position in the community and continues to educate the younger children of the local villages. An informal layout of chairs and tables now replaces the rows of old lidded desks but the teacher still hopes for a bright and cheerful answer to her 'Good morning, children'. A familiarity exists perhaps in the singing of hymns and chanting of prayers, although the chaos of multi-coloured coats hanging by the door is in stark contrast to the meagre jackets of old draped by the stove.

Pencils, notebooks and the influx of computers have replaced the squeaky slate as the school has entered the modern age. Even the midday dinners are calculated from the computerised attendance record. Would the children peering from the faded sepia of yesteryear long for this modern age – or are we all missing out on a simpler and slower way of life?

Top: 'Hansel and Gretel' rehearsal, 1951 on the roof of the old school on Park Street.
Bottom: Class III, June 1951.

THE SNOW LEOPARD

THEY COME TO THE AUSTERE BUILDINGS OF THE OLD GRAMMAR SCHOOL TO RECEIVE A GOOD EDUCATION. WEARING THE BADGE OF THE SNOW LEOPARD, PART OF THE DIXIE COAT-OF-ARMS, THEY PASS THROUGH THE OLD STONE DOORWAY WHERE EARLIER SCHOLARS LEFT THEIR MARK AS SCRATCHED INITIALS.

Carved above this same Gothic doorway is a saying of the Greek playwright and moralist, Menander: "Education is a good that cannot be taken from mortal man".

Today this might be more simply stated as "a good education is a gift that lasts for ever" – but what *is* a 'good' education?

Although loathing his time here, comparing his eventual departure as – "like getting out of jail", Samuel Johnson was the most famous man to teach in Bosworth. Writing later about the pursuit of wisdom, Johnson noted: "Integrity without knowledge is weak and useless, and knowledge without integrity is dangerous and dreadful".

Perhaps this defines the aim of every teacher – to gift not only knowledge, but also the integrity to use it wisely and conscientiously? Richard Willmott, Headmaster of the Dixie Grammar School, comments about one former pupil, Thomas Hooker, a 16th-century boarder, later known as the 'Father of American Democracy'.

"One of the first to hold a Dixie Scholarship at Emmanuel College, Cambridge and later a Dixie Fellowship, Hooker subsequently followed the Pilgrim Fathers to the New World. In 1638, in a powerful sermon in Connecticut, he preached – 'that the choice of public magistrates belongs unto the people, by God's allowance' and that 'they who have the power to appoint officers and magistrates, it is in their power, also, to set the bounds and limitations of the place unto which they call them'.

"So at a time when in England the Stuarts were denying the people by laying claim to Divine Right, a former Bosworth pupil was proclaiming democratic rights for Americans. And his ideas were echoed, over one hundred years later, in the Declaration of Human Rights – that governments derive 'their just powers from the consent of the governed'."

However, three centuries later the Dixie snow leopard was no longer seen on the blazers of pupils hurrying past the old black railings to attend their lessons. The medieval grammar school had been replaced by Market Bosworth High School and Community College, introduced under the experimental 1960s Leicestershire Plan.

After the abolition of the divisive 11+ examination, the aim of the High School was to provide a 'comprehensive' higher education for all pupils. David Fitt, the school's Vice-Principal, explains:

"Whilst the original principles remain, the school has changed dramatically since the 1960s. There are now over 600 pupils, who transfer to Bosworth College at Desford at the age of 14. In the past it was mainly 'chalk and talk' – blackboard and books, only listening and writing, with pupils' attention soon wandering. Now there are computers and TVs, videos and digital cameras, and very well-equipped laboratories for science and languages – much more variety, and children paying attention for longer."

Technology plays an important part in preparing children for life in today's world – some even e-mail their homework direct to the school. But not all their time is spent in front of a screen; teachers still stand in front teaching, and books and the school library are still equally important. Special support for children with learning or behavioural difficulties is also available, and funding allows time for individual assistance when needed.

"These procedures can also help with discipline, which is now more difficult since no power has been left with the teaching staff. Society is at fault for that, not the teachers. Children are encouraged to question everything, but defining the right line between questioning and recognising acceptable behaviour can be difficult. For example, we know that there is a school litter problem in the town, but surely more parental control is needed to help with this?"

Eventually the snow leopard returned to Bosworth after the High School vacated the old buildings, and the Dixie Grammar School re-opened as an independent school. Ancient and modern stand side by side in today's complex world, both striving to build those subtle relationships with students that allow teachers to provide "...the gift of a good education that lasts for ever".

Above: The front entrance to the Dixie Grammar School.
Right: Market Bosworth High School and Community College.
Previous page: The Dixie Grammar School and the old bank.

THE MOTHER CHURCH

"THE CHURCH OF ENGLAND PROVIDES CLERGY

FOR EVERY PERSON IN EVERY COMMUNITY IN

THE COUNTRY IRRESPECTIVE OF FAITH OR

BELIEF."

"The Clergy are involved in a whole range of activities essential to the community. When you need us, we are there, 7 days a week and 24 hours a day, free of charge...we are the original community service... and we now need your help."

Since medieval times an Anglican church has existed in most towns and villages, marking the English landscape with a pincushion of steeples: historic cold stone buildings, each with its own beauty and each served by a priest living off whatever rent was gathered from the church's glebe land.

This income could be very high – for example, Sheepy parish had the equivalent of £100,000 per annum, but many parishes yielded only meagre livings, with clergy as poor as church mice. The social status and wealth of farmer and clergy alike was judged by their houses – not just the prominent, substantial building where they lived but also by their other properties provided for servants and helpers, like St Peter's Park Street house where the church's widow washer-woman traditionally lived.

But social times and financial tides change and by the mid-20th century many of the big, neglected rectories were sold into private hands. Parish glebe land was exchanged for fixed stipends from the Church Commissioners, but this also meant taking on the responsibility for maintaining the church structure. John Plant, Team Rector for the ten churches in the United Benefice of Market Bosworth and Sheepy, explains the reasons for an appeal for financial support:

"St Peter's Church in Market Bosworth is a good example. It dates from 1325 and like many medieval buildings has seen good and bad times – the repair of the collapsed tower and derelict roof once had to wait until the landowners could afford to pay. Recently the local community raised over £100,000 for renovations and it's probably now in better condition than ever before. However, as an historic building it is subject to an architect's inspection every five years,

and whatever he reports we must complete in the next five years – at a cost of many thousands of pounds per year!"

Add the ongoing running expenses, and the £36,000 that St Peter's has to contribute annually to the Diocese and it is plain to see why the church needs financial help from the community. A recent appeal for 'planned giving' for St Peter's was very successful, but the church is about more than money:

"We do see our churches as the centre of each community. The Victorians filled the churches with pews, taking up space previously used for community gatherings. This led to more church halls – and many dance-floor romances – but it's not just about where people gather. People nowadays are more concerned with this life rather than the after-life – not the old Sunday School idea of the church. So our Alpha courses, the Millennium Men meetings (held in a pub) and the 'Churches Together' initiative – Anglican, Catholic and Free Churches all combining – even the ordination of women, these are all ways in which the church now tries to connect with life as it is lived today."

The Reverend Annette Reed, Team Vicar of the Sheepy group of the same benefice, was one of the first women to be ordained, and serves five churches:

"We only have Anglican churches in my area so we often have people from other denominations in church – for example two Catholics regularly attend Communion. Everyone is welcome. Two of my churches have no church hall, so we encourage people to use these lovely medieval buildings by holding concerts and special themed events – the World War Two weekend was very popular. We have also tried to bring back community activities by opening up more church space at Ratcliffe Culey and by using movable front pews at Sheepy Magna."

And are services changing as churches change? The 1662 Book of Common Prayer is still sometimes used, but whilst the readings still come from the Old and New Testaments, by and large all services now use the contemporary English found in Common Worship 2000. But one change seemingly common to all Anglican churches is the illumination of their steeples at night – perhaps to emphasise that the clergy really are there, seven days a week and twenty-four hours a day.

Above: An example of an Early English church window. Pencil drawing by Doug Lewis.

Right: The floodlit tower and spire of St Peter's Church, Market Bosworth.

LADY FLORENCE DIXIE

IN THE 19TH CENTURY IT WAS FROWNED UPON FOR A WOMAN TO DISPLAY ANY MASCULINE SIDE TO HER PERSONALITY, ESPECIALLY A WOMAN OF HIGH SOCIAL STANDING SUCH AS LADY FLORENCE DIXIE. SHE MARRIED THE 11TH BARONET, BEAUMONT DIXIE, IN 1875 AND WAS THE LAST IN A LONG LINE OF LADY DIXIES TO LIVE AT BOSWORTH HALL.

Florence was a strong and determined character, which became apparent at an early age when she would swap identities with her twin brother James, and insist on riding, swimming and climbing like him. In her twenties it was observed that "she can play a decent game of cricket, write a capital newspaper letter, beat most men at billiards and bivouac as well as any man". Her stubbornness shone through on her meeting with Queen Victoria, when she caused much concern on account of her appearance, and was later reprimanded by the Lord Chancellor who told her to "observe the rules in future". To this she was heard to remark: "I have preferred to keep my hair short and forego the pleasure of drawing rooms".

Literacy was certainly one of Lady Florence's passions. Many of her poems were published in 1902 under the pseudonym 'Darling', and she was the author of a number of books, two of which – *The Land of Misfortune* and *Across Patagonia* – were written in the early 1880s and describe her endeavours in South America. Florence returned with many treasured memories of those foreign climes, and also with a jaguar named 'Affums' who would accompany her on walks across Bosworth Park, much to the alarm of passers-by. After an unfortunate incident involving the killing of several of the Queen's deer she regretfully donated her pet to the zoological gardens in London.

Lady Florence Dixie was described as being emotionally unstable; this disposition was undoubtedly caused by the death of her father when she was 3 years old and the premature and tragic end to her eldest brother's life on the Matterhorn in Switzerland in 1865. She was, however, quite an unusual and a remarkably courageous woman in her day. At the time of the Boer War in the late 19th century she went to South Africa to report on the conflict: however, due to an armistice this assignment turned into a battle of conscience as she became involved in the fight for the freedom of the imprisoned Zulu king, Cetschweyo.

He later stated in a letter to her: "Although you are a lady, you have beaten men in your talking for me. This kindness I shall never forget".

In the grounds of Bosworth Park lies 'Beau Pool' which is named after Lady Florence's husband Beaumont. The last one hundred years has clouded not only the spelling but also the sentiment, which has resulted in the 'Bow Pool' we know today. Beaumont Dixie was a hopeless gambler and was mainly responsible for the demise of the Bosworth Estate, leading to its inevitable sale in 1885 when the Tollemache Scotts began to bring the estate back from its neglected state to its original splendour. Adjacent to the Hall, at the end of an avenue of graceful lime trees, is the Wilderness Garden which holds within its tangle of trees and shrubs a hidden testament to 'Smut', an Old English terrier who was close to Florence's heart. Composed in memory of him is a poem inscribed on his tomb, which is still in evidence today:

Forget Me Not

My little sweet companion, gentle friend,
Oh! Think not lying in thy lonely grave
My thoughts can wander or forget the spot
Where lies the last that earth can give to thee,
The dearest truest friend I ever knew.
Forget thee! Never! Never while memory lives
Can this sad heart do aught but dream of thee
And tend with gentle love thy last repose.
Beneath this soil, slow crumbling to death
Sleeps but the shell of all that was so dear –
Sweet little spirit dost thou hover round
With the old faithful love of former days.
Across life's dreary stage the veil that hides
That never-dying life that shone so clear –
Immortal in thy spirit await me where
When I have sought my last eternal rest
I can rejoin thee ne'er to part again.

Florence Dixie 1876

Right: Bosworth Hall. Watercolour by Andy Shore.

T H E   B E N O N I   E V A N S   f a m i l y

ARTHUR BENONI EVANS WAS THE HEADMASTER OF

THE DIXIE GRAMMAR SCHOOL IN THE MID-19TH

CENTURY. HE WAS BORN INTO A FAMILY OF

CLASSICAL SCHOLARS IN 1781 AND ORDAINED AT

GLOUCESTER CATHEDRAL AFTER OBTAINING A

DEGREE AT CAMBRIDGE UNIVERSITY.

The name 'Benoni', meaning 'child of my sorrows', derived from an uncle whose mother had died in childbirth. After a seventeen-year spell teaching officer cadets at Sandhurst and enduring an underpaid term as curate, Arthur met his wife, Anne Dickenson. It was shortly after this time, in 1829, that he moved to Market Bosworth to take up the position of Headmaster, which he continued up to the year of his death in 1854. His first impression of the school was recorded in his biography, *Time and Chance*, written by his grand-daughter, Dr Joan Evans.

"It was a bleak new building in Gothic style and set in a small cobbled square. The garden was a wilderness except for two old walnut trees."

Although the Dixie Grammar has changed little since that time, the school owes its continued existence to this remarkable man who was reported to have recovered its reputation from virtual ruin. With his unwavering consideration to the needs of the school, its staff and pupils, he proved to be an excellent head teacher. On his arrival he proceeded to sack the incompetent staff, raise the salaries and improve the school in general. Alongside the headship his other responsibility lay with the Church. He was a curate for Carlton, Cadeby and other villages and enjoyed traversing the lanes of the parish to help the poor and needy. The success and final stability of the running of the school enabled the Evans family to enjoy their surroundings and take long walks, when Benoni Evans introduced his five children – Arthur, George, Sebastian, John and Anne – to archaeology, botany and art through sketching.

Both the Howes of Gopsall Park and the Copes of Osbaston Hall became great friends of the family. The marriage of Sebastian Evans to Elizabeth Goldney, who was the sister of Lady Cope, secured this intimacy and during the deterioration of Benoni's son, Arthur, the Copes cared for him at Osbaston Hall until his death of consumption in 1850. The Evans' second son, George, also died of consumption, which was rife during this time. He was sent to recuperate in Madeira only to die, far away from his beloved family.

Benoni Evans' two surviving sons became notable scholars. With William Morris and the Pre-Raphaelites as his influences, Sebastian went on to become a painter and designer, exhibiting his stained glass at the Royal Academy. His sketch of the inside of St Peter's, Bosworth still hangs by the main entrance of the church. Although a troublesome child, it was John who brought fame to the family. He was considered too practical to attend university and was sent to work at his uncle's papermaking firm in Hemel Hempstead. It was there that he developed his interests in geology, palaeontology and archaeology. In 1892 he was made Knight Commander of the Bath (KCB).

John Evans' children became the third generation of Evans scholars. Most notable was Arthur who followed in both his grandfather's and his father's footsteps as a keen archaeologist. He studied at the Dixie Grammar School and is said to have engraved his initials on a pane of glass in a classroom window. In 1884 he was appointed keeper of the Ashmolean Museum in Oxford and sixteen years later, in 1900, he unearthed the lost palace of Knossos in Crete. He was responsible for the rediscovery of the Minoan civilisation, which was wiped out by the eruption of the volcanic island of Thera in 1628 BC. Evans named the Minoans after the legendary King Minos. Recorded as one of the most important finds of the century, his discovery led to his knighthood. Sir Arthur Evans last visited Crete and the site of Knossos in 1935 when a bronze bust of him was unveiled on the tree-lined slope there. He died six years later at his home in Oxfordshire, after presenting the Knossos site to the English school in Athens.

The Evans family had a strong influence in Market Bosworth. Dr Joan Evans, the sister of Sir Arthur Evans, continued to visit the town up to the 1960s when she presented prizes to the pupils of the Dixie Grammar School, under the headship of William Flower Gosling. Her grandfather, Arthur Evans, is buried with his wife and three of his children under the shadow of the south wall of St Peter's Church beneath a purple granite slab which marks his historic term at the Dixie School. The stained-glass window in the south aisle and the windows of the clerestory honour his memory by 'his friends both poor and rich as a tribute to his Christian worth. AD MDXXXLVI'.

Right: The Dixie Grammar School, founded in 1601 by Sir Wolstan Dixie, rebuilt in 1828. Painting by Margaret Atkinson.

THE MAN OF STEAM

"On April 1ˢᵗ 1986, the fire went out on one of the
best loved and respected men of steam"

These poignant words were written by Nancy Eames as part of the obituary to the remarkable Reverend Teddy Boston. Born in 1925, he was a 'Bevin Boy' in the coal mines, a Fellow of Jesus College, Cambridge, and for twenty-six years Rector of the Parish of Cadeby.

Teddy's father was a coal merchant who owned wagons on the railway and long boats on the canal, so as a boy these were his 'playthings'. Growing up in an age when steam was fast giving way to oil and electricity, Teddy seemed oblivious to such progress. He soon had a model engine room in the attic of their Solihull home, and this was followed by a model railway line in the garden shed when they moved to Cambridge.

Whilst in East Anglia he shared his growing passion for railways and anything driven by steam with the Reverend Wilbert Awdry, who later featured Teddy as the 'Fat Clergyman' and himself as the 'Thin' one in the 'Thomas the Tank Engine' books.

The two reverends became close friends and shared many railway expeditions together. The Reverend Awdry wrote affectionately of his visits to Cadeby, where he enjoyed Teddy's collection of steam engines. He recalled that a puffing 'Pixie' ran to and fro among the trees, and that 'Thistledown' rolled flat the rough places in the drive. Their shopping expeditions to Market Bosworth were also special: "...using a steam roller or traction engine by way of transport, parking as a matter of course in the town centre. Nobody batted an eyelid, they all knew and were fond of their Reverend Teddy Boston".

Many lines have been written about Teddy Boston and his eclectic and extraordinary life, yet perhaps few really knew of his interests away from the 'oily-rag and coal-dusted-cassock' image. He was also a musician, historian, photographer, archaeologist and theologian, and those who knew him well would confirm that he could say something constructive on almost any subject, even if occasionally his impish sense of humour spilled over into the comment. However, those same close friends would also say that above all he was a man of God, whose devotion to the Church outweighed all other interests.

The Domesday Book of 1086 records that there was already a priest at Cadeby and on the church wall is a list of most of the Rectors since 1250, but surely none could match this unusual man.

A stained-glass window in Cadeby church, installed in 1979, commemorates Teddy and his favourite steam engine 'Pixie', whilst Teddy, his wife Audrey and their dog Bonsie, also feature on a monumental brass. On this a railway wheel represents his passion for engines, and waves immortalise 'Bodger', the canal boat they built together and named after Teddy's first railway engine.

When Teddy died he was buried in the churchyard alongside earlier rectors of Cadeby, and Audrey recalls the occasion:

"A traction engine took us to church to be married, so when he died we steamed an engine to bring Teddy into his beloved church. Bonsie, our dog, was with us and the next morning he wandered into the church, walked up to the coffin, turned round, dropped his tail and ears and walked out again. He understood."

Above: Teddy Boston reading the scriptures.

Left: All Saints, Cadeby.

AJB

EFT

THE GREY LADY

SURVIVING THE STORM OF 1974, THE REMAINING COPPER BEECH TREE STANDS POISED BESIDE TOLLEMACHE SCOTT'S WROUGHT-IRON GATES. THE BROAD STEPS LEAD UP TO THE MAIN ENTRANCE OF BOSWORTH HALL WHERE A HUGE STONE FIREPLACE BEARS ABOVE IT THE LATIN TRANSCRIPTION 'MAY GOOD FORTUNE BE UPON THIS HOUSE'.

On the ceiling above this fireplace a rust-coloured stain has appeared over the years despite layers of paint. The age-old tale of Anna Dixie and the ghost of the grey lady always intrigues however, the horrific circumstances of her death, leading to this persistent mark, may still be a mystery to some.

Lady Anna Dixie was the second daughter of the 4th Baronet, Sir Wolstan Dixie, who lived at the Hall in the early to mid-18th century. She was entangled in a web of forbidden love with a servant from Osbaston Hall, and under the cover of darkness would hurry across the bridge over the moat to meet him in the Wilderness garden.

When he failed to appear one night, Lady Anna went in search of him but their secret liaisons had been discovered and her father, the Baronet, had set a mantrap. Although it was not intended for her, this barbaric contraption cruelly ensnared Lady Anna, and she was found at daybreak after a night of anguish and despair. She was carried to her bedroom above the main entrance hall on a door used as a makeshift stretcher, but sadly her wounds were fatal and the onset of gangrene took her to an early grave in the year 1758. She lost so much blood that it stained the hearth in the bedroom and seeped through the floor, leaving the mark on the ceiling below.

The family home was converted to an Infirmary in 1932, and renovated to become a hotel in 1987. At the time of the restoration it was suggested that the stain could have been caused by a rotten joist, as on replacement the mark seemed to disappear; however, it returned shortly afterwards with no apparent explanation.

Few stately homes are without some story of a resident ghost and Bosworth Hall is no exception. The fact that Lady Anna suffered such a tragic death has led many to believe that her unsettling but harmless spirit haunts the residents of the Hall. Today the wedding parties and guests at The Bosworth Hall Hotel pose on the bridge, lounge on the terraces and stroll along the lime tree avenue, oblivious to the distant tragedy some 250 years ago.

Above: The west elevation of Bosworth Hall in 1918. Only one of the two copper beech trees still survives.

Left: In spring a wonderful display of blue anemones can be seen amongst the avenue of lime trees behind the Water Tower.

EFT

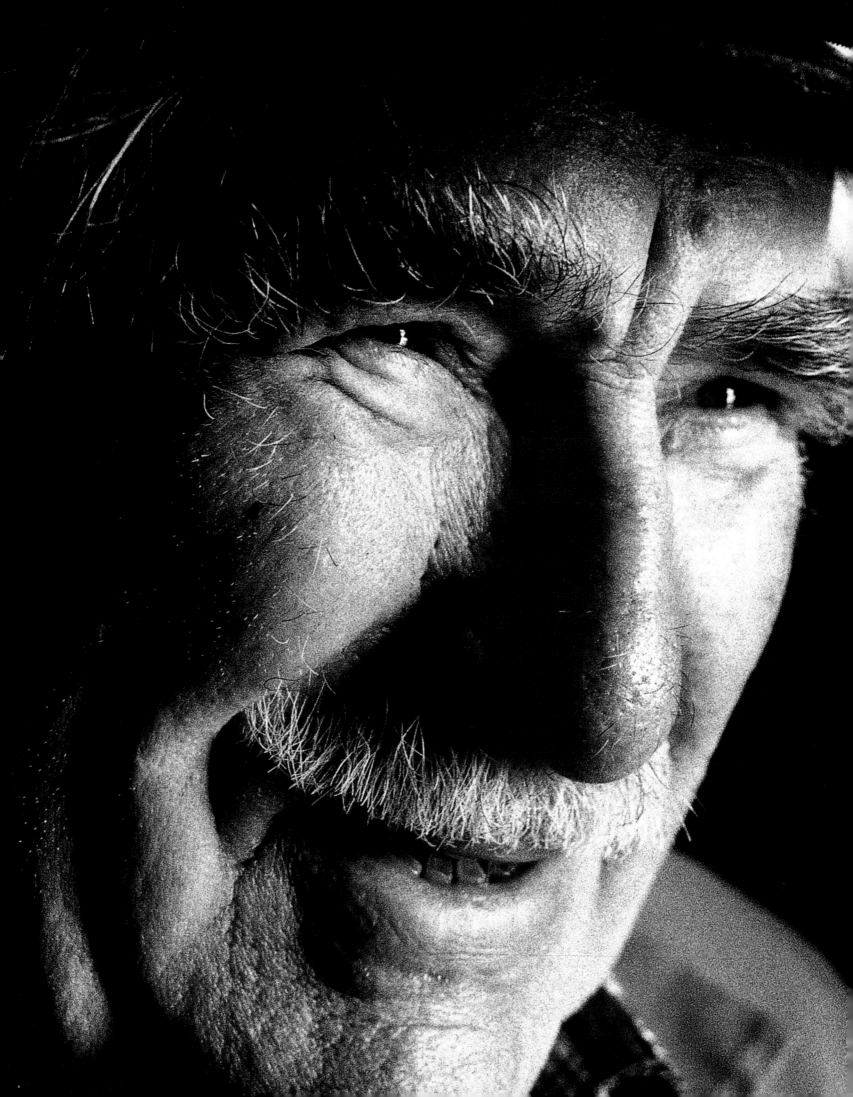

BOSWORTH INNS

THE EARLIEST MENTION OF AN 'INN' OF MARKET BOSWORTH IS TO BE FOUND IN DEEDS, DATED 1320, OF LAND AND PROPERTY CONVEYED TO ONE ALFRED FABER.

It is not quite known for certain which of the three inns named in the national survey of 1592 – The Bull's Head, The Unicorne and The George – this really was. However, it is fairly probable that this early reference is to The Bull's Head – papers dating 1558 referred to it as 'having lately been called the Signe of the Beare' and Hastings' survey of 1588 describes it as 'lying and beinge in the middest of the said towne of Bosworth and holding a pasture in the south field called beare close'.

It is thought that The Unicorne became redundant as a public house between the times of the 1588 and 1592 surveys. It probably stood in the marketplace on the site of the later Wheatsheaf Inn, once a coaching inn, which, until the early 20th century, occupied the building spanning the archway leading to its former stables, known today as the Wheatsheaf Courtyard.

The other inn, The George, was described in the Elizabethan survey as a veritable landmark and being 'a farme and freehold of Mr William Noell' quoting a Thomas Wright as the landlord. It stood on the site of the Dower House, whose large cellars could be those of the former inn itself. Records show that The George was still open until at least 1838 and it is therefore likely that it moved its location at the time the Dower House was built, sometime around 1770.

Market Bosworth's current complement of inns is four.

The Dixie Arms Hotel

Around 1824 the name of The Bull's Head Inn, which was then the chief hotel and public house in the town, was changed to The Dixie Arms in honour of the restoration of the squirearchy, the return of Sir Willoughby Dixie, the 7th Baronet, to Market Bosworth in the previous year. The building was also extensively renovated. Today's Dixie Arms exhibits a plain, stuccoed facade, which masks the older and lower structure of the inn, giving rise to low ceilings and window lintels and a large parapet above. The parapet was created as a result of the lifting of the old roof line to incorporate a third storey of attic rooms all lit by roof lights. Although there are typical features of the 1820s in the public rooms on the ground floor, the low height of the doorways and ceilings, on both this floor and the second storey, conflict somewhat with the building's apparent 19th-century appearance.

It is thought that the southern wing of the hotel, which has low ceiling beams and is constructed at a different level from the rest of the building and at an acute angle to the frontage, is of a much earlier date and may indeed be part of the original 16th-century Bear Inn. Across the inn yard is a tall, wide northern wing, which was built after 1824 and incorporated a large hall. The room displays features of its period, particularly moulded ceiling roundels where the chandeliers hung, a decorative cornice and impressive door frames of similar design to those installed in 1828 in the school across the way. During its life this particular room has been used for a whole multitude of purposes – civic functions, hunt balls, meetings of the magistrates and the Court Leet; for a short time it was even occupied by the Dixie School. However, its most bizarre function was to serve as the town's police station. What a useful facility the extensive beer cellars must have provided, as cells to house prisoners awaiting trial and sentence by the magistrates. The vaulted cellars mainly constructed of red brick, are a fascinating feature and weave an intricate maze below the majority of the northern wing of the building and part of the courtyard; they provide an interesting diversion for visitors to the hotel. It appears that the section underneath the courtyard, which was only rediscovered very recently, was sealed off from the main cellars, at the outbreak of World War Two, and treated with a waterproof lining material for use as an emergency water store.

The pattern of ownership of the historic Dixie Arms has turned full circle since it began life as 'The Signe of the Beare'. In 1886, after several hundred years of being part of the estate of successive Lords of the Manor, it passed, for a brief time, into individual hands when it was purchased by Samuel Moore for £2,200 following the bankruptcy of Sir Alexander Beaumont Dixie. In 1896 it ceased to be family owned when the brewery Ind Coope & Company Ltd bought it out. Finally, in 1992, following a series of corporate buy-outs, the cycle of family ownership of the hotel was restored when it was purchased by Michael and Anne Gibson, the tenants at that time. Although Michael and Anne have now moved on, the hotel remains in family hands, Andy and Wendy Knight being the current owners and proprietors.

Previous pages: Avril Hatton, Graham Pearson, Mr Poulson, Pam Nadin, Roger Jackson, Margaret Clark.

Right: A watercolour of the old bank and Main Street, with the Dixie Arms in the background by Andy Shore.

The King William IV

The detached building of the King William IV is the most modern of Market Bosworth's hostelries. It was built in 1938 to replace the old inn of the same name, which was demolished in 1937 following a serious fire and stands on a site very close to its former position. The original inn stood immediately adjacent to the roadside on the corner of Warwick Lane and Station Road and its door opened out directly onto the pavement. In the early part of the 19th century there was a large pond immediately across the road from the pub where carts were regularly washed. The old King William formed an integral part of an L-shaped terraced block, called Jubilee Terrace, which was made up of the inn and eight small frame-worker's cottages; at the rear stood parts of a three-storey building, which was once a hosiery factory then a carpenter's shop. All signs of these have long since gone, except that, if one looks very carefully, it is still possible to find some signs of the triangular area of the original building which opened out on to the street. At the end of the 1960s the new pub was extensively modernised with murals depicting scenes from the Battle of Bosworth painted by a Birmingham artist, Val Harris.

The Old Black Horse Inn

Little is known of the history of the Black Horse, which stands in a prominent position overlooking the marketplace. It is thought that the building was originally constructed as a group of dwelling houses, the oldest dating back to the 16th century. In the days when horse-trading took place in Market Bosworth, dealers would put them through their paces between the large elm tree, which stood outside the inn and underneath which the town stocks were positioned, and the bottom of The Square. The outer appearance of the inn dates from the early 20th century when the building was given a face-lift by the addition of a third gable facing the road and finials and dripstone courses over the windows. In the mid-1960s two older cottages adjoining its left-hand side were incorporated to form a restaurant area of the hotel.

Ye Olde Red Lion

The interior of the Red Lion is very old and is thought to date back to the early 16th century. Its exterior was the subject of extensive re-modelling in 1896, which is responsible for its present appearance. Two ancient cottages, all that now remain of a long terraced row, were also incorporated into the pub and on careful inspection can still be detected from the outside. The Trivett family kept the pub for over a hundred years until 1942, when the Hoskins Brewery took it over. By then the inn had a fine reputation for the quality and style of its beer, which was brewed in the brewhouse in the back yard of the premises and supplied many other local hostelries. The Trivett family also started a butcher's business and their slaughterhouse was situated at the rear. From 1919 the Red Lion ran Bosworth's first petrol station, two hand-operated pumps being positioned at either side of the entrance to the yard – the price of petrol at that time was one shilling per gallon.

Keith McCarthy

Above: A watercolour of the Black Horse and Rotary Cottages by Andy Shore

THE FIRE FIGHTERS

NONE OF THE CURRENT CREW CAN RECALL THE OLD

DENNIS WARTIME FIRE ENGINE 'BUT 146',

CONTROLLED BY THE MARKET BOSWORTH RURAL

DISTRICT COUNCIL, AND KEPT IN A GARAGE

ALONGSIDE THE DUSTCARTS BEHIND THE COUNCIL

OFFICES IN STATION ROAD.

However, they've heard the stories of how, with its open cab and single ladder, in the rush for the fire the separate trailer pump would sometimes get left behind!

The old engine got too old and was retired, and Les Goodwin is concerned that soon quite a few of the twelve-strong part-time crew at Bosworth will also have to go the same way. This would leave a problem, and unless new recruits can be found the unthinkable could happen – Bosworth might lose its Fire Station. Les comments:

"There are two extremes in our part-time crew: three real old-timers, holding the long service medal as part-time firemen – Dave Alesbrook has completed 32 years and Kevin Ginns and myself 25 years – but our newest recruit, Leanne Hampton, who is also our first woman firefighter, has only served for a few months. Chris Bostock, who retired from the full-time Hinckley Brigade, has joined us and his situation helps to explain our problem. He moved house to Market Bosworth into the ideal location – just over the road. You see, to qualify, new firemen must be 'locals' – living or working within four minutes of the Station, and there aren't many possible volunteers who do that nowadays. There is a scheme that allows for 'limited availability' – for example during working hours only – for those who work in Bosworth but don't live here, but as local factories close there are fewer and fewer of these as well."

Although today's modern pump is much more complex than the old-fashioned BUT 146, only six firemen are needed to make it fully operational – and it's still

the first six to answer the paged call who attend the incident. Competition is therefore fierce to be first 'in, on and out' in the five minutes that are allowed for the engine to be racing out through the Station doors, lights flashing and siren blaring.

"It's not just the equipment that's changed – the types of incidents we attend are very different. No doubt in the past fire-fighters went to many thatch, chimney, rick or barn fires, but these are now far less common. There is still the odd call for a cat in a tree, but road traffic accidents, house fires and hazardous material incidents are today's typical problems. So although we're only part-timers we have to learn how to use full protection suits, breathing apparatus and hydraulic cutters that can remove a car roof in just a few minutes. So our new title of 'Fire and Rescue' is deserved."

Watch a Tuesday night training session – hoses connected from hydrant to pump, ladders up to the 30 metre tower, the victim lowered swiftly to the ground – to see just how difficult is the real world of Fire and Rescue; this is not the artificial world of 'London's Burning'. And whilst praying you never need their services, even for something simple like your little boy's head stuck in the railings, be grateful they're there.

Above: Market Bosworth's fire crew.
Back row, from left: David Alesbrook, Chris Bostock, Chris Hooker, Andy Paton, Neil Harvey
Front Row: Leanne Hampton, Kevin Ginns, Richard Smith, Malcolm Padmore

C H U R C H E S ,   A N C I E N T   &   M O D E R N

THE LAND WAS DONATED BY SIR ARTHUR WHEELER,

HIS SISTER BROUGHT A MADONNA AND CHILD

FROM LOURDES, AND THE OAK ALTAR WAS MADE BY

FRED HEXTALL.

The original harmonium, donated by Mrs Trivett, was later replaced by a keyboard but the beautiful alabaster font, saved from a stonemason's yard, is still in use.

Before The Church of Our Lady and Saint Gregory was built in 1931, local Catholics began to meet to celebrate Mass in a house in Park Street and later at the Red Lion. The priest, Father Terry Fellows, explains:

"The purpose of the church is to proclaim Jesus Christ as God; to build the Kingdom of God in our world through the love of God and our neighbour. Our task is to make Jesus' message relevant today – for example by supporting Third World projects and being involved in justice and peace issues."

The Catholic Church has undergone many changes since the 1960s 2nd Vatican Council, which required the Church to reform. Mass is no longer celebrated in Latin and church buildings have been re-ordered, bringing the congregation closer to the altar and involving them in the way worship is conducted. Both priest and people are encouraged to be more outgoing and welcoming, in order to form closer bonds with other denominations.

"This is very evident in Market Bosworth where all who share the same faith in Jesus meet together as friends. The Council reminded us that we must all work together in ministry – with fewer priests, lay people need to be trained as leaders and teachers. Nowadays fewer people see the need of church – today's cathedral is the shopping centre – so we are challenged to face the modern age in new ways – as well as reconsidering some of the old ways."

Father Terry may not be alone in reconsidering some of the 'old ways'. Other local churches – Anglican, Free Church, Baptists, Congregationalists, Methodists – may also reflect on the way things were. However, the very new Elohim Church is still too young to have any 'old ways'.

The eight local people who prayed together in 1993 were most surprised to realise that God wanted them to start a new church, named 'Elohim', the Old Testament word for 'God'. Pastor Lynne Eveson and husband Brian never expected to start a church, but along with others they felt this was something they just had to do.

"The church is non-parochial and people come from afar to our Sunday service. This just flows, starting with prayer and communion. We have modern music, with a band, and some traditional hymns, but no sermon – instead we emphasise the teaching of God's word. A time for ministry, for those needing help or healing, is followed by fellowship together. Beyond the spiritual we try to hold everything in common, including money – we practise tithing, which means giving the first 10% of our income to God."

Practical help for the community is offered by the Elohim minibus – inscribed with the words 'Freely, freely you have received – and the Lord said freely, freely give'. Bought to offer Sunday transport for church members, it now offers help to anyone in the community – for trips to the post office, supermarket, surgery or hospital – all free of charge.

"One of our prime objectives is to connect with the community – to let our faith work through love to help people. For example, our Elohim Teens go out on Friday nights to find and talk, in a non-judgemental way, with other youngsters. Sometimes they find 10-year-olds, sent out for the night with £10 to amuse themselves – and needing to know that someone does care for them.

"Some of our youngsters also play in our football team, the 'Elohim Warriors'. They often have to explain what 'Elohim' on their shirts means, and why they pray before kick-off. They play to win, but not aggressively and no-one swears, and although they often lose they are respected by the opposition."

Another unusual activity is the weekend Prayer Clock. From 6 p.m. each Friday through to 6 p.m. on Saturday, different people elect to each pray for one hour throughout the 24 hours – for the Church, for the community and for solutions to world problems.

So not just free bus services, football, Sunday tea for the lonely, but a bold, hardworking, praying church, seeking to do God's will.

Two churches with very different histories, but both working together to serve the community.

Above: The west doorway of St Peter's Church, Market Bosworth. Pen and ink drawing by Doug Lewis.

HOLY BONES

THE VIRGINIA CREEPER COVERS THE TILES OF THE

ROOF IN SCARLET FROM THE BEGINNING OF

AUTUMN UNTIL THE WINTER WINDS BLOW THE

LEAVES DOWN TO THE WITHERING GRASS OF

NOVEMBER.

The house called Holy Bones casts a fairy-tale image sitting handsomely at the top of Church Street. It was built in 1861 when the Dixies owned the estate and displays the date of its erection and the Dixie crest of a snow leopard on a plaque above the front door. On a slight rise between the house and Bosworth Hall stands St Peter's Church whose immediate proximity gave the house its original name, Church Cottage. At that time the Dixies owned many properties in the town and the purpose of Church Cottage was to house the estate gardener. Some twenty-five years later the Dixies left Market Bosworth after selling the estate to Charles Tollemache Scott and his wife Lady Agnes. The house then became the comfortable home of their butler, William Dixon. At the rear of the cottage is a small window from which the estate workers received their wages.

Entering the churchyard through the wrought-iron gates past Holy Bones, two small boundary stones can be seen embedded, one on either side of the path. The initials C T S are engraved on the left, and on the right, S H P. The latter, Samuel Hunt Perry, lived at the house at the turn of the 20th century. In those days the church path crossed over his property, so he felt it necessary to mark his boundary. Church-goers were expected to pay a toll of one shilling in order to pass, in a tradition which was to continue for many years.

A house on the site of Holy Bones is recorded on both the Surveyors' Plan of 1824 and a Tithe Map dating back to 1848. This dwelling was known as The Cottage and was at that time probably part of the Bosworth Hall Estate. In front of the house was a patch of land called The Waste and opposite, some farm cottages which over the years evolved into what is now Beech House, Schwiening Language School.

The present name of the house has no known documentation, but its situation adjacent to the churchyard hints at its possible origin. During some excavation of the garden earlier this century a collection of bones was uncovered. These were perhaps paupers' graves or the remains of those unable to be buried in sacred ground. Is Holy Bones then the resting place for those lost souls whose bodies were buried unmarked?

Above: Holy Bones, Church Street, Market Bosworth.

BACK TO THE FUTURE

AT FIRST GLANCE IT LOOKS AS IF IT COULD BE A NUMERICAL ERROR — '...NOT TO BE OPENED BEFORE 8TH DECEMBER 2101...'

BUT THEN THE WORDS 'MILLENNIUM TIME CAPSULE', FOLLOWED BY 'BURIED 8TH DECEMBER 2001' — RE-FOCUS, AND THE MEANING OF THE SMALL PLAQUE ON THE WALL IN THE PARISH FIELD BECOMES CLEAR.

The more mature amongst us, especially those with very long memories, might just be able to recall a little of how life was a hundred years ago, at the beginning of the 20th century – but a very vivid imagination is needed to forecast the lives that our progeny will experience at the end of the 21st, when this capsule should be opened. Consider the world of someone born in 1900 – before television, penicillin, frozen food, plastic, contact lenses, video, frisbees and the Pill. No radar, credit cards, split atoms, lasers, ballpoint pens, jet aircraft, dishwashers, artificial hearts, disposable nappies, mobile phones (hurrah?) or instant coffee.

The chip was a piece of wood or a fried potato, hardware meant nuts and bolts, and since there were no PCs or Gameboys, software wasn't a word, and nor was 'gene'. It was fashionable to smoke cigarettes (though not so fashionable to smoke Wills Woodbines), grass was mown, 'coke' was kept in the coal place, a 'joint' was meat for Sunday dinner, and 'pot' was something to cook in.

So what will those born late in this new century make of all that emerges, when this concrete cylinder is dug from its six-foot grave, the half-ton lid is prised up and the capsule's seal hisses open?

How will their sense of humour see the jokes in the 2001 *Dandy?* Will the ingredients still be to hand to try a recipe from the local cookbook – and might

they ask 'What is an Archbishop and what's a Canterbury?' when they read his *New Aspect* Millennium Christmas Message?

Might they marvel that such a small town could exist at all – only 2,000 people – with individual families boxed up in those quaint little houses – and all above ground! (How did they cope with the heat?) And those funny little metal cars running on *wheels*! And metal 'money' – from all over the globe: how was that used? *Phantillestich!*

Fantasy? Perhaps, but for sure, whether it's your great-great-nephew or someone else's grandson, whoever it is that digs it up will have lots to go at – a copy of the 2001 census which included the personal household data from Bosworth parishioners, including one family tree dating back to 1780, lists of children and staff at all of the schools, and of all Community College groups, clubs and societies. Will they wonder how we had time to go to work?

Unless all future planning applications fail they will need the 1999 Bosworth street map, and Sue Styche's guidebook, to identify where all of the businesses used to be – the comprehensive list defining what they did, who ran them and who worked there, will help – or might they gaze into the quartz crystal donated by Ore Inspired, thinking it some antique telesponder that will open a window to the past?

And of course there's more, some fading memorabilia of our distant age: a lottery ticket, beer-keg tops, the *Hinckley Times*, *New Aspect*, *Just Seventeen* and other magazines and daily papers. (What *was* the latest news on Saturday 8th December 2001?)

So thanks to all who helped, with information, ideas and money, muscle and the will to do it and see it through, right to the end. They'll never see the capsule again – or will they? As genes are sorted, twisted, bent and reorganised until, who knows, we all live longer – some of us might just make it to 8th December 2101.

Top: Sunset over Far Coton.
Bottom: St Andrew, Carlton

"...I TAPPED HIM ON THE MOUTH WITH MY STICK BUT HE STARTED BACKING UP, ALL THE TIME, BACKED

UP RIGHT THROUGH TWO FIELDS, TILL HIS BUM WAS IN THE HEDGE, THEN SUDDENLY — WHOOF — HE

CHARGED ME. I FELT HIS HORNS COME OVER MY SHOULDER AND I FELL."

S A L V A D O R

Eugene Salvador was head cowman at Coton Priory for 27 years, looking after up to 300 head of pedigree-attested Friesians, including a prize-winning bull, Bertus. But he talks here of a problem with another bull.

"Mr Roland Smith was very proud of his herd of Friesians, and would only buy the best accredited bulls, some of them worth thousands of pounds, and he won many prizes at the Bosworth shows. One prize-winner was Bertus: he wasn't big when he was born, but fully grown he must have weighed a ton and a half.

"But one of my worst things was the fright I had with one of the other bulls – Zwortman. He came from the Scotland AI Station, but might have had some Dutch blood. He'd served some heifers and his time was up, so four of us went to bring him in, one on each side, one at the back and I was leading in front, but he wouldn't come up, started to make a fuss, bellowing. I tapped him on the mouth with my stick – but he started backing up, all the time, backed up right through two fields, till his bum was in the hedge, then suddenly – whoof – he charged me. I felt his horns come over my shoulder and I fell. Three others were with me – not one of them moved an inch!

"My pipe was still in my mouth when I got up and I gently picked up my stick, backed away and sent for a tractor – but he charged that. Eventually the vet, Nadin, came and asked what was up and he tried to put the staff through his ring, but he banged the gate with one horn, so I said we would leave him in the field to calm down. I fed him daily and on the third day I managed to staff him. I whistled for Freda Grewcock to open the gate and he walked up all gentle again. It's surprising just how strong cattle are; even a newborn calf heifer, taken from its mother for de-horning and castration and being fed by hand, can lift a man when he tries to push its head down to the bucket."

Eventually, in 1973, the cows were proving too demanding:

"It was so quiet without the cattle, so Mr Smith looked at running ostriches, but common sense took over when he realised how many alterations would be needed, so he bought a herd of deer. For twenty-two years we had seventy fallow and red deer, although if we had a year with too little rain we had to buy feed for them, so they were culled to about sixty. We killed some for venison, but only for the family – they were kept for pleasure, not run as a business. We also had some peacocks to wander around the place.

"Turkeys were kept as a business – about a thousand breeding hens for eggs, Bronzes and Whites. One male turkey went broody, so we sat it on some guineafowl eggs and after they hatched it was still broody so we sat it on turkey eggs – there's a picture in the *Leicester Mercury* with this big twenty-pound turkey, watching where it puts its feet because of all the little turkey chicks running around."

Looking at their old farming photographs – the first combine harvester in the district; a grinning young bronzed and mustachioed Eugene leaning on his hay-fork; the Smith family with Peggy, the spaniel dog – reminded Eugene and Roland Smith's niece, Eunice Beard, who also lives at the Priory, of some of those long-gone days:

"Mr Smith was a tall man, like his father, who used to be a gamekeeper for the big-wigs, but we never had game on Priory Farm – though the previous owner did – he used to shoot in Hook's Covert, now gone. Eunice's grandad used to take the horse and float to Bosworth Market every Monday with Mr Furbey from Lower Farm, Coton, and they would see Sir Wolstan Dixie in his corner at the Black Horse."

Eugene Salvador is a remarkable man who has continued to move forward as times have changed around him. For someone who in the 1940s used to walk to the prisoners' huts at Sutton Cheney for a haircut by an Italian barber, who was torpedoed *en route* from Italy to Sicily, wounded by a bomb in Tobruk, survived a train crash in Egypt and a lightning strike in an aeroplane, he has not been deterred from travelling around the world. He has been to Ecuador, Brazil, Argentina, Peru, Colombia, Venezuela, North America, most European countries and Egypt, but has always found most pleasure at Coton Priory where, like his trees, his roots are deepest.

Left: Eugene Salvador.

Right: Coton Priory.

L O C A L   I N D U S T R Y

THE DEEP-ROOTED MANORIAL SYSTEM, BASED TOTALLY AROUND AGRICULTURE, THAT ONCE

ALLOWED RURAL SELF-SUFFICIENCY, EVENTUALLY CHANGED, AS SLOWLY AS THE SEASONS,

WHEN INDUSTRIAL ACTIVITY BEGAN TO BLUR THE DIFFERENCES BETWEEN TOWN AND COUNTRY.

The blacksmith's hammer still rang, the carpenter still sawed, millstones slowly ground, but new sounds were drifting out from cottage window and garden workshop.

Perhaps it was the rattle and squeak of the treadle of a new-fangled knitting frame, as the cowman-turned-knitter slowly made the small piece of knitted worsted that his dairymaid-turned-seamstress wife would sew up as a woollen stocking; or just along the lane, the needlemaker's urgent swish-swish of polishing as he finished the needles needed by the framemaker later on that day. Below the hill, the glow of a kiln lit the evening air as sweating labourers fashioned bricks and tiles from greasy clay.

These new industrialists may just have shivered slightly in their sleep as ghosts of Roman workers, laden with Bosworth-made nails or coins or pots, passed down the hill that led to Lichfield. But even in their wildest dreams could they imagine the sounds of industry today? What would they make of keyboards tapping over the quiet hum of the computer, the grunt and grind of caterpillar track on quarry gravel; the whine of drills and saws, the buzz and spark of welding, the deafening thump-thump of a road drill, or the steady thwack of a nail gun? How could they comprehend that where the station brickyard once stood, now Churchill's turn out metal blades to power the fiery turbine engines for the Tornados that roar and flash across the hill? Or that in the station yard there are now so many cars, and just next door the sound of motorbikes being tuned to racing pitch?

But as they looked around there'd be some recognition here and there: no cattle walking down the lanes to Congerstone, but beasts aplenty trucked through the gates of the Dawkins brothers' abattoir. The forge is there in Park Street; a leatherworker is at his bench; there's still a sawmill; and a butcher's cleaver cuts and chops. Might Barton's old clockmaker, Samuel Deacon, smile to see the Clock Shop in the marketplace – but frown at the prices of those old things in the antique shop's windows?

So much has changed, but much too remains – so we examine, in the next few pages, the good and the bad, and reflect on how all rural workers' lives have had to change.

Above: Frame-knitters' cottages, Barton Road, Market Bosworth, now demolished.

Right: Carlton Mill on a foggy November evening.

AJB

RAILWAY GHOSTS

THE PLATFORM THAT ONCE ECHOED WITH THE SHOUTS AND LAUGHS OF EXCITED CHILDREN, AS DAY-TRIPPERS JOSTLED TO BOARD THE HISSING STEAM TRAIN WAITING TO RUSH THEM TO BLACKPOOL OR SKEGNESS OR DUDLEY ZOO, STILL VIBRATES TO THE RATTLE AND CLATTER OF THE OCCASIONAL TRAIN STEAMING SLOWLY PAST.

Not heading now for distant seaside or zoo, but to Shenton or Shackerstone stations, passengers can only gaze at the cars and vans waiting silently for repair or sale at Station Garage.

Soon after 1963, when Dr Beeching's axe fell, killing branch and trunk lines and decimating LMS, LNER and all the other British railway networks, Market Bosworth station was left deserted. With peeling Victorian waiting room, ticket office and porter's room, dusty coal-fired grates and brick chimneys, rusting engine shed, weighbridge and cattle pens, it eventually had to turn its back on the rails and face a future based on roads – rubber tyres replacing iron-clad wheels.

In the town, two old hand-operated Shell petrol pumps standing guard at the entrance to the Red Lion yard were already obsolete, and Kelly's, at the top of Station Road, was the only garage. The main station buildings were, therefore, converted to offer car repairs and sales, but the other old railway facilities were left to decay; the cattle pens and weighbridge dismantled and sold, and the engine shed left empty.

Some time later, Kelly's town garage changed hands, and as the car became king of the road, with motorists demanding service to match the increasing speed of their vehicles, most petrol stations changed to the faster, more impersonal self-service system. However, Ken and Vivien Coleman, the new owners of Kelly's, decided that the pace and demeanour of Bosworth's still mainly agricultural lifestyle required the personal touch. Attended forecourt service remained, and the Market Bosworth Service Station flourished, becoming the town's important chat-shop, where hot-gossip was quietly exchanged as pumps surged and petrol gurgled. Eventually Ken, who as a lad had once helped drive cattle down to the old cattle pens, and his new business partner Ken Reeves, were also able to purchase the old Station Garage. However, pumping petrol and confidential conversations were not the only action seen on the service station forecourt. Once an exhausted fox, chased by baying hounds, went to ground under the paraffin tank, and the Master of the Atherstone had to be firmly reminded, by Vivien, that "this is private ground, and no place for horse or hound – there will be no fox's blood spilt here today, so kindly move – be on your way!" They went – and the lucky fox survived.

To the regret of many Bosworth residents, time does not stand still. Supermarkets drew more shoppers away from local stores, tempting them with cheaper goods and cheaper petrol, and tongues wagged when the garage remained closed on Sundays. Later, after the complete closure of pumps and garage, and the transfer to car servicing down at the old station site, the chat-shop was finally silenced.

But despite being more remote, things still happen there. The old weighbridge office exchanged hundredweights for kilograms when Scottish international swimmer, Teresa Davis, living at the old Station Master's house, pumped iron there; steam locomotives were replaced by modern engineering machines, renovated and sold from the old engine shed; and ex-Ministry of Defence cars, once driven by neatly-uniformed and shiny-shoed WAAFs, Wrens or Pongos, are sold on to Nike clad, designer-stubbled civvies.

No Bosworth petrol, no town-based chat-shop, and the only steam from a mid-morning brew-up – but still enough hammering, spannering and polishing to please the railway ghosts?

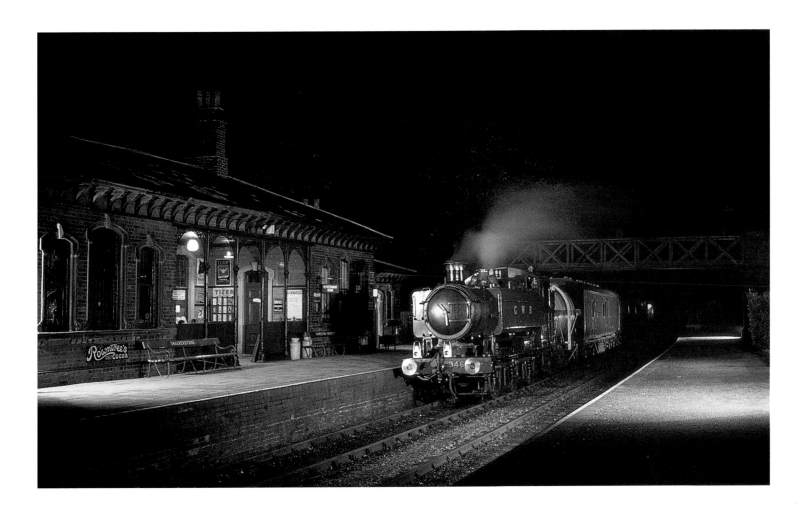

Above: Shackerstone Station at night. The engine is GWR Pannier tank 9466.
Photograph courtesy of Neil Hudman.

DIGGING UP THE PAST

NARROW, TWISTING AND TURNING, BRASCOTE LANE APPEARS TO BE LEADING NOWHERE, AND COULD EASILY BE MISSED BUT FOR THE FOREST OF SIGNS AT CADEBY CORNER.

But the 1349 'Black Death' plague touched this corner of Leicestershire and as a result the small village of Naneby, whose inhabitants had quietly minded their own business at the far end of the lane, was abandoned. Brian Griffin, one-time owner of Naneby Hall Farm, thought he could see the faint remains of the village and the site of plague-victim graves, as he flew over the area in his light aircraft.

Today the site is overlooked by, but protected from, the massive excavations of Cadeby quarry, now operated by the Tarmac Company but started by Braithwaites in the mid-1960s.

John Lancaster was born in Bosworth and has worked at the quarry for thirty-nine years. His dragline bites out 5 tons at a time from sand and gravel which lie in layers up to 30 feet below the surface. His collection of fossils suggests that these deposits may be 200 million years old derived from debris laid down by rivers, glaciers and the sea. Could Bosworth once have been beside the sea?

The site now covers more than 500 acres, with conveyors up to two miles from the processing plant; the eleven employees excavate and supply thousands of tons of materials annually to local construction companies. However, although each area of land may be excavated for several decades, the land must eventually be returned for farming. Rightly proud of their reputation as good environmentalists, the quarry-owners backfill the holes with quarry waste, finishing them off with original topsoil.

The quarry's closest customer, literally on their doorstep, is the concrete products company that was started by two other local men, Roger and Alan Jackson. No strangers to Cadeby, since the family owned land at Church Farm from early last century, Alan as a teenager raised poultry and pigs in buildings rented at Naneby Hall Farm. He was therefore on the spot when Brian Griffin sold the land for quarrying having discovered the sand and gravel deposits there. Alan and Roger set up on the very edge of the excavations, using the sand and gravel to make specialist concrete products – in friendly competition with their father's concrete business in Ibstock. The year 2000 marked their 30th anniversary, but in their first year, using only traditional muscle and sweat

methods, the two of them made and supplied nearly 2,000 tons of fencing posts and other concrete products.

Nowadays, whilst the same 'work hard' ethic still exists, modern equipment means fewer blisters and less sweat in supplying up to 30,000 tons of specialist products per year, as varied as terracing for West Bromwich Albion's new football stadium, security fence supports for the Glastonbury Festival, floor decks for Sheerness harbour, and platform copings for Luton Airport.

However, concrete work still seems to build men of concrete – witness Derek Jelley, an ex-Jackson Precast Ltd employee now turned regular first team front row forward for the Leicester Tigers!

A busy and industrious place, Brascote Lane. It no longer buzzes with the sound of Brian Griffin's light aircraft, the growl of his Maserati, or the chatter of Kirkby Mallory race-track parties. Now it's a relatively quiet road despite the extensive and continual industrial activity that has replaced them – and the odd laugh and giggle from the nearby children's nursery school or a few barks and growls from the kennels.

Also, judging by the number of rabbits scampering about, it seems to remain a haven for wildlife. With the 1,000 trees recently planted to screen the concrete plant, and other measures taken by these environmentally aware industrialists, neither quarry nor concrete plant seem to detract from the visual beauty of nearby Cadeby.

Above: Ammonites found at Cadeby quarry by John Lancaster.

FIREPROOF

THE NAVVIES WHO ORIGINALLY DUG THE ASHBY

CANAL ADJACENT TO THE OLD GASWORKS SITE

MIGHT BE SURPRISED TO KNOW THAT 220 YEARS ON,

THE NAVY STILL BENEFITS FROM THEIR LABORIOUS

EFFORTS.

The Timber Fireproofing Company traditionally sold fireproofed timber to the Admiralty, for use in Her Majesty's fighting ships including the *Ark Royal* and many modern frigates. So perhaps it was no coincidence that when relocating from London in 1910, they sited themselves alongside water? Of course the canal, and the adjacent Ashby-Nuneaton railway, were ideal for shipping timber in and out, and both have remained important to the company during its long stay in Bosworth. Water has been especially important since it is used in the treatment processes – and has allowed at least one employee to spend his lunch break fishing in the canal.

London Underground have been customers for fire-proofed timber, but their engineers might have blinked with astonishment at the unique on-site rail transport system at Bosworth. The timber to be fire-proofed is stacked on trolleys running on narrow-gauge rails that are mounted on top of a 50-foot long bogey. This bogey, running on wide-set triple rails, is shuttled to and fro between pressure vessels by an old farm tractor. A fork-lift truck pushes the trolleys into each treatment vessel, but once the process is complete an ancient rope-and-pulley device hauls the trolleys out again after treatment. All looking rather Heath Robinson, but effective and efficient despite being almost a hundred years old – and only stopped occasionally by snow on the lines!

So how is such a readily combustible material like wood made resistant to fire? The answer, for some of the more dense, heavier woods, is very, very slowly. For example, a heavy balk of close-grained mahogany, first needs high-pressure steam for 24 hours to open the pores. All moisture is then removed under vacuum before it is 'pressure cooked' for several weeks to impregnate it with a non-toxic mix of ammonium and phosphate salts under high pressure and temperature. After drying for a few more weeks, in kilns heated by a sawdust-fuelled boiler, it can eventually, perhaps almost three months after treatment started, be returned to the customer – but not before samples have been flame-resistance tested.

If the treatment time is often lengthy then so is the life of some of the equipment – most of the 'pressure cookers', or autoclaves, were installed in the early 1900s. Tested annually for safety, the oldest of these enormous inches-thick pressure cylinders – up to 40 feet long and 8 feet in diameter – are still giving good service after almost a hundred years. The oldest one needs a massive 'key' with a two-man, 6-foot handle to rotate and lock the 8-foot diameter convex door which weighs over a ton. Only once has there been a problem with this mighty giant, when, only partly latched for a steam-cleaning process, pressure blew the door open, bending the 10-inch thick hinges.

Fortunately not all of the wood treated by the old Timber Fireproofing Company takes months to process. The softer, less dense wood like the Gaboon plywood from Africa, only needs a week or two, whilst the soft pinboard, made from re-cycled newspapers and used for school noticeboards, takes even less time.

So from school noticeboards to Navy ships, coal mines to concert halls, buses to aeroplanes – the company's products are in use anywhere that Health and Safety regulations require fire protection for timber. And fire protection is only a part of the activities at this old site, since the same impregnation can be used to rot-proof red cedar and other timbers, whilst a timber-mill makes other bits and pieces for the building industry.

The Timber Fireproofing Company was eventually taken over and although renamed Palgrave Brown it has always been known simply as 'Fireproofing' but whilst both the canal and the Battlefield Railway line survive, and even thrive, it seems this 'fireproof' company may not. Not even all the water in the canal may be enough to save it from being engulfed by the flames of progress.

Above: Dark clouds over Palgrave Brown.

TURNING FULL CIRCLE

A UNIQUE MIX OF MOTIVE POWER EXISTS IN A QUIET CORNER OF MARKET BOSWORTH. CANAL, RAIL AND ROAD TRANSPORT MERGE WHERE THE OLD ROAD TO LICHFIELD PASSES OVER TWO BRIDGES, AND A LIGHT AIRCRAFT FROM WHARF FARM OCCASIONALLY BUZZES OVERHEAD.

But when a fighter-bomber zooms overhead across Godsons Hill targeting St Peter's Church spire, and shattering the peace, the engineering wheel turns full circle – for the whine of compressor blades made at Churchill's factory combines with the roar of the jet engine.

Was it an 18th-century blacksmith who introduced 'engineering' to Market Bosworth when he started to make special parts for the new-fangled knitting frames? Perhaps bearded needles, or jack sinkers – precisely fashioned and smoothly polished so that the worsted yarn would not snag on any burrs or roughness?

Whoever it was, local engineering started as little 'factories' opened to cut and hammer, file and polish; developing the same engineering crafts we see today on Bosworth's small industrial estate – home to a surprising number of specialist engineering companies, from dental technicians who 'engineer' artificial teeth, to a world-class, world leader in the manufacture of aerospace components.

In 1938 Walter Churchill started making parts for Armstrong Siddeley aircraft engines, and his company was soon deemed vital to the war effort. When a direct hit destroyed the factory roof, leaving an unexploded German bomb to be unceremoniously dumped in the adjacent canal by the somewhat foolhardy night shift, Walter was required to re-locate away from blitzed Coventry. He moved the company to Market Bosworth, initially to the Dower House and then to the old gas-plant site, before finally settling at its current home on the opposite side of Station Road, adjacent to the canal.

Walter Churchill, DSO and DFC, served as a fighter pilot in the Battle of Britain and lost his life whilst helping to defend the George Cross island of Malta. His son, James Churchill, brings the story up to date:

"In today's world, when so many people think nothing of flying, it's strange to think that the jet engine is still only 60 years old. My father worked with Sir Frank Whittle, making the special compressor blades for his unique engine, so our company's work on jet engines pre-dates even Rolls Royce. We go to extraordinary lengths to precisely fashion and smoothly polish each blade, because any tiny burr or roughness can cause the engine to fail and the aircraft to crash. We are very proud of our safety record, which shows that in sixty-three years there has been no single loss of life attributable to our compressor blades.

"Our blades are used in most Boeing and Airbus civil aircraft, Concorde and military aircraft including the Harrier jump-jet and the Tornado fighter-bomber. Having fighter aircraft occasionally zoom over our factory roof reminds us how important our quality standards are.

"We use very, very precise co-ordinate control in everything we do, and can guarantee zero defects in every one of each million blades made – something that none of our competitors has yet achieved. Some of our leading-edge machine tools, networked by computers direct from production control to the shop floor, work unmanned and run so fast that it's impossible to see what they're doing."

It may be leading-edge technology, but it is shared with the local community in a Lunchtime Technology Club. Some of Churchill's employees have helped a group of local schoolchildren to create a working aeronautical model, to be displayed at Loughborough University. Churchill's staff are equally proud of some of their other products:

"We make other items as well as blades – precision cutting tools, mechanical assemblies for diesel engines, and missile propulsors. The last are used to drive military torpedoes, and whilst not designed as lawnmowers, we do have a rather battered prototype which, after speeding at about 70 mph along a Scottish loch, following the failure of the torpedo's flotation valve, chewed its way across a field and killed a cow!

"My father introduced the ethic of hard, satisfying work and loved a challenge, and we like to think that we have maintained this tradition. However, he also insisted that work should be fun, and although we sometimes find it hard to keep smiling if we have just lost the annual Bosworth Raft Race, we do try! Bosworth is a lovely place to live and work and since we have plenty of room for expansion, we expect to continue to enjoy its benefits for a very long time."

Above: James Churchill at his home.

Left: Shackerstone – home of James and Maggie Churchill.

WULFS, TOADS, DONKEYS & CONKERS

NO DOUBT THE SANDS-OF-TIME STILL RUN UNDER THE VILLAGE, BUT THERE CAN BE NO MORE FREE-WHEELING DOWN CHURCH HILL TO CLIFF HOUSE.

The old house no longer exists but the company now occupying the same site develops video games that have replaced the football skills and 'one-armed' rabbit shooting that once took place in Twycross.

Once part of Earl Howe's Gopsall Estate, and always a quiet, slow-to-change village, an earlier resident, Jack Phillips recalled how it once was.

"As boys we used to free-wheel down the main road from Church Hill almost to Cliff House. The field opposite the rectory is where my father trained the prize-winning football team. One day my father and his men dug out a hole for a 500 gallon petrol tank, only to wake the next morning to find the tank at ground level. The running sand under most of Twycross had floated the tank to the surface overnight.

"The post office was kept by Mr Prince, the ex-butler from Cliff House, and the postman, Mr Webb, was a one-armed 1914 war veteran. At harvest-time he and a legless ex-serviceman, Harry Smith, would form a shooting party to kill rabbits escaping from the corn binder. A marvellous sight!"

Times have changed in the village. It now hosts a famous zoo, an agricultural tractor company, a few old cottages on the increasingly busy A444, and a small independent school. The 13th-century stained-glass in the church windows, saved from the French Revolution, must be amongst the most ancient and rare artefacts, but the company Rare Ltd must be one of the newest and most unusual additions to the village. Built on the site of the old Cliff House, and now one of the world's leading computer games companies, it was started in the late 1970s by the Stamper brothers. When Tim found himself helping older brother Chris to convert Space Invaders boards for arcade games, neither could have forecast just how popular home computers would become. Having launched the company, Ultimate, from their small terraced house in Ashby-de-la-Zouch, they soon needed more space for the fast-growing company, so moved to Manor Farmhouse in Twycross – more used to disc harrows than floppy discs.

With names that still smack of a Flash Gordon movie – *Jetpac, Lunar Jetman, Sabre Wulf, Underwurlde and Alien 8* – Ultimate developed games for Sinclair Spectrum computers that outsold all competition and led to the establishment of Rare Ltd, which quickly became the world's leading-edge computer game company.

The more advanced systems that superseded the relatively simple Spectrum demanded more sophisticated games and eventually led Rare into the home video game market. Games like *Marble Madness, Battletoads* and the famous *Donkey Kong Country* kept the Twycross company in the limelight and led to a unique honour.

The Nintendo Company Ltd offered Rare the first fiscal partnership outside Japan, leading to even more global success. *GoldenEye 007,* based on the Bond film, made even more profit than the original film. *Mickey's Speedway USA* was the first in a high-profile deal with the Disney empire, whilst *Conkers Bad Fur Day* was the most recent release, ahead of the anticipated GameCube system from Nintendo.

No free-wheeling today down Church Hill and certainly none at this unusual and exciting high-tech company – but perhaps the quiet rural location was inspiration for some of their games – with *wulfs* and *toads* and *donkeys* and *conkers?*

Some company – some growth – some brothers.

Above: 'Conker' the computer game character developed by Rare Ltd

V I R T U A L   R E A L I T Y

"LIKE AN ORANGE BOX ON GIMBALS... A BIG
HANDLE STICKING OUT OF THE BACK, WHICH A MAN
LOOKING OVER THE TRAINEE PILOT'S SHOULDER,
WOULD PUSH OR PULL. THIS SHOWED THE PILOT
WHAT EFFECTS WOULD BE PRODUCED WHEN HE
MOVED THE JOYSTICK IN A REAL AEROPLANE."

This is how Terry Rowley, who moved to Market Bosworth in 1972, describes the
early flight simulators – not at all like the complex all-singing, all-dancing,
all-shaking, computer-controlled systems that are used to train pilots nowadays.

Whilst working with Marconi in Leicester, Terry helped to develop the techniques
for 'virtual reality' (VR) simulation devices that are used to train, amongst
others, supertanker and container-ship captains and the aimers of naval
weapons. So how does he describe 'virtual reality'?

"The real world around us is perceived by decoding our sensory inputs using a
world model which we have each constructed from all of our experiences since
birth. If we put ourselves in a position where the real world sensations are
blocked out by a compatible set of sensations generated by computer, this
'virtual world' replaces our real world and becomes a 'virtual reality'. Not all of
our sensory inputs need to be replaced – the usual ones are sight and sound.

"The earliest flight simulators were introduced to try to reduce casualties, caused
not so much by flying aeroplanes, as by not knowing how to land them. Getting
down was not that difficult – it was being able to walk away from the getting
down that was proving difficult!"

The development of low-cost, high-speed computers, coupled with realistic
computer graphics and trackable head-mounted displays, allowed virtual reality
to be introduced into education and entertainment. Terry set up his own
company, Educality Ltd in Market Bosworth, and the old lofts at Stables End
Court were used to develop and demonstrate educational applications of VR
systems produced at the company's Leicester office.

"The first device was a 'stand-up system'. You put on a head-mounted display
and special belt and having grasped a hand-held controller you carefully
stood up. You then found that as you moved around you could do things in
'virtual space'. For example, you might see four doors. By 'opening' one and
going through it you could find yourself standing on the top of a high cliff, with
a river below and a meadow opposite with a letter hanging in a tree.

"Your task was to retrieve the letter, so you stepped off the cliff, pressed a button
in your hand and looking up you saw a parachute open above you. As you floated
down you could direct yourself to land on a raft moving down the river, get the
raft to the river bank and retrieve the letter – when you would then find yourself
transported back to try one of the other doors! This system was used by Fabergé
to promote their products – set up in public places, it offered people a chance to
enter this strange new virtual world."

Terry's company not only used Bosworth as its base, it also used places in
Bosworth as the basis for one of its VR educational developments.

"A recent system, developed to help teach languages, uses a model village built
within the computer that includes scenes from Bosworth's marketplace. The
student, using a head-mounted display, can 'move' around the marketplace to
purchase things from the shops, but only by using the language being taught.
For example, the interior of one of the 'virtual' shops is an art gallery, and the
pictures on the wall are the watercolours produced by Michael Warr and used in
the recent Market Bosworth guidebook. By 'walking' into the gallery and
pointing to one of the pictures the student will be told all about it in the chosen
language. Various kinds of help can be offered and the total immersion in the
virtual world ensures a very high level of attention."

For a while the company moved away from Bosworth and Terry is now 'virtually'
retired, but he still enjoys living here – and helping out at the Bosworth Drama
Society. Play acting aims to create an impermanent 'virtual' world on a real stage
– to delight, amaze and entertain – and Terry's back-stage skills have helped
many of the Drama Society's illusory productions. Perhaps these might be
thought of as 'real reality' in a place where 'virtual reality' was developed?

Above: Virtual Reality – to delight, amaze and entertain.

NO. 9 MAIN STREET

THE DOUBLE-FRONTED SHOP ON MAIN STREET APPEALED TO IKE AND LUCY BAMFORD WHO THOUGHT THAT THE QUIET, SLEEPY TOWN OF MARKET BOSWORTH WOULD OFFER THEM GREAT PROSPECTS.

The year was 1960 and although the shop had seen different proprietors since the early part of the century, from the Drackleys to the Beales, the Quinceys to the Tebbuts and finally to the Bamfords, it had changed little. It no longer advertised horse and cattle medicines or the extraction of

teeth but did still remain an old-fashioned village store. Almost anything could be purchased – Carters seeds in springtime, chicken and rabbit food at any time, freshly sliced ham and bacon, a selection of proprietary medicines and a wide range of beers, wines and spirits.

An old polished mahogany counter, complete with its original till drawer, stood on the patterned tiled floor. A beautiful Huntley & Palmer's biscuit stand still displayed its wares in glass-topped biscuit tins. Row upon row of glass sweet bottles were arrayed over a counter, which was chock-full of liquorice laces, gobstoppers, sherbet fountains, Wagon Wheels and lucky bags – all tempting schoolchildren to part with their pennies. And housewives would patiently wait while a tin was filled with a gallon of paraffin, or whilst an ounce of snuff for Grandpa was carefully weighed and folded into a small triangular bag.

Ike and Lucy set about making a few improvements but tried to retain the friendly character of the shop. They offered quality merchandise, free delivery around the villages and a very personal service, often opening up after hours to serve regulars who seemed to know neither the time of day nor even the day of the week. To make more space they moved their living accommodation upstairs, allowing a small craft and coffee shop to open in the old front room. Here, it was claimed on the opening day, just before Christmas, a child's fox-head hobby horse was sold to a bespattered huntsman, still in his pink, who proudly walked off with it, unwrapped, down Main Street.

Right from the early days of the Drackleys, No. 9 had kept its traditional village shop appearance but since Ike and Lucy retired in 1976 many changes have taken place. Eventually the original shop became Elizabeth Ann's Hair Salon, the coffee shop is now Lloyds the Chemist, whilst the old storage rooms have seen dress shops, wicker-basket makers, antique and furniture sellers and, more recently, accountants and a bistro restaurant.

Where does Grandpa buy his ounce of snuff now?

Above: A collection of old cigarette packets.

BOYTON WILLIAM JELLICO

THERE WERE FOUR GROCERS' SHOPS, TWO GREENGROCERS, THREE BUTCHERS AND THE CO-OP IN THE CENTRE OF MARKET BOSWORTH — ALL WHEN THE TOWN WAS SMALLER, BUT NOT THAT LONG AGO.

Someone recently claimed to have counted forty different businesses, shops and offices in and around The Square, so commerce in the town has radically changed. Now there is a much reduced choice of foodstuffs – bread and butter groceries from the Co-op, apples and pears from In Season All Seasons, olives or *fois gras* from Peppercorn Cottage and fresh beef, lamb and pork from Lampards, the only remaining butcher's shop. Not only meat, of course, as Boyton William Jellico Lancaster, the butcher and proprietor, explains:

"Ashley Garratt introduced cheese a long time ago and we added bread, since the one thing Market Bosworth lacks is a baker – there used to be two, and when my dad was a lad he used to help Amos Fletcher with his bread round.

"When I started thirty years ago I was thrown in at the deep end making sausages. After two days the boss, James William Lampard (Billy) – we had to call him 'Sir' – told me to come to work the following day in a tie as I was to go out in the van. Robert Jarvis was taken on to do the butchering; he taught me all I know – where to cut with the knife so the meat looks right."

In those days butchering meant seeing it through, from the hoof to the shop floor, since Lampard's did their own slaughtering in the abattoir behind the shop. Animals bred and raised on local farms were sold by auction at the Bosworth cattle market, so Billy Lampard – and later his son, Jim – had to bid for up to 35 lambs, 3 beasts and perhaps 5 pigs that were needed each week. Jim Lampard, who lived 'over the shop', always liked 'a bit of black' on his cattle – the Friesian/Hereford cross – since he felt that it gave good conformation and good eating meat. Nowadays leaner cuts are preferred, so it's usually a French Charolais/Limousin cross – often purchased from Ron Wyatt at Barton in the Beans until he sold his herd. Bill Lancaster continues:

"Jim Lampard was a character, always chatting and charming people. When they stopped using the van I had to serve in the shop, which in the early days I never really wanted to do. I guess I picked up a lot from him. When you've got a shop full it's like being on stage – you have to perform your skills with the meat but also spiel away – give it the patter, all the gossip and some leg-pulling – this is what a village is about. Without the chat it's not a village any more. There again you can sometimes drop yourself into a big hole, but that's part of the fun. I once told a guy to cheer up – had his wife left him? He looked so sad – and she had!

"The shop is central to village life: you don't go to Asda and have a chat with the lady on the till – you probably have to tell her to cheer up. This is what we lose when a village shop closes."

Bill comments about how much the commercial atmosphere around The Square has changed: there are now so many different types of shops. Because there are more motor cars and supermarkets, and Westhaven and the Infirmary have closed, quite a lot of business has been lost. He thinks it's good, therefore, that Bosworth has grown a little because without that expansion the shops wouldn't have survived – but it must not grow too much or it will lose the character that makes it such a good place to live.

Bill, a true local having been born in one of the wooden bungalows on Godsons Hill, no doubt had his leg pulled at school about his names: Boyton after one of his father's best friends from Barton in the Beans and Jellico after a famous Admiral. Bill's grandfather, Harry Grewcock, was also famous – twice Champion Hedgelayer of Great Britain and Northern Ireland.

When Bill was younger many happy days were spent on motorbikes. He once slid a 750 Suzuki down the road, and not daring to go home he went to Jim Lampard's, and Shirley – Jim's wife – patched him up. Often frequenting the Paddocks at motorbike races, he made friends with lots of riders; the father of one-time world champion, Barry Sheen, once stayed at his home and helped make burgers in the back of the shop!

"I love the Isle of Man, but I couldn't live anywhere but Bosworth: I was born here, I have so many friends here and my roots are too deep, but if I had to move that's where I would choose."

Above: Harry Grewcock, twice National Champion Hedgelayer. He moved from Norton-Juxta-Twycross to Park Street Market Bosworth, opposite The Forge, before finally living for the rest of his life in a cottage at Coton Priory.

AJB

THE SMITHY

WITH BRAWNY ARMS AND SINEWY HANDS HE STOOD IN HIS LEATHER APRON IN FRONT OF THE GLOWING EMBERS. THE BLACKSMITH WAS AN ESSENTIAL MEMBER OF THE COMMUNITY, AND THE RINGING OF HAMMER ON ANVIL A FAMILIAR SOUND OF VILLAGE LIFE.

Market Bosworth's forge on Park Street, dating back to the late 18th century, was run by the Wothers family from 1840 but belonged to the Tollemache Scotts as part of the Bosworth Hall Estate. The Wothers bought the establishment in 1918, when Scott's daughter sold the entire barony, and continued to live and work at the forge until 1933 when it was sold again after the tragic suicide of Mr Bill Wothers. A public auction was held at the Dixie Arms and it passed into the hands of Mr Clement Phillips, who became an admired and familar figure about the village. In his time he produced some intricate and beautiful pieces of work which can still be admired on the gates of both St Peter's Church and the Memorial Garden at the top of Park Street. After his retirement in the late 1960s, the smithy became dormant and would remain so for some 30 years.

In the summer of 1997, the Oakley family bought the house at No.15, along with the adjoining forge and outbuildings, amazed that it was all so perfectly preserved. Only a few restorations were required. The chimney was cleared of sticks from years of jackdaw habitation, the dusty and stiff bellows coated with neat's-foot oil, and new belting installed and connected to the lathe, pillar drill and grindstone in order for the mechanisms to resume their duties after years of slumber.

Like many ancient country crafts, the art of the blacksmith has severely declined during the last hundred years, possibly due to the modern-day mass production of ironware which has created a limited market for the work of the traditional craftsman. At one time the horse played a very important role in rural England and a farrier was situated in most villages. However, in the hustle and bustle of the 21st century, the quiet and tranquil style of living has been lost and the horse is used mainly for recreational purposes.

In its heyday the blacksmith's forge was at the heart of the community, and beneath the meagre shade of the tree growing close to the wall, the horses would stand patiently flicking their tails. The men, waiting for their horses to be shod, passed the time in idle discussion, while the village children pestered to pump the huge bellows that stood in the corner. It was a winter treat to warm their chapped hands by the welcoming fire on the way home from school.

Lost in the haze of fading memories, The Forge on Park Street now holds its breath on what once was. With both the echoing clop of hoof on cobble and the sweet smell of horses long drifted away on the wind, it has taken on a new role and is now the interesting setting for an art and photograph gallery. This wonderful piece of history continues to draw interest and still holds a special place in the community, offering to both residents and tourists a treasured glimpse into the past.

Left: Brian Oakley at The Forge – photograph by Roy Illston.

Above: The Forge. Pencil drawing by Alan Spencer.

'BEAN'

PREVIOUS OWNERS OF THE GOPSALL ESTATE

PLANTED THE PARKLAND WITH MAGNIFICENT

TREES, SO TIMBER WAS ALWAYS ABUNDANTLY

AVAILABLE FOR EARL HOWE'S CARPENTERS.

They felled, seasoned and crafted this local wood into many things, including furniture for the Hall, and occasionally as wedding or retirement gifts for the Earl's retainers.

However, the Estate eventually declined and almost nothing now remains. Local antique dealer, John Thorp, known locally and affectionately as 'Bean', confirms that he rarely finds any items from Gopsall, although he does know of two old chairs in the locality.

One, an attractive Windsor chair, carved with a stylised 'H', for Howe, was made on the estate using locally grown wood, and presented as a retirement gift. The smooth seat and arms have that deep gleam resulting from continual

use and loving care over very many years. The other, a Victorian easy chair of the mid-1800s, stands square on polished but blackened mahogany legs and retains its original horsehair padding. This venerable and comfortable wing-chair was once a wedding present to one of the long-serving Gopsall housekeepers.

Old and treasured items have been offered for sale for many years in Bosworth – in the marketplace at the Miss Shepherds' shop, the 'Old Weighbridge Furnishings', and at the Lycett's shop, where Bob and Jill Roberts now run 'Corner Cottage Antiques'. Grace and Marianne Thorpe originally owned 'The Corner Cupboard' antiques shop in Main Street, and although no relation, this is the shop bought and now run by John Thorp as 'Bosworth Antiques'.

Although he rarely displays any Gopsall memorabilia, to gaze into John's shop window is to peer into an Aladdin's cave. Displayed on polished pie-crust tables, curvaceous Art Deco sideboards and barley-twist stools, are china plates, pewter mugs and glass jugs, enamelled metal boxes, all glinting in reflected light. And so much more – yesterday's pictures framed in heavy gilt; doilies, dollies, doorknobs and dinner knives; all manner of what-nots, knick-knacks and trinkets. All silently waiting, as so often before, to be lovingly taken and proudly displayed in yet another home, another stage on that journey that started so long ago in their maker's skilful hands.

Whilst having no particular favourites in the world of *objets d'art,* John does get special satisfaction in helping to identify items that have both aesthetic and financial value.

"There are no complete experts on antiques. Some do specialise in one particular field, but you have to be open to learn something new every day. A lady once brought in some silver to be valued, including a lovely old silver bullet teapot. She thought it might be worth something but had no idea and was in a bit of a hurry. I explained that it was a good piece, but I needed to look it up, and eventually, though I didn't buy it, I was able to tell her that it was worth two to three thousand pounds. It's nice when that happens."

John's grandfather, who once kept the Red Lion, rode to hounds with the Atherstone. John followed him into the saddle, so perhaps he has, at some time, hunted amongst the few remaining old trees at Gopsall. The same trees that may, even now, be waiting their turn to be made into desirable antiques of the future.

Above: John Thorp enjoys a laugh when reminded of his nickname 'Bean'.

Right: Bosworth Antiques, on the corner of Park Street and Main Street.

THE   WOODMAN

STROLLING AMONGST THE TANGLED PILES OF TREE
TRUNKS WAITING TO BE SAWN INTO BEAMS OR
PLANKS, ONE OF JOHN FINNEY'S CUSTOMERS
SUDDENLY STOPPED, STARED AND EXCLAIMED THAT
HE NOW HAD POSITIVE PROOF OF LIFE AFTER
DEATH, FOR HE COULD SEE NEW SHOOTS AND
GREEN LEAVES GROWING ON AN OLD TREE TRUNK
THAT LOOKS SO ANCIENT THAT IT MUST BE DEAD!

John, who runs the Verdon Sawmill, did not disagree, although he knew that whilst that tree trunk was quite old it could not be considered dead – it was a spring-felled tree, and the sap would keep rising long after felling, often creating new shoots and small leaves. He also knew that no wood should ever be considered 'dead'; since as a naturally grown material, even after felling, sawing, planing and shaping it will always retains some 'life' – and this gives wood both structural advantages and allows it to retain its visual beauty.

Starting life in Shackerstone in the 1940s, the sawmill moved via Parson's Yard in Verdon to its present site in Newbold Heath in the late 1950s, where the installation of modern machinery saw the death of the traditional sawpit. Thereafter the youngest employee was spared the slow, hard, tedious work, as in the bottom of the pit, blinded and choked by falling sawdust, he laboriously pushed the blade of the long two-handled saw back up through the log on which his older mate balanced as they sawed plank after plank, all day long.

The site – containing an old pond which is rumoured to have been fished, for their Friday meal, by the Newbold Heath monks – supplied lagging boards, lids and cutter-nogs for use on underground railways, but as Coal Board work died away, other products needed large amounts of imported timber. However, a wide range of English-grown timber is still used, and the yard is full of close-grained ash, straight-backed firs, beech, lime, poplar and coarse-barked oaks.

The mill's rather unusual practice of still sawing logs complete with their bark, led to an interesting diversion. A film crew was making a film about a German artist who, hounded by the Nazis, needed to conceal his massive 24 foot painting depicting the horrors of war. The film would show the artist effectively killing the picture on a saw table as he cut it into small pieces. However, his family hid the bits until after the war, when it was brought back to life by re-assembly. The cutting-up scene needed to be shot in an authentic sawmill that still cut logs in the old-fashioned way, complete with their bark, and Verdon Sawmill was ideal.

John enjoyed this brush with the film industry; although he takes his work very seriously, he is something of a romantic, and likes to occasionally indulge in unusual activities. The enormous totem pole standing at the entrance to the mill illustrates this. These traditional tribal emblems are often associated with the giving of life back to long-dead ancestors – perhaps reflecting John's instinctive feeling for timber? The totem stands 25 feet tall, alongside the head of an Indian chief complete with full feather head-dress. Both the totem and the head were carved with a chainsaw and rasp by local tree surgeon Tony Gardner, and painted by his brother.

Sadly, amongst the tangled pile of tree trunks in the yard are the remains of what was probably the last sessile oak in the county of Leicestershire. Felled only recently in Sutton Lane, Market Bosworth, with the sap still rising, it will remain alive and trying to support new growth – perhaps like village life which, despite the felling of so much from the past, will, whilst thoughtful and caring people supply its life-blood, continue to support new growth and live on and never die.

Right: The totem pole at Verdon Sawmill.

MINERAL / WATER

"THE HORSES IN THE FIELDS ALWAYS REMINDED ME OF THE PIT PONIES ON THEIR ANNUAL ONE-WEEK'S HOLIDAY ABOVE GROUND. THEY WOULD PRANCE AND KICK AND RUSH AROUND LIKE MAD THINGS, AND THEN RESIST LIKE HELL ALL EFFORTS TO GET THEM DOWN AGAIN. THIS WOULD MAKE ME ENJOY MY QUIET TIME ON THE WATER ALL THE MORE."

"Working underground at Desford Pit for all those years, I needed fresh air, and to hear the birds singing in the peaceful countryside, away from all the dirt and noise and bustle, and twenty years ago this simple stretch of canal was just right – you could be out all day and perhaps not see another boat."

So says Joe Goode, who moors his old narrowboat *No. 3 – Josh* at the old Bosworth Wharf, and who has enjoyed twenty years of narrowboating on the Ashby Union Canal. But he doesn't rate the pleasures now as great as they once were:

"Sadly that's now changed, it's more like driving on the roads – there's too much traffic, and the real peace and quiet's all but gone. There are no locks on this part, but on the Severn Trent or the Grand Union, you might queue for one and a half hours just to go through a single lock. And some of the people are so inconsiderate, not stopping to chat, not bothering to help someone in trouble. That's taken away so much – and that's why I don't go to the big get-togethers any more – I know lots enjoy it but for me there are too many boats, too many people and too much fuss."

The canals and the Midlands' coal mines are lasting monuments to the Victorian engineers and entrepreneurs. Joe recalls that the miners and engineers he worked with were great innovators:

"Desford was an experimental pit, and we had engineers visit from China, Russia and America. The first hydraulic pit prop, which replaced the old timber prop, was invented by Matt Smith, a local mines safety engineer. He slotted together two conveyor rollers with a leather seal and pumped it up, and it worked. It was called the Desford chock. The Beckeritt monorail system was also invented and first used here. I used to work on the cutting face, and I was one of the last ones to leave when the mine closed – I transferred to Whitwick."

Tied to the coal industry since its opening in the early 1700s, the twenty-two miles of the Ashby Canal carried coal from the North Leicestershire mines to

Above: Ashby Canal with St Peter's Church, Market Bosworth in the distance. A watercolour by Andy Shore.

Coventry and beyond. Coal was also unloaded at Bosworth Wharf, often spilling into the water from the overloaded barges, to be fished up later by local lads diving head first from the parapet of the bridge. So when Joe moors by Station Bridge, might he just imagine, within the spreading ripples of a rising fish, the pale reflection of a boy's hand triumphantly lifting a dripping piece of coal, grubbed up from the murky bottom?

In 2001 Joe did visit the popular Shackerstone Steam and Canal Festival, to meet up with an old mate he hadn't seen all year because all leisure activities on the canal had been halted by the foot-and-mouth epidemic.

Amongst the hundreds of boats at the festival was one belonging to Pete, who demonstrated coal-loading techniques – he believes his is the last remaining working boat still moving goods on the Midlands canals. The last commercial load on the Ashby Canal – rolls of paper – was shipped from Gopsall Wharf in 1970.

The gathering of more than one hundred boats included *Adamant,* one of the few remaining steam-powered narrow boats, and also *Helen,* a renovated ice-breaker, which originally would have been pulled by a team of steaming horses while men frozen by the cold, rhythmically rocked the boat from side to side to break a channel through the ice.

While the coal mines and this short length of canal were once major employers in the district, now the canal provides only leisure attractions for tourists. The canal, with its hump-backed bridges, steep-sided cuttings, aqueducts, and reportedly red-eared terrapins where the Midlands West Coast Railway crosses the canal, is growing in popularity. There are plans for an extension beyond the Snarestone Tunnel up to Europe's best preserved iron-smelting furnace at Moira, and also for a sixty-berth marina at Bosworth.

Coal, water, steam and railways – these are all constant reminders of those busy Victorian engineers, and still, two hundred years on, they provide some employment.

Above: Playful horses running free.

LEANER TIMES

THEIR FATHER USED TO WALK CATTLE AND SHEEP ALL THE WAY BACK FROM THE

ASHBY SALE YARD AND, RATHER NOSTALGICALLY, DAVID AND JOHN REMEMBER,

AS TEENAGERS, WALKING THEM BACK FROM BOSWORTH TO CONGERSTONE.

It was never easy and took time and patience. Someone had to lead the way to make sure that all the field gates were closed, to seal off road junctions with waving arms and shouts, and to look out for the occasional car.

John Dawkins accepts that those days have gone forever. Giant double-decker cattle wagons, carrying up to 40 animals each, are now needed to bring in the large number of cattle that are processed each week at the Dawkins' slaughterhouse. He often

Above: Limousin cross.

wonders, though, what the two brothers who started the business almost 250 years ago would make of today's world. In those distant peaceful days of 1755, driving cattle along deserted country lanes would have been quite normal, since all of the beasts would have been reared on local farms. Perhaps even the kicker, or 'best cow', sold at Bosworth Fair by Joseph Moxon on 8th May 1798 for £15. 19s.* might have been bought by the two Dawkins brothers, slaughtered at Congerstone, and the meat taken around the district by horse and cart to sell to local housewives.

Although the business now is different, there are still similarities. Up to 500 cattle and 3,000 sows, bought in from Scotland, Wales, Cornwall and the Isle of Man, may be processed each week, so 45 employees are needed rather than the 5 or 6 family members in 1755. The pole axe has been replaced by humane automated machines, but carcasses are still hung for 12 hours before being chilled, with the entire process and environment being computer controlled. John explains:

"Whilst the way the abattoir operates has not changed much, the quality and control standards are now very much higher. For instance, we have to pay for an army of inspectors and for a vet to be on the premises all day and every day, testing for everything – bacteria, hormones, BSE, etc."

This guarantees the quality of the product, though strangely enough the meat produced and sold five generations ago, when farming and the countryside was so much more natural, was probably just as good. Also, the skills of the slaughtermen – and women since it's no longer a job just for men – haven't changed in many years.

"In recent years the customer has wanted very lean meat, but some of the retailers, like M & S, are now responding to customer requests for more traditional meat – if it's too lean it doesn't eat so well."

In the 1970s David and John's business, expanding into the export market, merged with a specialist export packing company, but then BSE came along:

"We were exporting mainly to Italy – up to 1,000 cattle per week – but overnight this dropped to only 25 animals, so we had to re-focus on the UK market. Many abattoirs were forced to close, but we survived and recovered, and are pleased that we are still recognised as being amongst the top level of abattoirs in the country."

John still sometimes looks back to happier times, recalling with amusement an old guy on his blue tractor, absolutely sozzled after a Bosworth sale day, but never failing to bring back the stock in his trailer. However, he prefers to look forward with anticipation to better times for the farming community and all who live and work in the countryside.

Above: Champion! David Dawkins celebrating an early award.

* from *A Truly Honest Man* by Peter Foss and Timothy Parry.

'CLOCKY' DEACON

THE OLD CLOCK ON THE FRONT OF THE CONGREGATIONAL CHAPEL AT NEWTON BURGOLAND IS QUITE UNIQUE. THERE ARE TWO FACES — ONE ON THE OUTSIDE FACING THE SECULAR WORLD AND ONE ON THE INSIDE FACING THE WORLD OF PRAYERS, HYMNS AND SERMONS.

The man who made this clock was not only a renowned local clockmaker but also a very devout 18th-century Baptist pastor. As a very intelligent and thoughtful man, might Samuel Deacon have used this clock as the basis for one of his sermons? Perhaps to reflect on the daily temptations faced in the sinful outside world, and how they could be resisted by time spent face to face with God inside the chapel?

The early part of the 18th century witnessed a massive evangelical revival which, despite stormy opposition, swept from Wales through the Midlands and right into Barton in the Beans. Taking root there, a strong Baptist tradition slowly spread its influence far afield, causing Samuel Deacon's father, also named Samuel, to lay down his scythe and decide to become a Baptist pastor.

Young Samuel was sent to Normanton le Heath, apprenticed to a clockmaker who was also a Baptist pastor. He instructed Samuel not only how to regulate clocks but also how to find an acceptable balance between his secular and religious lives. In 1771, young Samuel, married to the daughter of one of the first seven members of the Baptist Church at Barton, came to live there and to set up his own clockmaking business. His first sermon, preached in the chapel in 1777, was so well praised that he was invited to be co-pastor along with his father, old Samuel.

Baptists recall young Samuel's claim to be a minister first and a clockmaker second and point to his easy-to-read pamphlets and telling sermons, sometimes preached at the old nearby gibbet post. However, in horological circles he is best known for his clockmaking skills. Eventually, employing several journeymen in his workshop, he produced a wide range of clocks and watches. His old turret clock from Market Bosworth church now chimes in the Leicester Museum, whilst his musical masterpiece was a clock for the Vicar of Hinckley. This could play fifty different tunes, with hymns on Sunday, and included a band of mechanical musicians. The number of longcase clocks still tick-tocking around the country is testament to Samuel's craftsmanship. Clocks that originally sold for £4 to £6 now regularly sell for £7,000 to £12,000.

The simple mechanism of Samuel's early clocks was no different from those of most contemporary makers. A chain of gears, driven by descending weights, that needed pulling up again every few hours or days, drove the hands and a bob-weight pendulum regulated the time-keeping. His father-in-law made the wooden cases, in oak or mahogany, whilst the painted dials were made in Birmingham. His clocks are usually simply signed as *'Deacon, Barton'* but as a skilled engraver many of the mechanisms include engraved faces. He is reported to have been a happy man, prepared to work very long hours whilst existing on bread and small beer, but the 'Clock Clubs' he ran showed him to be an astute businessman. A number of people would agree to pay so much per month until the price of the clock was met when the members might then draw for that clock. These clubs were also treated as social gatherings, as two of the 'club rules' would seem to indicate: 'Members to pay 4/- per month and 3d to be spent on ale.' (Ale then cost $1\frac{1}{2}$d per pint), and club hours were – 7 to 8 in the summer, 6 to 8 in the winter.

Buried with his father in Barton chapel, young Samuel's memorial tablet recalls him as 'a most luxuriant inventor, a ready wit, a fluent utterance and a striking aptness at appropriate metaphor' and he is commemorated by the many visitors who visit this very important chapel each year.

The Romans, once in this area, may have founded the old village name – Barton Fabis (Latin for bean) – and may have tracked time with candles ringed to mark each hour of burning. And so much later, workers in the many bean fields – so many that Leicestershire folk were known as 'Bean Bellys' – may have told the time by church bell chimes. But then along came young Samuel. As a farm boy he set up simple sundials in the fields to tell the time – an upright stick in a circle scratched on the ground – but as a man he left his mark for all time in this quiet rural place.

Left: Barton Baptist Chapel which in 1841 cost almost £900 to build.

N A T U R E   &   E N V I R O N M E N T

ONE DAY A LARGE PART OF THE MIDLANDS, RIGHT
ON OUR DOORSTEP, WILL BECOME AN INTRICATE
PATCHWORK OF MATURE FOREST AND FARMLAND
— A NEW NATIONAL FOREST.

In the very heart of England this very ambitious long-term environmental project will return 200 square miles of land to a green swathe of millions of trees, perhaps reflecting the way things were in days long past. For once this area was so abundantly afforested that noble lords and kings hunted in deep shade for deer and boar.

But strong oaks were felled to help build England's naval might, while ash and willow armed her doughty bowmen. Trees were slowly burnt to charcoal which then fed ever-glowing forges, where smiths wrought armour, swords and pikes.

Later, in more peaceful times, much wood went underground as pit props, whilst charcoal continued to feed the forge for harness, plough and scythe. The sawmill buzzed all day to create rafters, fence posts, lintels, floorboards, chairs and sideboards, coffin planks and the lych-gate for the church.

Until at last the farmers had to have the land to meet the ever growing call for food. Factories too needed space to grow, and faster ways to move their goods than country lanes – so roads evolved through carriageways to motorways, until it seemed that concrete was everywhere.

Fortunately, not all of the forests, woods and spinneys, or even all the hedges, were sacrificed. This quiet corner of the old Sparkenhoe Hundred is amongst those areas still blessed with pleasant countryside, and in the following pages we reflect on the infinite variety in our local environment today.

Farming is beset with problems which must, to some, seem insurmountable, and the new millennium started badly when foot and mouth returned early in 2001. And not just farmers suffered, since all whose interests mean their shoes are stained with country mud were badly hit. While many backs are turned upon the land, others move into the country, barns fill with designer kitchens, and fields are reshaped as country estates for the *nouveaux riches*.

However, not all is doom and gloom, and farming is only part of the country scene. The experiences related here by a former vet are both humorous and serious, as are the rural reminiscences of a one-time 'Resident of the Year'.

Gardening changed and changed again during the 20th century and with 'everything organic' now back in favour, the roles of the garden centre and organic kitchen garden are compared.

Old and new are so often found side by side in nature. Summer visitors to Market Bosworth are drawn both by its history and the floral displays that now enhance the town. Lady Agnes Drive, developed by Tollemache Scott for his wife, starts at the edge of the new Country Park Arboretum. Fungi, amongst the most ancient of all growing plants, are considered and explained, whilst a new development on old neglected ground in Shenton Lane is reviewed.

However, it is trees that add so much to any English countryside. So we also look at Osbaston's 200-year-old beech tree; at the hundreds of trees planted and nurtured at Coton Priory by Eugene Salvador; and at the work of a local tree surgeon.

The wonderful English countryside is to be revered, cherished and enjoyed, as in the opening words of Laurie Lee's 'Home from Abroad':

So do I breathe the hayblown airs of home,
And watch the sea-green elms drip birds and shadows,
And as the twilight nets the plunging sun
My heart's keel slides to rest among the meadows.

Laurie Lee.

Above: Red squirrel. Pen and ink drawing by Glyn Croman.

Right: Copper beech tree at Appleby Magna.

MANOR FARM, BARTON

UNTIL RECENTLY THE COWS FROM MANOR FARM WALKED THROUGH THE VILLAGE, DOWN TO THE CROSSROADS AND UP THE ROAD. THEN THE COWS CAME FIRST IN VILLAGE LIFE — BUT NOT ANY MORE.

Today, Barton's last remaining dairy herd hurries quickly across the road so as not to hold up the traffic. Village life and the farmer's place in it have changed much as we enter the new millennium.

From respected 'post-war feeder of the nation' to 'over-subsidised and feather-bedded', 'farming in crisis' is now the familiar headline. Farms and farmers have slowly disappeared. Increased efficiency, over-production, the power of the supermarkets: whatever the reasons, the effects on farming have been dramatic and the village has changed forever.

In the 1950s there were seven working farms in Barton. All were mixed farms employing village labour, sending children to the village school and supporting the cricket team that played at the farm. It is perhaps too easy to look back at this as a rose-tinted 'Golden Age'. Some changes have been for the better and as a location the village is no doubt on the up. Now there are but two farms left and the school and cricket team are long gone. Although the acres farmed in the village are still the same, the land has been amalgamated and the farmhouses and farm buildings sold off or converted. One-time cowsheds now contain designer kitchens, and four-wheel drives fill the one-time farmyards (more horsepower is needed for the school run than was ever needed for the farm). All this, so familiar now, would have been inconceivable to our grandfathers' generation.

Manor Farm has so far resisted the temptation to convert and is now farmed by the fourth generation of the Jackson family. The question is, will it be the last? Over the years Manor Farm has grown, and now comprises also parts of the old Yew Tree, Sycamore and Grange Farms. The farm has recently converted to organic production, specialising in organic milk.

Roger Jackson

Above: Friend or foe?

Right: Manor Farm, Barton in the Beans.

BOSWORTH IN BLOOM

1985 WOULD MARK THE QUINCENTENARY, SO DECISIONS HAD TO BE MADE ABOUT HOW TO CELEBRATE THE 500TH ANNIVERSARY OF THE BATTLE OF BOSWORTH.

Suggestions included a medieval dinner, coats-of-arms in The Square, commemorative litter bins, shop assistants dressed in period dress, and flowers to brighten up the town centre.

The Parish Council, chaired at that time by Jackie Atkinson, liked this last suggestion from Joy Brookes of the Inner Circle, and the town was duly bedecked with flowers. Joy had also heard of the Britain in Bloom competition and it seemed sensible to enter that at the same time. Surprised to be announced winners of the East Midlands class and joint winners in the All-England class, it was decided to try again in 1986 – and Bosworth in Bloom was born.

Living in the The Square, regularly to be seen clearing litter or sweeping the gutters, Dick and Blanche Symonds have been closely involved since the first year:

"A small committee was formed to plan each year's display and without these enthusiasts the organisation wouldn't have been so successful. John Rawson and Peter Bayliss are now the main advisers on plants, but innumerable volunteers collect, sort, plant, water, feed, weed, dead-head and eventually, at season's end, help to dispose of each year's display. They also help to bring in the money with our raffle, plant sales and second-hand books which are sold right through the year. Costs have risen each year from less than £1,000 in 1985 to almost £6,000 nowadays, and these are always met by public donation."

Although it is hard work the rewards are very satisfying. In fifteen years, Bosworth in Bloom has won the Regional award fourteen times and competed in the National Finals ten times. Having won the National in 1988 Bosworth was chosen along with Bognor Regis to compete in the Entente Florale, and was awarded an honourable third place by the European judges.

"The committee act as hosts when the judges call to inspect, but it's not just the flowers, because only 25% of the marks are awarded for those. They also check to see if the town is tidy, verges cut, rubbish bins empty, streets clear of litter and dog dirt, no graffiti and no fly posting. We have to show photographs of springtime flowers and they ask how many children are involved; is this a true community project; is there any permanent planting; and so on."

This is why so many people help – Brownies, Cubs and Play Group planting spring bulbs and High School children pulling up weeds by the school railings. The town benefits from the tourists who come to see the flowers – many of the local organisations give generous donations and are also actively involved.

"Many businesses in the town arrange and care for their own displays – Mrs Williamson always took special pride in her geraniums – and the busy-lizzy towers at the town entrances are watered and dead-headed by people who live close by. It's a real community effort right through the season – the landlady at the King William, for instance, waters for Tin-Tin when they go away – and one man donates two big nets of bulbs every year. Some people say community spirit is dying in Bosworth but that's not our experience.

"We both love Bosworth and couldn't live anywhere else. We're saddened that there are so few residences left in The Square – it has changed the character. Parking remains a problem, of course, but the Wheatsheaf Courtyard is a delightful spot – difficult to imagine when that was just Mr Hatton's barber's shop and a cafe."

Left: Cherry tree and tulips, Barton Road.
Above left: Lily.
Above right: Petunias in front of St Peter's Hall.

AJB

'OLD BEASTY'

LOW IN THE BRANCHES OF ONE OF THE FINEST TREES IN THE AREA,

A MISTLE THRUSH RAISES HER HEAD AND CALLS TO THE CRISP

MORNING AIR.

"She returns every year", says Mr Gordon Earp, who lives at Osbaston House Farm.

This magnificent copper beech seems to embrace the old house and, over a span of nearly one hundred years, it has witnessed the growth of three generations of the Earp family.

'Old Beasty' was planted about two hundred years ago by Mr James Thorpe, who is buried in the churchyard at Nailstone. Through the years of wind and rain, only one of its largest branches has been lost. A remaining huge bough stretches 20 feet parallel to the ground 6 foot above the cobbles of the yard and when the tree is bursting with purple foliage, the Earps place a large prop under it to support the extra weight of the leaves.

The whiskers of 'Old Beasty's' crown rise high above the roof of the house and during the summer months it is a wonderful sight to see it cast tiger skins of dappled sunlight on the side of the building. The copper beech tree was possibly grafted onto a common beech which accounts for a raised ring at waist height on the trunk. At this point the girth measures an impressive 14 feet.

It is certainly one of the most beautiful trees in the Market Bosworth area and in reaching this grand old age, out-living the man who planted it by 134 years, it is a shining example of one of the giants of our English natives.

The name 'Old Beasty' seems a fitting title but when asked about the origin of the name, Mr Earp laughed, "No, no, old BEECH tree!"

Above: An old giant – photograph by Erica Tomlinson.

'DINGLE DELL'

FOR OVER 30 YEARS ALBERT AND GRACE GUTTES LIVED IN THEIR OLD BUNGALOW WITHOUT MAINS WATER AND ELECTRICITY. TEATIME MEANT A TRIP TO A SPRING OR LOCAL DITCH AND EVENINGS WERE SPENT IN THE SOFT FLICKER OF CANDLES OR OIL LAMPS.

Their near neighbours, Jackie and Alice Smith, lived in an old caravan just down the road. Their water supply was also a spring in the nearby field, but it was piped into an old brick cattle-trough behind the caravan.

Albert, who came to England from Estonia when in his early twenties, and his wife, Grace, have lived in their bungalow for well over forty years, but now, through the concern of Shenton villagers and the local council, enjoy the benefits of mains water and electricity from a generator.

Jackie Smith, employed by Bosworth Council as a roadman, and Alice lived alongside the railway for many years, often adding bits and pieces to their caravan and to a collection of ramshackle sheds until the whole site became what would have been Heath Robinson's pride and joy.

When Jackie died, Bill and Violet Orton, Alice's daughter, moved in for a few years until, eventually, the old buildings were cleared away to make space for the storage of reclaimed building materials. Then, in 1999, a 'For Sale' notice went up at the old farm site.

Most of us would have walked past without any thought of buying such a neglected and derelict plot, but for Brenda and Norman Gould, it was the answer to their dreams, as Norman explains:

"We had built our own house in Stoney Stanton twenty years ago but we felt it was time to move on. We had just missed buying a bungalow in Market Bosworth when I saw this advertisement in the local paper. I used to run along the canal towpath with the dog, so I knew Shenton Lane and as soon as we looked over the site we knew it was where we wanted to live.

'After we moved to live in a second-hand 'seaside caravan', a mate asked what on earth made us want to live at such a dump. We laughed and told him that he had to look at the potential and not what it was then. We already have mains water but still rely on a generator for electricity. The garden is slowly beginning to take shape, although Brenda thinks the temporary flower beds I made for the plants we brought with us look more like graves!"

The Goulds are an unusual couple. Brenda loves the peace and solitude of their new home yet is an Eddy Stobart lorry fanatic. One very special birthday treat was a ride to Chesterfield in a Stobart lorry with her son at the wheel. But Norman's gift of a picture of Brenda in front of one of Eddy's lorries, painted on an old milking churn, was even more special.

Norman and Brenda both love the great outdoors. They have walked the Pennine Way together and love mountains and lakes. Some time ago Norman completed three London Marathons, benefiting the Great Ormond Street Children's Hospital, and he expects to run in other local events in the future.

When they first moved in they took down the old *Dingle Dell* sign from the gate and renamed the site *Wood View*. Their old 'seaside caravan' has been replaced by a new mobile home, and trees planted to encourage more wildlife, and when interviewed they were both looking forward, in Brenda's words, to the 'miracle of spring'. When asked to say what is so special about living there, Norman simply opened a window and said: *"Listen – silence, except for the birds singing – that's why we're here!"*

Above: Young tawny owls. Pen and ink drawing by Glyn Croman.

GREENFINGERS

"...THEY USED TO MAKE BRICKS HERE — IT WAS CALLED BRICKYARD FARM ON THE DEEDS. PEOPLE WOULD CALL TO ASK IF THEY COULD DIG FOR OLD BOTTLES, BECAUSE AT ONE TIME IT WAS ALSO AN OLD VICTORIAN RUBBISH TIP."

In 1976, when Brian and Sandra Claybrook moved in, Tilcon were still extracting sand from the Cadeby quarry just over the road, right opposite the 2.5 acre site. There was only a small bungalow and a few old farm buildings, but Brian and Sandra needed the ground to grow flowers.

Brian had opened his first greengrocer's and florist's shop before he left the mines and now with five shops to stock, the site quickly bloomed with chrysanthemums. However, flowers grown from cuttings, back-breakingly rooted in open ground and carefully nurtured whatever the weather, still sold on Coventry Wholesale Market for only 10p a bunch.

Holland had been the centre of the European flower industry for many years and was supported by massive subsidies. Imported Dutch flowers soon began to undercut even these low prices, and supermarkets were starting to hit the corner greengrocer's pocket, so Brian and Sandra needed to think again:

"It became obvious what would happen, so having invested in our first glasshouse, we started to sell bedding plants grown from seed. We had no thoughts of a garden centre, because at that time they just didn't exist. Keen gardeners sold their surplus home-grown produce at the roadside and nurseries mainly supported the big country houses – they were the only ones with real ornamental gardens.

"Gardeners went to nurseries for their seeds, cabbage plants and the like, and perhaps a few wallflowers, but that was all. We still sell a few cabbage plants, but fifty times more flowering bedding plants, plus trees and shrubs and all of the composts and pots and gravel and water features – everybody wants so many different things. It's all a big change from when we started to sell bedding plants from pallets on the front lawn."

Heavy snow in 1990 caused some of the glasshouses to crash and gave problems not only to Greenacres but also to Bosworth in Bloom:

"We have supplied Bosworth in Bloom right from the first year, but when the electricity failed during a heavy snowstorm, we couldn't save the plants in our glasshouses. Normally you turn up the heat and the snow slides off the warm glass, but that year we lost all our plants and couldn't supply anything. Sandra and her team still make all of the hanging baskets for each year's competition and for other customers in the surrounding villages.

"Winter can be a difficult time. In the summer and autumn, shrubs fill the space vacated by the earlier bedding plants, but from November to March there's a gap. At one time nursery staff would be laid off over the winter months, but as we don't want to lose them we've built up our Christmas displays, which everyone seems to like.

"The garden programmes on television are changing garden fashions. Once it was all conifers – Leylandii – now it's laurel and the like. Ten years ago you couldn't sell a big plant, but now young people want instant effect: bigger and bigger shrubs and trees, and all those decks and bright purple paints!"

What would the staid Victorians, throwing away their old bottles in the tip, have made of this demand for 'instant' gardens? Or of Brian, telephoning his plant order to an agent at an Amsterdam auction, knowing that a successful bid will guarantee immediate shipment and arrival at Greenacres within 24 hours!

Right: A display of tulips.

LADY AGNES DRIVE

A LARGE LIME TREE SHADES THE ENTRANCE TO
LADY AGNES DRIVE. STICKY WITH WINTER MUD
AND CHOKED IN THE SUMMER WITH HOGWEED, THE
PATH OPENS UP TO DISPLAY A VARIED COLLECTION
OF TREES INCLUDING BEECH, OAK AND SYCAMORE
WHICH DRIP THEIR CRIMSON AND GOLD INTO THE
AUTUMN PUDDLES.

Charles Tollemache Scott bought the Bosworth Hall Estate from the Dixies in 1885 and built the tree-lined ride not long afterwards to commemorate his wife. The drive leads to Wood House, the old shooting lodge, then known as Park House, which lies between the Old Fox Covert and Spring Wood behind the present Bosworth Park. A few remaining cobbles still peep between the moss and grass as a reminder of those affluent days of gentle strolls and high tea in the summerhouse which stood adjacent to the Old Fox Covert. A building still stands in the same field which may have once been a deer hide but is now crumbling and bursting with elder.

Each season brings its own beauty to this enchanting spot, and through May the wood towards the top of the path becomes a mist of blue as spring lays its carpet of bluebells. Scott had a keen interest in rehabilitating the woods and coppices on his estate, and this thoughtful restoration is reflected in the character of the woods we enjoy today. The Oak Ring, half-way along Lady Agnes Drive, just before the Looking Glass Lake, is particularly lovely during spring with its generous explosions of pink rhododendron blooms under whose twisted stems lies a plaque which reads: *Planted in 1886 by Charles and Agnes Tollemache Scott.*

The half-timbered lodge was built in 1886 by Tollemache Scott, replacing an earlier Keeper's House. The wooden lintel above the main entrance bears the inscription CTS. These initials are a familiar sight throughout the town as Scott was responsible for many of the improvements to the estate, not only to the parkland but also to the buildings of Bosworth. Many were superfluous additions and it is these buildings which proudly boast his initials and coat-of-arms.

During the late 19th century Bosworth Park was abundant with deer and was home to both a herd of rare Black Old English fallow deer and a smaller herd of red deer. A large and varied collection of game thrived on the estate, providing the visiting gentry with their recreational pleasures. The walls of the lodge would have been crowded with portraits and trophies of Scott's successful shooting parties. As a keen huntsman, he held great respect for his horses. This particular tribute, engraved on a shrine south of Beau Pool in Bosworth Park, echoes his heart-felt sentiment:

In memory of SCOTT'S GREY, 10 seasons without a fall. Born 1876, Died 1892. A trusty steed, a faithful friend, makes good the journey to the end.

Silhouetted against the Southwood Park, in view of both Lady Agnes Drive and Sutton Lane, stands the solitary statue of Hercules, dramatically posed subduing the Nemean lion which was the first of his twelve labours. It is believed that the 4th or 5th Baronet Dixie brought him back from a grand European tour in the late 18th century. At that time it was common practise for the aristocracy to return with souvenirs from foreign countries, often in the form of a statue or bust to enhance the estate parkland. After the departure of the Dixies some years later, the new squire of Bosworth Hall, Charles Tollemache Scott, named his racehorse after the monument and the Hercules Inn across the fields in Sutton Cheney was, in turn, named after the horse!

Above: The statue of Hercules subduing the Nemean lion.

Right: A beech tree in autumn splendour.

THE SHOW

THE 2001 FOOT AND MOUTH EPIDEMIC CAUSED HAVOC AND MISERY, AFFECTING MOST PEOPLE IN SOME WAY BUT DEVASTATING THE FARMERS AND ALL WHOSE LIVES DEPEND ON FARMING.

Also badly affected were those whose livelihoods needed the countryside to be 'open' and available for recreation and leisure pursuits.

Among the list of casualties caused by this terrible disease was a local one that, sadly, may never fully recover.

Cancelled by the same disease twice before – in 1912 and 1966 – the 2001 Bosworth Show, held since 1896 at Bosworth Park and more recently on the Bosworth showgrounds, could not be staged.

Arthur Tomlin has been a committee member for the Show for many years:

"Today's younger farmers are too busy trying to make a decent living out of the land, and may have insufficient time or interest to devote to a Show that now seems more entertainment than agriculture.

"Perhaps it's got too big. Do we need to re-introduce more stock, to balance the equestrian events? Costs are now so high – £52,000 for the 2000 centenary year, and even the Marines Band cost £4,000. We now have to deal with all of the VAT headaches, yet we could only donate £3,500 to the Hinckley Scanner Fund.

"I'm sad about the changes, since the old Bosworth Show was an important meeting place for farmers, where they could look at and buy the latest farming implements – there would be 200 yards of them all laid out on display. Of course, tradition demanded it always rained on Show Day, and once it was so bad that the showground was cleared after lightning struck the Secretary's tent – Finlay Salmon at that time."

Arthur, now in his eighties, hopes the Show will continue, and not follow the Bosworth Sale Yard into oblivion. Some of his favourite memories relate to these two local institutions, and to his father's Shire horses.

"One Show morning one of the Shires loosened a shoe, and my Dad said to run around to Clem Phillips, the blacksmith, to ask if he could re-nail it. However, Mrs Clem opened the door and told me to 'Clear off – my husband needs his day off for the Show'. I never knew such an antagonistic woman! She also made me miss my dinner one Saturday morning. I had walked a pair of Shires from Wykin to Bosworth to be shod and Clem, a lovely mild-mannered helpful man, had finished all but a few nails. However, it was almost 12.30 and on the dot Mrs Clem called to say it was dinnertime. Clem said that he had just four nails to do and would be there in a minute, but the reply came immediately: 'Do you want your dinner now or do you want it in the bin?' Clem grinned sheepishly and went for his dinner. I had to wait another hour and a quarter, then walk the horses back home and I missed *my* dinner!"

Arthur also recalls the importance of the Bosworth Sale Yard, when all the farming news and gossip would be exchanged around the pens or around a free dish of mushy peas set on the bar at the Black Horse.

"Lady Dixie owned the rights to the Sale Yard as well as The Square and collected the tolls during the Cattle Market. One of the auctioneers, Tommy Marsden, who lost a leg in World War One, always wore a top hat when he was selling. Bosworth May Fair, always held on the 8th of May, grew to be one of the largest in the country – sometimes running for two days.

"At one time 80 to 100 breeding bulls would arrive by train and had to be led, each by the ring in its nose, up Station Road to the Cattle Market. Lots of stock walked in by road and one time a neighbour asked if I would walk in some of his calves along with my Ayrshires. They'd been reared in a barn and had never seen daylight, so were almost blinded, and were uncontrollable – into the hedges, people's gardens, all over the place – we didn't get there till after dinner, almost too late for the sale."

Arthur's quite a man – he was Hinckley and Bosworth 'Resident of the Year' in 1998 and he once came fourth when he 'ploughed for England' in an international competition held near Chester. Having learnt to paint and draw as a boy whilst convalescing from tetanus – "… a terrible time, hardly able to move for weeks, everything locked up – even my eyes – and with cupfuls of serum into my bum twice a day" – he has since painted or drawn 45 local village churches and country houses, all featured in the local press.

Left: The entrance to Bosworth showground.

AJB

THE TREE SURGEON

ON AN OLD MAP DETAILING PROPERTY FOR SALE BY AUCTION, AYLESBROOK COTTAGE WAS SHOWN AS AN ISOLATED HOUSE ON THE EDGE OF THE VILLAGE.

The age of the property is not known, as it was part of the Bosworth Hall Estate which was broken up in 1918, but parts of the house are thought to date back to the 1600s when it was probably built for an estate worker.

Tony Gardner, the owner of this pretty picture-book cottage, takes up the story:

"To a Leicester lad, moving to Bosworth almost 25 years ago, it was like taking a holiday – we couldn't believe our luck. Everything was here we could possibly want and everyone said 'hello'.

"Our cottage, which was recently re-thatched, is unique. It's the only 'straw' house in Market Bosworth, since Rainbow Cottage and the old almshouses in the Market Square are thatched with reed.

"We were a bit worried when opposite us the old Westhaven garden wall was demolished and a new building started, but then we realised that living in a thatched house opposite a fire station might not be so bad after all! We were grateful to have help so close at hand when a bad chimney fire had the thatch smouldering and the whole roof was threatened, but Terry Parnell, the then Fire Chief, and his part-time fire-fighters, saved the day."

At first sight Tony's garden might appear to be typical of most old English cottages, until you notice the wooden sculptures. All made using only a chain-saw and rasp, they include not only animals native to our shores – owls and otters, but figures too that would perhaps be more at home on Easter Island or other tropical shores. Tony again:

"I always wanted to be a gardener – perhaps something to do with my name? – but when I applied to Leicester Parks Department the only vacancy was for a trainee tree surgeon. I was 'apprenticed' to an old man who over the next year or so taught me all he knew about trees. I take a real pride in my work and feel privileged to be able to spend most of my time with trees, which I really love – it's much more than just a job. Every day I know that there will be new challenges – the type of tree, its location, neighbouring roads and buildings and all of the safety considerations.

"I can understand why passers-by are interested to watch when we're working up a tree, but it still amazes me that they often ignore my groundsman's warning and still walk right under the tree when we're cutting. An old oak tree can weigh 4 to 5 tons, and cut branches are deceptively heavy and potentially lethal.

"Originally we used only a bow-saw and no ropes or safety devices. You simply free-climbed just like a young boy would do, and I had an early scare when a heavy Lombardy poplar branch suddenly split, threatening to crush me as it swung violently towards me. Eventually we started to use simple hemp ropes but nowadays modern synthetic ropes and safety harnesses are used. But don't ask me to lend you any of my safety gear – my life depends on it when I'm 100 feet above the ground!

"We now use chain-saws and these have allowed me to extend my passion for trees and timber by carving free-hand sculptures – recycling waste wood into what I hope may be seen as simple environmental art. I also hope that my demonstrations of this technique at country fairs may help youngsters to take a deeper interest in trees. It's yet another thing that I look forward to when I drive back through the park gates – I know I'm home, back to my cottage and family, and the chance to relax and think about another sculpture."

Above: Silhouette of pines above Market Bosworth Rectory.

Right: Aylesbrook Cottage. The exact date of the property is unknown, but it is thought that parts date back to the 1600s.

T H A T C H

THATCHING IS THE OLDEST BUILDING CRAFT IN THE COUNTRY AND HAS BEEN USED FOR MAKING ROOFS FOR OVER 2,500 YEARS.

It reached its peak in the Middle Ages and has changed little since. In the days when wheat was harvested by hand it was the cheapest method of roofing. However, when materials became too costly for the working classes, corrugated iron was laid over the worn and tattered roof as a makeshift barrier against the elements. The art of thatching had come under threat and the thatched roof started its decline.

Norfolk reed is the hardiest of thatching material and if laid properly can last up to 80 years but due to the drop in availability and the inevitable rise in cost, it is not always the first choice. Long straw is a local resource in the Midlands so is a fitting option for the re-thatching of Aylesbrook Cottage on Station Road, Market Bosworth. The crop is grown especially long to accommodate the needs of a thatcher as today's modified crops encourage shorter straw for easier harvesting and less susceptibility to storm damage.

Aylesbrook Cottage in Market Bosworth is a quaint little house and displays a fine example of thatch. The old roof has been replaced by long straw, enhancing its existing charm and transforming it into a picturesque little dwelling. A roof thatched in this way has a more natural and almost untidy finish compared with a roof covered in reed. Its appearance is very distinctive and offers a wonderful natural finish in contrast to the manicured look of Rainbow Cottage, the Rotary Cottages in The Square and No. 9 Sutton Lane, which are all reed thatched. The ridge of the roof is cut into points and scallops and decorated with liggers and crossrods, which are fixed into place with spars. Hazel wood is used to make these essential implements, as it is flexible and easy to work with.

Joe Wykes is the talent behind the roof of Aylesbrook Cottage. He is a true craftsman, dedicated to his chosen trade, and takes unusual pride in his work. Thatchers must be a hardy breed as they work outside, up and down a ladder for most of the day carrying tons of reed and straw. The job can take many months and must continue during harsh weather conditions. Joe commented that in his early days as a thatcher he would suffer with hard calluses on his hands, and if one was to peel off he would 'superglue it back' as a soft sore spot was unbearable. These days his hands are as tough as leather!

Recently the thatch has made a welcome come-back. Rural areas are becoming commuter hot-spots, bringing wealth into the countryside, the once thatched cottages are claiming back their original status. In Bosworth a plot of land has been pinpointed for a possible development of new thatched houses and in many parts of the country, architects are incorporating thatched roofs into their designs. Its handsome appearance and excellent insulating properties perhaps encourage this new-found popularity. It is cool in the summer and warm in the winter and almost totally soundproof, which is hardly surprising under 4 feet of materials! This natural, ancient craft will perhaps take root once more and flourish in the environment to which it belongs.

Above: An old thatched house. Pen and ink drawing by Doug Lewis.

Right: A 16th century thatched cottage on Sutton Lane, Market Bosworth.

THE SECRET GARDEN

STRETCHING THE DISTANCE FROM OSBASTON HALL TO HOME FARM AT THE CROSSROADS, IS A TALL 18TH-CENTURY RED BRICK WALL TENTATIVELY BRUSHED BY THE GRACEFUL BOUGHS OF AN ANCIENT BEECH TREE. CONCEALED BEHIND ITS IMPOSING STATURE IS A HIDDEN TREASURE.

As children growing up in Osbaston, we didn't like to play down the lane towards the home of the formidable Guinness family. This secluded part of the village was damp and dark under the trees even during the summer months, so we would gladly retreat to the warmth of the red brick and the exciting glow of the unknown. It was a 'secret garden' and we longed to get over the wall to where we knew the raspberries grew.

A rambling apple tree stood to the side of the double white gates, its boughs gnarled and twisted, tempting us into its branches with the rosy cheeks of its fruit bobbing and shining.

Up until the last few years, Osbaston kitchen garden was kept exclusively for the residents of the Hall, but under the ownership of the de Lisle family it has opened its gates to the eagerly interested public. For a small fee one can enjoy the beauty of a scene seemingly lost in this modern age, and wander between the flourishing shrubs and swaying hollyhocks.

Flick, the gardener, voluntarily dedicates much of her time to the upkeep of this garden, which is a true testament to the efficacy of organic gardening without the use of chemicals and man-made fertilisers. The inevitable presence of nettles and other weeds encourages butterflies and insects which are of great importance for the survival of native garden birds. Tucked away in a quiet spot overgrown with long grass, a pile of breeze-blocks accommodates a family of coal tits which return every year to raise their young.

This idyllic garden is open to the public six times a year, giving visitors the opportunity to escape from the present day and step back into a place where time has stood still.

Previous pages: Osbaston kitchen garden.
Above: The east elevation of Osbaston Hall.
Right: Blossoming apple tree at the entrance to the garden.

Above: The old veterinary surgery, built by William Beck for John and Pam Nadin in 1956-7. Watercolour by Keith Johnson.

THE VET

As a young veterinary surgeon from a busy Coalville practice I first drove into Market Bosworth one beautiful sunny September morning in 1951 – and what a lovely peaceful and unspoiled place it was. I was getting married in three months' time, and thought how wonderful it would be to live here.

The practice at Bosworth dealt predominately with large animals – dogs and cats were almost unknown. Now, owing to the sad decline in agriculture, the tail wags the dog. Dairy cattle were our mainstay with some pigs, sheep and horses, which in those days included pit ponies. Then we had to make up most of the medicines ourselves from basic ingredients. Our horse embrocation, containing turpentine, was very popular with the miners for their bad backs. In the early 1950s the practice was 80% art and 20% science; now, the opposite applies.

One evening a lady came into the surgery with a shoebox, which she informed me contained one of her pet budgies, Percy, who according to her was as good as dead. I removed the lid with less than the usual caution. Whoosh! Luckily the surgery window was shut. I remarked that Percy appeared far from dead and was informed that the budgie flying around was Freddie whom she had brought along to keep Percy company. Poor Percy was beyond treatment. In 1967, on Michaelmas Sunday, I received a telephone call that a client was worried about three or four of his cows. On arrival at the farm a close inspection left me in no doubt that here was Leicestershire's first case of foot and mouth disease. Fortunately it turned out to be the only one. No Michaelmas goose that day!

Market Bosworth had a fatstock market every Monday and we held a surgery for a short time, first in the Black Horse and then at Bakery Cottage. We had our own telephone line, 226. There were many small family farms in the area, now all sadly gone. Most local villages had four or five, some had more – Market Bosworth had seven (nine if you included Coton). Many still employed a horse or two.

In 1954 I was fortunate to be able to purchase a small field in Barton Road, and built a house and surgery there. It was a dream come true. William Beck, whose yard is now Warwick Close, built the house. In the early 1970s I purchased the adjacent Old Parks and Old Park Spinney from Mrs Bruxner, Randall's Estate. The Spinney was badly neglected and the lake was silted up. This was cleaned out and stocked with fish. With the able help of Glyn Croman, a lot of scrub was cleared and paths made, bird hides constructed and many nest boxes put up. Within a very short time many species of waterfowl appeared. One Boxing Day a very rare bittern appeared. Unfortunately in the 1980s the dreaded mink came and the waterfowl disappeared, as did many of the other birds.

In 1995 we sold the house and land and retired to a house nearer The Square. During our time here we have made lots of wonderful friends in the farming community and locally.

This is a wonderful place to live.

John Nadin

Above: John Nadin.

THE   GREEN   MANTLE

THEY LINE THE ROAD ALL THE WAY FROM THE RAILWAY BRIDGE AND ALONG THE NARROW, GENTLY RISING LANE THAT LEADS TO BOSWORTH, ENFOLDING, LIKE A SOFT GREEN MANTLE, A HANDFUL OF COTTAGES AND A MELLOW 16TH- CENTURY PRIORY: HUNDREDS AND HUNDREDS OF TREES — ALL PLANTED, NURTURED AND LOVED BY ONE MAN, AN EX-PRISONER OF WAR.

In April 1943 Eugene Salvador was pleased to be re-located from the prisoner-of-war camp near Tamworth, to work at the Smiths' farm at Coton Priory, where, in his words:

"Everywhere was a big mess. The nettles were taller than any man on earth, and nobody seemed interested in doing anything about it – not only at the Priory but on most of the farms too. The farmers were producing food for the war, but were not rich enough to do the other priority jobs. There were about ten workers on the farm, which was mixed – arable and stock – and while I was not allowed to do whatever I wanted I was allowed to make some changes.

Above: Salvadore's trees along the road to Far Coton.

"The house was a lovely old 16th-century priory, built in three stages, but no-one knows for which religious order or whether it was for monks or nuns. There was a coach house, stables and a duckpond and there may have been some sort of moat – the telephone men found slurry at about 4 feet down when putting in a pole and had problems getting it anchored. At that time the road went right in front of the house, which had a small front garden with railings. Mr Frank Smith and his wife were very kind people, with two lovely daughters, Evelyn and Ivy, and a son, Roland."

After the war Eugene had to decide if he wanted to return to his home in Italy, but he felt that he had no real choice. When asked about the best thing that happened to him during his life he immediately replied:

"There is no doubt – love; I fell in love with Coton Priory and with Miss Ivy, and there is nothing nicer than love. Love is love. If you love somebody, or something, you are the richest man in the world. It's got to be followed by good health and some money, but love is the key thing. That's why I worked on this place.

"When I came there were only three trees at the Priory, and they are still here– an ash, a plum and a pear tree – and the house looked as though it needed a drive, a bigger garden and more trees. Now my father, at my home just north of Venice, was a countryman, and I always loved anything that grows and anything that moves – animals and trees and flowers – so I asked Mr. Roland Smith if I could move the road, dig a fishpond and plant some trees, and he agreed.

"So I moved the road and made the drive and built the walls; dug the fish-pond, bought and placed the statues, which are all mine, as are the fish in the pond – goldfish and dark grey carp and Golden Orfe – and later, after we saw a man passing with a bucket under his arm, we seem to have got some perch. It's a lovely place to sit, and the fish know me and come to the side when I feed them every day. We had some trouble in the early days with herons, but now the trees are so big, they can't fly in and out, and they can't see what's in the pond."

The trees. That's the real love story. Digging the long drive and the 50-foot pond must have seemed like moving a mountain, but planting and caring for the trees has been, and remains, the real labour of love.

"Everything you see here I planted – and there is a lot, lot more that you can't see at first. There are hundreds and hundreds of trees. They were mainly grown from cuttings and seedlings, and they start near the railway bridge, go halfway up the lane towards Bosworth, and are all round the house and cottages. There

are all sorts – conifers, oaks, larches, a thorny acacia, beeches, yews, poplars, a handkerchief tree, Cupressus, chestnuts, a *Sequoia dendrum gigantum* (these can grow for several thousand years), and a walnut tree. I grew the last from the hardest walnut you can imagine. It was so thickly packed inside you couldn't get it out to eat and it came from my father's tree in Italy. When the tree here matured, I took its seed back to my brother's farm in Italy: now that tree is mature too and I have planted its seed back here, so there are now four generations of this international tree – and the latest nuts are softer and easier to eat.

"I also planted a grove of conifers – this is my favourite place, because that is where Ivy, Evelyn and I used to picnic. Ivy was a lovely girl; she didn't enjoy good health but worked hard on the farm and was a good tractor driver. We never married but I loved her, and miss her now she's gone."

Above: Coton Priory, with one of Eugene's statues in the foreground.

THE TREE GARDEN

DAVID HARDWICK THINKS OF THE ARBORETUM AS A 'TREE GARDEN' — A COLLECTION OF TREES, SOME NATIVE TO THE UK AND SOME EXOTIC.

"In the early 1970s there was an upsurge of interest in the environment and in particular in trees – remember 'Plant a tree in '73'?"

Certainly at that time, after acquiring 90 acres of the Bosworth Hall Estate, the County Council decided that an old woodland area, below the boat-house in the new Country Park, would make an ideal arboretum.

This small area, once planted as an 11 acre wood by Squire Delius, brother of the composer, was later developed by Mr Loseby as a *pleasaunce*. After careful landscaping he and his guests could walk amongst shady trees, elegant shrubs and flowers, following a softly tinkling stream to the ancient fish stews that were alive with flashing dragonflies and water boatmen.

Unfortunately, in the 1960s this area was all clear-felled and left to stagnate, until the decision was made to reclaim it as an arboretum. Since soil and climate were suitable there would be a unique collection, featuring different species of oaks and maples, plus other hardwoods, conifers and wetland trees, all selected for leaf colour. The fishponds, once used to breed stock for local lakes, and the stream and cascade from Beau Pool, would be retained, as would the cleft-oak fencing that once bounded the 400 acre deer park.

Planting continued through the 1980s, but sadly some species of maple were a disappointment. Local conditions were thought to contribute, but both honey

fungus and grey squirrels undoubtedly caused some of the devastation, as David explains:

"Neglect after the earlier clear-felling allowed the fruiting bodies of this very aggressive and persistent fungus to appear each autumn, attacking the roots and eventually killing the tree. This problem has now eased but a growing population of grey squirrels is a more recent threat. They cannot resist the sweet maple sap and so strip the bark to get at it, causing the top branches to die. Hares and Muntjac deer can also damage the lower trunks, but once the tree matures this is less of a problem."

David and the other Park Rangers are responsible for the care and well-being of the Arboretum as well as the Country Park and Bosworth Battlefield. At one time the Country Park was managed almost like a town park – with the grass kept short-mown and everything neat and tidy. Eventually it was recognised that this was wrong, that a country park should reflect the countryside, with natural areas where wildlife could flourish, and where visitors feel closer to nature than to the town.

David's team welcomed this change and now are also progressively changing the Arboretum to make Mother Nature feel more at home.

So ragged robin, yellow flag and skullcap proudly stand, masking and softening the margins of the fishponds, where waterlily cups and water-soldier blooms float gently on still green water. And as frogs and newts search hungrily for food, dodging lazy carp and bream, they themselves are hunted down, along the water's edge, by slithering grass snakes quietly waiting for their meal.

Tomorrow's plans, which will echo and sustain this quiet shady spot, will also add more of man's and nature's older ways with trees. Already alive in springtime with yellow primrose, daffodil, and even the small sweet violet, the area's native and exotic trees will be pollarded, forming sweeps of trees where children may run and play. Groups of willow and hazel will be coppiced, cut and harvested, showing how our forebears bent and shaped these into fences, baskets, hurdles and shady arbours.

And David Hardwick has the last few words:

"We are just outside the new National Forest – its boundaries are a few miles away – so we don't qualify for many grants, but we are very fortunate to have the continuing support of the County Council for both the Park and the Arboretum. There is still a lot to do to make the area even more attractive, but if it had been left as it was, or simply landscaped into the parkland, we would have lost this enchanting tree garden."

Previous pages: Bosworth Park.
Above: Maple leaf.
Right: Maple trees in the Arboretum.
Overleaf: A frosty Beau Pool.

FOOT AND MOUTH

Number of confirmed cases:

2,030

Official number of animals
slaughtered:
(Government statistics)
4,068 million

Unofficial number of animals
slaughtered (compiled by the
Meat & Livestock Commission)

10,849 million

FEBRUARY 2001, WHEN THE FIRST CASE OF FOOT AND MOUTH SINCE 1967 WAS CONFIRMED IN NORTHUMBERLAND, WAS A BLACK MONTH FOR BRITISH FARMERS.

Up to the time when the British Isles were officially declared free of the disease in November 2001, there were 2,030 officially confirmed cases. Almost 10,000 farms in 30 counties were involved and for months the countryside reeked with the stench of rotting or burning carcasses, whilst the air was blackened with the smoke from hundreds of funeral pyres.

Government statistics show that just over 4 million animals were slaughtered, but figures compiled by the Meat and Livestock Commission indicate that the total number was over 10 million.

Farmers saw generations of work, and their livelihood, wiped out in just a few weeks. It has been estimated that 10% of them will leave farming as a result of this epidemic and official government statistics indicate that between 1997 and 2002 more than 64,000 farmers left the industry. The total cost of the foot and mouth epidemic to the British economy has been calculated to be over £20 billion, including a cost to the tourist industry of almost £5 billion.

Leicestershire escaped the worst of the epidemic, suffering only a few confirmed cases, but even so many farms were affected. Local farmer Richard Lawrence, of Upper Coton Farm, commented on his experience in an article in New Aspect:

"On 25th February 2001 there was an immediate ban on movement of all livestock throughout the United Kingdom. We were very fortunate that all of our livestock were housed indoors at the time and not in the fields away from the homestead – we hadn't yet started lambing. On 28th February there was a local confirmed case at Fenny Drayton and this was really bad news since it was too close for comfort. We decided to shut the gates, to cut out all unnecessary journeys and to accept that for the time being our social life would be non-existent. We were really grateful for the telephone since this was to become our main lifeline.

Right: Two of Tertius Perry's cows down Coton Lane.

"Our business virtually closed. A cancelled sale at Lincoln meant that three breeding bulls that had been prepared for this sale had to remain on the farm. We needed their pen for cows calving but it was not to be and we had to find a way around the problem. The buildings were quickly getting full with ewes and lambs, cows and calves but nothing could be moved to grass because we were not allowed to take stock across the road. The official advice was to keep animals inside to reduce the risk of catching the disease but we had no option: there was nowhere else for them to go.

"Soon foot and mouth appeared out of control, no matter what the politicians were saying. We just kept hoping we would stay clear as we have been breeding Texel sheep for twenty-three years. Some of the northern farms where we used to buy our stock rams unfortunately went down with the disease, so this will give us problems in the future. During the epidemic the public were very co-operative. They seemed really concerned with the situation, and we were grateful that they obeyed the signs along the footpaths and the canal tow-path, although it remained unnaturally quiet in the lanes."

The farm at Upper Coton fortunately did stay clear of foot and mouth, but tragically the disease claimed one human casualty locally. Thomas Waring of Barwell died following a fall from the roof of a Stoke Golding farm building whilst washing it down to help control the spread of the disease.

Restrictions were eventually lifted in May 2001 on 1,904 farms in the Hinckley and Nuneaton area.

F U N G I

WHEN THE LIGHT EVENINGS ARE DRAWING TO A CLOSE AND AUTUMN BEGINS TO NIBBLE AT THE TRAILING EDGE OF SUMMER, THE WOODLANDS AND MEADOWS OF BRITAIN BECOME HOME TO A WIDE VARIETY OF FUNGI. THEIR LITTLE FLESHY BODIES POP UP OVERNIGHT TO DANCE ACROSS THE GRASSY FIELDS AND GATHER EXPECTANTLY AROUND THE SHALLOW ROOTS OF TREES.

The Romans named fungi 'vapours of moist soil'. They were a mystery to these early natural scientists who considered them to be the work of dark powers as they seemed to 'mushroom' out of the ground with no explanation. The purpose of fungi is now more certain. They are nature's recyclers responsible for clearing away dead plant matter and reconditioning it to become nutrients for other organisms. They reproduce by spreading their spores on the wind and after firmly establishing themselves, continue to reappear in the same spot for many years.

A fairy ring is a fine example of the tenacity of fungi. The myth suggests that fairies use the rings as meeting places for dancing and the toadstools on which to rest! The most common type of fungi to grow in this formation is the Fairy Ring Champignon (*Marasmius oreades*). Some of the rings date back as far as 700 years and can measure 50 feet across. The toadstools grow in a circular formation, feeding on a hidden radial system underneath the soil. This is a system of white threads, called mycelia, which are thinner and more delicate than a cobweb and are present in the soil throughout the year. The natural phenomenon of the ring is relatively rare but does exist in areas of Bosworth Park, in the grounds of Bosworth Hall and in a few domestic gardens in the local villages. The Clouded Agaric (*Clitocybe nebularis*) and the Wood Blewit (*Lepista nuda*) are common in the area and also flourish in this pattern.

When Squire Delius re-planted Tollemache Scott's arboretum in Bosworth Park in the early 20th century, some of the older and dead trees, situated around the perimeter of Beau Pool, were felled. Many species of fungi thus began to thrive on the remaining stumps, for example Deadman's Fingers (*Xylaria polymorpha*), Many-Zoned Polypore (*Trametes versicolor*) – favoured by flower arrangers due to their colourful stripes – Sulphur Tuft (*Hypholoma fasciculare*), Brown Roll Rim (*Paxillus involutus*) and Glistening Ink Cap (*Coprinus micaceus*), which have all been spotted and correctly identified in recent years.

Protruding from the bark of the birch trees seen along the lanesides and footpaths is the bracket fungus, Birch Polypore (*Piptoporus betulinus*), also known as Razor Strop fungus as it was used by the Victorians to sharpen razor blades due to its smooth texture when old or specially dried. One of the most well-known toadstools is the Fly Agaric (*Amanita muscaria*), with its scarlet cap and white spots.

Above left: Parasol Mushroom (*Lepiota procera*) - photograph by Erica Tomlinson.

Above right: *Coprinus atramentarius*, related to the Shaggy Ink Cap *Coprinus comatus* - photograph by Erica Tomlinson.

Although it is often depicted in children's stories, and used as seats by garden gnomes, it is in fact a poisonous fungus and, if consumed can prove fatal, in rare cases. Thriving under silver birch trees it can also be spotted in Bosworth Park's arboretum, and some will be lucky enough to find it in their gardens.

There is a wide variety of fungal species in this country, many of which are delicious if picked when fresh, some which are liable to give you hallucinations, and others that should be regarded from a safe distance due to their deadly properties. The Death Cap (*Amanita phalloides*) and Destroying Angel (*Amanita virosa*), fortunately uncommon in this area, are the most lethal of British fungi and are fatal if consumed. The very unpleasant symptoms presented by these almost scheming little organisms can occur up to twenty-four hours after the fungus is eaten. By this time the toxins have been thoroughly absorbed by the body, so any preventative measures undertaken, such as vomiting and stomach pumping, are in vain. The victim remains conscious throughout the ordeal and endures a brief period of remission, which is then followed by the realisation that death is beating at the door.

The appearance of a mushroom or a toadstool can be deceptive as many edible specimens have poisonous replicas. It is imperative when collecting – either for studying or for consumption – that your identification is correct. If in doubt, *don't touch!*

Above: Fly Agaric (Amanita muscaria) – photograph by Erica Tomlinson.

ANCIENT ROOTS

THE OLDEST TREE IN THE MARKET BOSWORTH

AREA IS UNDOUBTEDLY THE ANCIENT YEW IN THE

GROUNDS OF BOSWORTH HALL.

As yews can live for thousands of years this tree possibly stood witness to the original Manor House, now the site of Bosworth Hall. Hiding under a mass of laurel and rhododendron it exists almost in a world of its own. The yew has a close connection with the churchyards of Britain, perhaps grown to ward off evil spirits and to watch over the dead. In the hamlet of Goatham near Osbaston an ancient yew tree stands at each end of the village.

Between Market Bosworth and Far Coton a beautiful oak tree standing at around 60 feet grows in the hedgerow. Its magnificent boughs throw long shadows over the lane, sheltering the passing Romanies with their painted caravans and shire horses. Not always conjuring a romantic image, the oak sadly often stands uncomfortably beside a settlement of modern itinerants who leave in their wake an unsightly collection of metal and waste.

The oak tree's age can be gauged by the width of its girth, which spans an impressive 17¼ feet. It has probably stood on this site for over 200 years, possibly planted in the late 18th century by a farmer or agricultural labourer in order to mark the boundary of the land. Surviving storms, gales and blizzards it has suffered the loss of only two of its main branches.

There are many remarkable trees in the Market Bosworth area and a number of the surrounding villages too have their own magnificent specimens. The beech overhanging the perimeter wall of Osbaston Hall is a rich blend of gold and russet in the autumn and standing opposite but out of sight is another beech, over 150 years old, with inscriptions carved into its grey bark. Less obvious to the public eye is the giant redwood in Cadeby, towering above the roof of the old rectory, and behind the houses of Barton Road, Market Bosworth are a group of beech, sycamore, oak and lime trees which once formed part of the parkland of the Bosworth Hall Estate.

Floodlit and eerily ghostly on a foggy night is the copper beech at the gates of Bosworth Hall. The following piece of writing was written for *Aspect* by Matron Mole in 1974 as a tribute to its lost companion.

THE FALL OF A FRIEND

"On Friday 11th January at 1.20 am, during the height of a storm, a large copper beech tree in the front courtyard of Bosworth Park Infirmary crashed to the ground.

"The tree, which is thought to be over 300 years old, was struck by lightning in 1963 after which some of the larger branches appeared to be dead. A few years later, borings were taken by a dendro-chronologist and every effort was made to save the tree but unfortunately later reports received indicated that in the interests of safety the copper beech would have to come down. Staff and patients were saddened to think that we were to lose a beautiful tree, then nature in her wisdom did it for us. Almost every branch was completely lifted off, as if by a giant hand, and deposited in the courtyard causing no damage to either the ornamental ironwork or surrounding wall.

"Often as I walk from the nurses' home to the hospital I have thought of the man who planted the two copper beech trees. As he planted did he think of the pleasure those trees would give to so many people for so many years? Their matching symmetry and beauty in all four seasons were a joy to behold. We feel we have lost an old friend."

Matron Mole from the Park Infirmary (now Mrs Alice Long)

Left: An old oak at Carlton.

Above: One of the oldest oak trees in the area on Coton Lane.

APRIL RISE

If ever I saw a blessing in the air
I see it now in this still early day
Where lemon-green the vaporous morning drips
Wet sunlight on the powder of my eye.

Blown bubble-film of blue, the sky wraps round
Weeds of warm light whose every root and rod
Splutters with soapy green, and all the world
Sweats with the bead of summer in its bud.

If ever I heard blessing it is there
Where birds in trees that shoals and shadows are
Splash with their hidden wings and drops of sound
Break on my ears their crests of throbbing air.

Pure in the haze the emerald sun dilates,
The lips of sparrows milk the mossy stones,
While white as water by the lake a girl
Swims her green hand among the gathered swans.

Now, as the almond burns its smoking wick,
Dropping small flames to light the candled grass;
Now, as my low blood scales its second chance,
If ever world were blessed, now it is.

Laurie Lee.

LEISURE TIME

This interesting comment by Benjamin Disraeli might still appeal to many because whilst recognising the need for work, the prospect of more money and more free time is very attractive.

Free time is time away from the humdrum toil that for so many is work. It is time to do as we please, to think or just to daydream. And perchance whilst quietly daydreaming a whisper of verse may suddenly slip into our minds, for it is claimed that everyone, at some time, writes at least one poem. No-one knows how, why or when the muse will appear, but poetry does seem to be just one of the by-products of that time we most enjoy when not at work – our leisure time.

In his poem 'Leisure', William Henry Davies spells out how much we lose if we are deprived of our free time, starting as it does with:

> *What is this life if, full of care,*
> > *We have no time to stand and stare*

And Philip Larkin, in the opening few lines of his poem 'Toads Revisited' seems to agree:

> *Walking around in the park*
> > *Should feel better than work*
> > > *The lake, the sunshine*
> > > > *The grass to lie in.*

> *Blurred background noises*
> > *Beyond black-stockinged nurses*
> > > *Not a bad place to be ...*

However, and rather strangely, Larkin is not simply extolling the pleasures of leisure for he continues by stating a preference to be at work:

> *Yet it doesn't suit me...*
> > *No, give me my in-tray,*
> > > *My loaf-haired secretary,*
> > > > *My shall-I-keep-this-call-in-Sir:*
> > > > > *What else can I answer?*

A sentiment probably shared by few. Work has to have its place – but in this modern time-pinched, consumer-driven, hectic, work-all-day world, how can we find time to stand and stare? With *too much work*, who can make time for *Jack to play* and so avoid becoming a *dull boy?* Fortunately in the Bosworth area many people do take advantage of an almost infinite variety of social, cultural and leisure opportunities on offer.

A quick glance through the pages of *New Aspect* reveal much of it: clubs and societies for everything – the Women's Institute, the Flower Club, Natural History Society, Scouts, Rotary Club, the Royal British Legion, the Drama Society celebrating fifty years...

And anyone for tennis? Or rugby, soccer, cricket, judo, sailing, fishing? You might prefer a winter wildlife guided walk, or to ride a horse, or even double-dig that overgrown allotment bed.

But still there's more to do and see. Visit the Battlefield or Country Park, let off steam at the Railway Trust, drift in a narrow-boat on the old canal, polish up that rusty French, or quilt a quilt, or build and fly an aeroplane, or practise scales, or pot a pot, or paint that distant scene.

Or quite simply spend your leisure days like Larkin, just quietly musing, or even writing a poem.

> *Days*

> *What are days for?*
> > *Days are where we live.*
> *They come, they wake us*
> > *Time and Time over*
> *They are to be happy in.*
> > *Where else can we live but days?*

Right: The Meet at Osbaston Hall.

THE PILOT

COULD THE PROBLEM-SOLVING SKILLS OF ROMAN
ENGINEERS WHO SETTLED IN THESE ISLANDS HAVE
BEEN PASSED DOWN THROUGH SUCCESSIVE
GENERATIONS TO SOME OF TODAY'S INNOVATIVE
ENGINEERS?

If so, then Les James could be of Roman descent. He is a very unusual engineer who, by small coincidence, was born beside the famous Roman road leading north from London – Edgware Road. He now lives at Wharf Farm in Market Bosworth – a small corner of Leicestershire where road, rail, water and air transport all combine.

His interest in aircraft started when he was an apprentice at de Havilland Engines, increasing in the Fleet Air Arm and later with Armstrong Siddeley in Coventry. Although he started flying training at Elstree, he later had to give it up and concentrate on his engineering business, but about twelve years ago the bug really bit.

"I forgot about aeroplanes for about thirty years, but did race motorbikes for a while – at the first meeting at Mallory and on the Isle of Man – and I didn't do too badly. Bike racing really gets the adrenalin going – takes years off you – but I eventually stopped to help bring up the family. Then Janet bought me a trial flying lesson and that was that – I signed up for a course and eventually got my private pilot's licence.

"I then decided to build an aircraft. This was an American Kitfox – a high-wing monoplane, all aluminium tubes and spars covered with Dacron fabric. You stretched out all the wrinkles by heating it with a domestic iron. I eventually built six of the same design, including some that I repaired from accident-damaged aircraft."

The Romans and the railway engineers, like Les, joined metal with rivets, but there was a difference. The early engineers heated iron rivets to avoid them cracking, but Les uses thousands and thousands of refrigerated aluminium rivets in his aircraft, each one used 'cold' to ensure maximum strength.

"I never intended to build so many light aircraft – it must be about seventeen by now – but it became a passion. Pilots are all nut cases! Flying itself is not difficult or clever – anybody can do it: it's the instructors that make you what you are."

Wharf Farm, where Les has built a hangar and where he flies his current Glastar high-wing monoplane, is underneath the flight path of the fast military jets that roar low over Bosworth at irregular intervals – does this present any problems?

"I do have to be aware of military aircraft but in reality I can just jump in and go. There is a number you can ring, but the onus is really on you to tell them that your field is operating – Wharf Farm is mapped as an official airfield. The risk for the few seconds when I am climbing to my altitude is very low – it's probably more dangerous driving up Station Road."

Although Les' head is often in the clouds, his feet are not only firmly on the ground but have at times also been in the water. As well as creating his own lake at Wharf Farm, he also helped with the design and development of the lakes at Bosworth Water Trust.

"When my good friend Nigel Ryley told me about his project I offered to help. I had no civil engineering training but it seemed fairly straightforward – a question of level, and banks at the right angle to resist the water pressure – so we researched it and had a go. Now it's maturing nicely and I think it's a real asset for the town.

"I'd hate any of this to sound boastful, because that's not what it's meant to be. We know we are very, very fortunate to be able to walk out of the back door and jump into an aeroplane – somebody up there has really been looking after me. I wouldn't want to live anywhere else but Bosworth – it's a relatively civilised place to live and just feels like home."

The Romans may have used the old Lichfield Road, the coal entrepreneurs built the canal, and the railway carried goods and passengers – and now, from these same few acres, Les James takes to the air.

Right: An inviting sky.

LIVING HISTORY

EVERYONE AGREES ABOUT THE DATE, BUT EVEN AFTER MORE THAN 500 YEARS THE PLACE OF THE BLOODIEST FIGHTING AND THE FIELD WHERE THE LAST KING OF ENGLAND WAS TO DIE IN BATTLE, ARE MUCH DEBATED.

Most agree that the battle raged on waste land, with a marsh and a hill, and that King Richard III did camp the night before on Ambion Hill, whilst Henry Tudor was at Whitemoors to the west.

But no-one knows for sure, and the surrounding villages have all, at some time, laid their claim to the famous battle that, on 22nd August 1485, ended the Wars of the Roses.

"Richard **did** pray at the tiny Sutton Cheney church, yes, but the large cache of weaponary and skeletons unearthed at Dadlington **prove** the battle was there – perhaps – but Henry VII **was** crowned at Stoke Golding, on Crown Hill – and then the Earl of Oxford's archers were based at Shenton before the battle!"

Despite all claims and counterclaims, the battle is historically remembered as 'The Battle of Bosworth', and the County Council decided that the Battlefield Visitor Centre and Country Park *were* to be at Ambion Hill.

After 500 years, of course, nothing remains to prove where this bloody and historic conflict was fought. The marsh has been drained, woodlands established and open fields and wasteland enclosed by hedgerows, and during the last 200 years a canal and a railway line have been built on what is now pleasant and tranquil farmland.

At one time there was only one memorial to this famous battle: on private land, near Ambion Hill, a small stone cairn marked the lonely and remote spring where the King supposedly quenched his thirst before the battle – King Dick's Well. However, in the 1950s and 1960s new battles raged between the farmer and pilgrims wanting to visit this site, and these were only resolved when the Visitor Centre opened in 1974.

No other royal presence followed King Richard onto this field of battle for 500 years, until, in 1985, Prince Charles and Princess Diana opened an extended exhibition to mark the quincentenary celebrations.

Since then countless visitors, reliving that infamous day whilst tramping along the waymarked paths, have stared at Richard's and Henry's giant standards fluttering in the breeze, or watched breathlessly the annual August re-enactment of the battle. Showers of arrows cascade indiscriminately among fierce soldiers and mounted knights who, following Richard's White Boar or Red Tudor's Dragon, fight hand to hand, sword to sword, pike to pike beneath the smoke and roar of belching cannon.

And not just once each year – hundreds of schoolchildren relive and revel in events that are frequently staged by the re-enactment society *Les Routiers* as 'Living History'. Within a tented, smoky, medieval camp, children help a combatant prepare for battle by buckling on his chainmail, breastplate, and helm. He teaches them the skills and art of ancient warfare – broadsword, buckler, pike and mace – before, conscripted, armed and dressed in Richard's or Henry's colours, the warrior children are drawn up in battle lines and fight, with valiant shouts, to win the day. But Henry always wins!

Now a major tourist attraction, the battlefield hosts many weekend events. Visitors arriving by road, canal or rail may hear the thrum and thud as arrows hit the straw, shrill cries of hunting hawks, the chip of adze on wooden beam, and the strange 'phfff' and flash of a muzzle-loaded gun, or talk of 'archaeological digs and finds' as heads nod sagely at the accompanying guide.

But do they also feel the chill surrounding 'Desford Bill' – a wicked medieval weapon of a type most probably in use in 1485, found at Desford years ago – and now displayed in a gruesome exhibition of 'Weaponry and Wounds', with a skull from a mass grave from the Wars of the Roses?

Perhaps it is as well that no-one knows where gory ghosts might haunt the fields and lanes around this now untroubled land.

Left: St James, Sutton Cheney, where King Richard allegedly took his last Mass before the battle.

Right: Members of the Leicestershire re-enactment society, *Les Routiers de Rouen*, marked the 550th anniversary of King Richard's birth by marching from Castle Park in Leicester to Bosworth Battlefield. Picture courtesy of the Leicester Mercury.

AJB

M A G I C   L A N T E R N S

WITH A FACE SIMILAR TO A SIAMESE BUT WITH A

SHORT CURLY COAT LIKE THAT OF A LAMB, THEY

START LIFE WITH THEIR VERY LARGE EARS ALREADY

FULLY GROWN — SO RATHER BEMUSINGLY THE

KITTENS LOOK ALL EARS.

The Devon Rex is an unusual breed but having a very affectionate nature, they are rewarding pets.

John Finney, with ten of these cats, devotes some of his spare time to writing a new encyclopaedia about the breed. However, most of his free time is taken up with his real passion – the Magic Lantern Society, for which he is the publicity officer. This is not so surprising since the projected image, or more correctly, 'film', featured early in John's life. One of his aunts owned the cinema that once stood behind the Newbold Verdon garage, and another relative owned the Barlestone cinema. He recalls how after showing the first reel of a film at Barlestone, a boy on a bike would race with it to Newbold, returning later with the second reel – always hoping for no delays or punctures!

Of course, the magic lantern pre-dates moving pictures by a long way. Invented by a Jesuit priest in the 1600s, it projects only still images, although John advises that a simple 'slip-slide' system allows very basic movement – for example a man will lift and lower a spade. John's collection of over 200 lanterns spans many years, from the earliest of the 1850s to the most recent, made in the 1950s. The former was rescued from an old cinema-turned-strip-club, where it was used to show the name of the next 'artiste'.

Running out of room for the collection, despite having built their own home cinema for magic lantern shows, John and his wife now spend their time looking for old magic lantern slides, especially sets of slides that tell a simple story.

One of their favourites is a tale of life and death: 'The Curfew Shall Not Ring Out Tonight'. The story starts with the capture and sentencing of a young soldier, who is to be put to death when the curfew bell rings. However, the soldier is kept alive after his lover climbs the tower and grimly hangs onto the bell clapper while the deaf sexton tries to ring the curfew. The story closes after Oliver Cromwell has granted a pardon, and the lovers walk off arm-in-arm into the sunset!

John is a real countryman at heart and whilst recognising that more homes are always needed, he regrets that the old villages are losing the character that he loves. The over-zealous application of clean-cut straight lines and too tidy grass verges often, in his opinion, leads to litter and vandalism, at the expense of hedges and roses. The churches and chapels still survive and people still help to look after them, but so much of the old life is dying – too many of Verdon's lovely old farmhouses and barns, filled with cart-wheels and traction engines, have gone.

Above: A splendid old magic lantern.

Right: John Finney's collection of magic lanterns and phonographs.

2 — 1 AT TACHERTING

THE BIG ONE, THE MATCH OF THE SEASON —

GERMANY VS ENGLAND!

THE SPECTATORS SHOUT AND CHEER AS THE

PLAYERS RUN ONTO THE PITCH, EACH NAME

BELLOWED OUT ON LOUDSPEAKERS:

ALESBROOK — HOLDSWORTH — LEAROYD...

The national anthems 'God save the Queen ...' and 'Deutschland uber alles...' are proudly sung by each team... handshakes, a word from the referee ... and Market Bosworth 2000 kick off!

This was not the German National Stadium but the Sports Centre at Tacherting, Bavaria, during the visit of the Bosworth Junior Football Club in the summer of 2001. The team was drawn from the Bosworth Club's three squads of Under 11s, 12s and 13s and in their orange strip they were more Holland than England. They may not have won the game but, cheered on by parents and friends, they maintained the stout old English tradition of fighting hard right up to the final whistle.

Then after changing back at their camp, the evening's celebrations started – soft drinks for the boys and something stronger from the town's own brewery for the dads.

Having been invited by the Mayor of Tacherting, those on this mini European Tour enjoyed outstanding hospitality during a very hot week of sport and excursions, and left wishing that some of the magnificent facilities at the Tacherting Sports Complex could be duplicated at home.

Some of those dreams might come true, because with only two seasons of playing behind them, they already have local kit sponsorship, a recent Lottery Award, bags of player and supporter enthusiasm and also the right organisation and ideas.

For this is not the kick-and-rush soccer we all played as kids on the local rec. – pullovers for goals and a soggy old leather ball. All of these youngsters are registered with the FA, they must abide by the club's Code of Conduct, pay match fees and for training – and if nominated as Man of the Match or for Special Effort they get to keep a trophy for a week.

Managed and coached by John Alesbrook they are hoping to improve their playing skills with extra coaching from Leicester City Foxes. So who knows, we may one day see a David Hill, or a Chris Plant, celebrating on the pitch at the German National Stadium having beaten Germany 5–1 yet again!

Oh, and the best and worst scores at Tacherting?
Germany 2 – England 1
Germany 1 – England 2 – after a 5–3 penalty shoot-out!

(But Bosworth lost the Dads vs Dads match 7-6)

Top row from left: Matt Brooke, Tony Learoyd, Phil Holdsworth, Chris Plant, John Stansfield.

Bottom row left: Callum Duncan, Tom Alesbrook, David Hill, Mitchell Brown, Joe Coney, Tom Wilford.

THE 'BOZZY BOYS'

STANDING QUIETLY ON THE CORNER OF PARK STREET AND MAIN STREET, WHO WOULD GUESS THAT THE RED LION'S ALE ASSISTED IN THE FATHERING OF A CLUB WHICH, AT THE TURN OF THE MILLENNIUM, CELEBRATED THIRTY-FIVE SUCCESSFUL YEARS?

As Bill Oliver stated in the 1987 Leicester Rugby Union handbook:

"The details of finding a squad, arranging games and finding pitches were argued and agreed at a local pub, thus ensuring a plentiful supply of the lubricant conducive to clear thinking and the fearless resolution of problems which might otherwise have appeared insurmountable."

It seems that the small group of 'keep-fit' enthusiasts who first decided that Market Bosworth needed a rugby football team, and who recruited (or was it press-ganged?) players, also decided that in the absence of a clubhouse, the Red Lion bar would be a suitable venue.

Their early games were played on the Bosworth school pitch and later on a local farm field, but in 1973 they purchased six acres of land in Cadeby Lane. Three pitches were established, though whoever volunteered to mark them out also had to remove rather smelly droppings left by occasional grazing animals.

The Red Lion, and later the Dixie Arms, remained the club's spiritual – not to say 'beeritual' – home, with an upstairs room acting as committee room, changing room and after-match 'snap' room. The Cadeby Lane clubhouse only became possible after enough profitable post-match beer had been drunk and enough players' fees collected.

The Club soon managed to field four teams on most winter Saturdays, with the third and fourth teams comprising, not unsurprisingly, some of the real characters. These included those who traditionally not only propped up the bar, but also what was laughingly called the 'front row' of the scrum.

Those who flaunted the paunchiest of paunches and the most tawdry of tackles, whose enthusiasm quickly ebbed along with their flagging fitness, always needed, as opponents' scores soared, a smutty joke or desperate quip to keep them stumbling around the pitch, at least until 'no-side' at half time.

There were players like daffodil-eating John Bailey who seemed to prefer either flower or bulb to meat pies, and who always 'borrowed' the opposition's Christmas tree after December away matches. Or Paul Ringer, whose party trick needed a live goldfish – and of course, the original 'Tel-e-tubby', Terry Parnell, one-time Fire Chief, County Cricket umpire, and regular supporter of the Isle of Man TT races.

Packing down alongside, or behind, 'El Tel' was some experience – a man who left a deep impression, not only on the opposing front row's shoulders, but also on everyone he met. Terry, despite his long-term heart problems, was determined, in his own words to 'live life to the full', and a special annual memorial fixture against the Hinckley Rugby Club still keeps his memory alive.

The first and second team players were, by comparison, paragons. They knew almost every rule and won matches, progressively raising the Club's reputation and position in local leagues. The Club still runs three senior teams plus a colt's team, and all players happily stump up their fiver a game – to play, that is, not to be paid. There are no big professional salaries at this level.

Many of those early players, from both the good and the ugly teams, are now retired but still support the Club in running both the senior teams and the County Championship-winning Colts. With their help, hundreds of local children have progressed through the mini-rugby echelons to the senior game. Winter Sunday mornings will normally see up to forty 'six to sixteen' cubs chasing that funny oval ball.

And cubs grow up, if not quite into Lions then certainly into Tigers. The current Leicester Tigers Rugby Club can field at least four ex-Bosworth players – Derek Jelley, Dorian West, Oliver Smith and Ben Buxton – three of whom are full or 'A' England Internationals, whilst past Tigers players include Ronnie Budulis, John Brown, Ian Bates, Richie Robertson and Darren Grewcock.

So play up you cubs and colts – we'll see you all later in the Midlands Two East League – or even at Twickenham one day, if the club maintains its remarkable record of three league promotions in only four seasons!

Right: Matt Gadsby wins the ball for Bosworth Rugby Club. Printed by kind permission of the Hinckley Times. Photo Will Binns.

AJB

THE TWITCHER

"HE WOULD SIT IN THE PARK WITH A LINNET IN A CAGE, TRYING TO GET IT TO LEARN TO SING BY COPYING A LINNET IN A TREE. HOWEVER, HE DID GET ANNOYED IF THERE WAS A GOLDFINCH IN THE TREE AND THE CAGED LINNET STARTED TO SING LIKE THE FINCH."

Ken Reeves' grandfather bred British birds for best breed competitions that required them to both look good and to sing properly. However, bred in captivity they picked up the wrong songs and it was by accompanying him on these 'singing lessons' that Ken's interest in birds developed.

This interest developed into a passion, and not just one for *watching* birds, because often he and his fellow 'twitchers' may only be able to hear but not see their prey. Ken comments about the fascinating topic of bird song:

"We get almost as much pleasure from listening, because there is so much variation. One professor, using a sonograph to analyse the sounds, recorded 122 different noises – songs and calls – from the great tit. Also, although the British chaffinch looks like and, to the human ear, sounds identical to the French chaffinch, there are differences – so the French chaffinch appears to have a French accent!

"Again most people – even Shakespeare in 'A Midsummer Night's Dream' – would say that the owl's call is 'twit-twoo', but this is not so. Each owl only

calls with a 'twit' or a 'twoo – and another owl will answer. Strangely, if the first call is 'twoo' the answering call will be 'twit'."

Guided walks, offered by Ken and fellow enthusiast Bern Gibney and advertised on their Internet website, cover bird-watching, wild flowers, wildlife and local history:

"On a recent guided evening Owl Walk in Bosworth Park, several of the children turned up dressed as wizards in cloaks and pointed hats, hoping, I think, to find Harry Potter's owl Hedwig. We know where the owls normally roost, so by using taped calls we were able to get them to respond, and then point them out with a lamp for just a few seconds – not enough to disturb them. That night we found tawny owls, little owls and a barn owl – about eight or nine in all, juveniles and adults, all roosting in the Park. We go back two nights later to check that they are still on the same roosts, so we know we haven't disturbed them too much."

Ken, who as a naughty young boy once swam across the canal at Blaby in his underpants to get swans' eggs for his collection, now recognises the survival problems facing the bird population in Britain, especially farmland species.

"The grey partridge is down by 90%, the skylark 80%, the corn bunting and linnet by about 70% – all affected by changes in farming methods – although perhaps we are all at fault in wanting cheaper and cheaper foods from the supermarkets. Fortunately the decline in garden birds – really woodland birds – is not so bad, and the raptors, like the sparrowhawks and kestrels, are marginally increasing since we stopped using DDT."

The Scilly Isles – "for the American vagrants passing through in the autumn" – and Norfolk are Ken's favourite places to watch birds. Norfolk is directly in the path of the northeasterly winds that bring all of the Scandinavian birds and northern geese to overwinter in the east of Britain.

However, he cannot choose a favourite bird since there are so many, and all have so many interesting features and behaviour patterns:

"The long-tailed tit is rather special. They pass through in the winter, always in small groups that consist only of family members – mum, dad, grandma, grandad and the kids, the whole shebang. This is unique behaviour for any British bird – fascinating!"

With a total tally of 464 different birds seen in the area, perhaps it is not surprising that Ken has a devoted following for his guided walks and illustrated talks, his written articles and monthly talks on Radio Leicester.

Above: A European Eagle Owl.

THE WATER PARK

THE CRACK OF THE MAYOR'S GUN STARTLED THE GEESE AND WITH MUCH URGENT HONKING AND SPLASHING, LONG NECKS OUTSTRETCHED AND WEBBED FEET FURIOUSLY PEDALLING LIKE PADDLE STEAMERS, THEY HEAVED THEMSELVES INTO THE AIR.

Forming a ragged 'V' they disappeared into the east and the island seemed to shiver as other birds dropped silently back to hidden nests in the long grass.

As the first wave of fifty swimmers rushed headlong into the water, they appeared to be thrashing some enormous hidden carpet, but slowly, as the strongest pulled ahead, it became clear that this was a race. The first leg of Biddy Foord's annual Terrapin Triathlon at Bosworth Water Trust was under way.

Biddy organised her first triathlon eleven years ago to raise money for a specialist bone disorder charity, and the following year was asked to organise the National Junior Championship at Bosworth. She tries to use local services in organising the event, so each year it brings considerable benefit to the area.

The mayor usually starts the event, the Council provide the winners' medals, and local sportsmen and women provide safety and security services. With over 200 competitors, and often up to 3,000 spectators, Bosworth is full to overflowing during the Triathlon weekend, and Biddy is proud that the event still proves so popular:

"Not all of our events are championships. The usual triathlon course at Bosworth, centred at the lake, involves a 750 metre swim, and 21 km cycle race followed by a 5 km run – three laps around the lake. The best competitors – who include Olympic and Commonwealth athletes, and even the several times women's world champion triathlete, Dr Sarah Springman – finish in less than one hour.

"The top competitors use high-tech equipment – so you can imagine how surprised we were one year when this 80-year-old gentleman arrived with an old sit-up-and-beg bike complete with a basket and saddle bag. We all thought it a bit of a joke, but he was allowed to compete in the slightly shorter novice event and Mr Patrick Barnes, retired British Airways accountant, finished successfully, albeit in a much longer time. He still comes back most years, although he is now the grand old age of 88!"

Old and young are equally welcome, and a children's triathlon, held with the help of David Fitt at Bosworth College, was a great success:

"The swim took place in the school pool and there were forty-three competitors, although only two from the immediate area. If we ever organise another one we would hope to attract more local children because so many youngsters use and enjoy the marvellous water park. We are fortunate that Jo and Nigel Ryley are always so helpful in letting us run the major events here."

In 1989, when farming was already struggling, Jo and Nigel decided that they should start the Bosworth Water Trust. Nigel had always loved water, the local council was in favour, and with lots of help from a neighbour the new leisure facility was designed and constructed in just twelve months.

"We had already established a small and successful pond for coarse fishing, and decided we should provide two new lakes for sailing, wind-surfing and canoeing. But it wouldn't have happened without our friend and neighbour, Les James, who overcame all of the many difficulties – he was marvellous.

"Although the lakes are relatively small and quite shallow, they have proved very popular, attracting not only watersports enthusiasts but lots of caravanners as well. The triathlons are the most popular and best supported events, but we have attracted quite a few other national championships – the open water swimmers, lifeguards, the first round of the World Model Sailing Boat Championships, and even an American car rally."

The preparation of the lakes created a lot of local interest. Two shallow depressions had to be scooped out, but one early visitor didn't understand the purpose of all this work.

"The excavations were finished, the sides puddled and the newly landscaped grass areas were showing green, when someone popped in to ask when it would be opened. On being told not until next spring, he immediately replied: 'Oh hell, you can't get a round of golf anywhere at the moment.'"

Above: Bosworth Water Park in winter.

AJB

Above: Market Bosworth's original Rectory, built for the Rector John Dixie *c.* 1690. Demolished *c.* 1848. Pencil drawing by Doug Lewis.

THE GRANT OF ARMS

To help pay for the costs of the Napoleonic War, Prime Minister William Pitt was forced, in the late 1790s, to introduce several unusual taxes — on windows, dogs, carriages, servants, hair powder — and on the display of armorial bearings, or coats-of-arms.

As the local Chief Constable, Joseph Moxon had the duty of collecting such taxes. His diaries note the reluctance of Squire Willoughby Dixie, whose family coat-of-arms was very clearly displayed on the drainheads of Bosworth Hall, to pay this tax.*

The Dixie coat-of-arms is based on a lion rampant and is displayed on a remodelled 'Jacobean' fireplace in the old Bosworth rectory, along with three other armorial bearings of Richard III, Henry VII and Robert Harcourt. Complete with carved dragons and gargoyles, the fireplace has five panels and Brian Wilson, the present owner of the Rectory, was uncertain about what to display in the fifth panel.

"I wanted to display the Dixie coat-of-arms alongside those of Richard and Henry, because it was John Dixie, rector at Market Bosworth for thirty-four years, who in the 1690s rebuilt the previous rectory – next to the church, and in such a lavish style that it almost rivalled the Hall. It was described as "...a palace – one of the best Parsonages in England".** The Harcourts were also very influential locally, so their arms needed to be displayed but I couldn't decide about the final one until a friend suggested I should consider approaching the Royal College of Arms to see if I could have a Grant of Arms – my own armorial bearings.

"They agreed and eventually accepted the design you now see, which features some of my interests. The two flanking tobacco pipes represent my collection of meerschaum, porcelain and hookah pipes, with a central black panel to represent my black belt in judo – I'm proud to state that I trained at the same club as the ex-world champion Neil Adams. The Latin inscription reads *Non orbium lumine sed mentis* – Sight is not necessary for success but vision."

The beautiful but austere heavy wooden 'Jacobean' staircase in the Rectory hall was possibly moved from John Dixie's former Parsonage. It probably appealed to the Reverend Nathaniel Pomfret Small, who built the Old Rectory on its present site in 1848, for he was thought, by the then headmaster at the Dixie Grammar School, to be "meticulous, responsible and dry – with no heart for friendly attachments".** Perhaps this nature was also reflected in his design for a rather ordinary dark red brick Elizabethan-style building, with a Tudor-style porch and plain interior. The site was, perhaps, chosen not only for its splendid views over the open lawns and the glebe field to Sutton Cheney, but also, as Peter Foss comments, "for its independence from hall and town, its austere isolation and grandeur" – an isolation perhaps now emphasised by the new metal gates at the entrance to the sweeping paved drive.

The rector's study, with its heavy metal-doored vault that once housed precious church silver and ancient church records, must have witnessed innumerable plans for christenings, weddings and funerals, as well as agonised hours seeking inspiration for Sunday sermons. The splendid back parlour, with its deep frieze of summer fruits, will have hosted hundreds of tea-cup-rattling-sponge-cake-eating Mother's Union meetings, while the Rectory lawns were often trampled under the tiny feet of pirouetting, perspiring and aspiring young ballerinas, hopeful tombola-ticketed mothers and gleaming, grunting fathers bowling for a pig at the annual garden fete.

Those days have long since gone. The new Rectory, positioned once more as close to the church as its 1690 predecessor, has no view over open fields, no spacious lawns for a summer fete. Rector John Plant's Sunday texts are now, no doubt, picked out on a computer keyboard, while winging e-mails unite team members of the Benefice – but friendly and charitable hospitality is still to be found at both the old and the new rectory locations.

Above: The south front of the Old Rectory on Rectory lane, built in 1848 for Nathaniel Pomfret Small.

* From: *A Truly Honest Man* by Peter Foss and Timothy Parry.
** From: *The History of Market Bosworth* by Peter Foss.

AJB

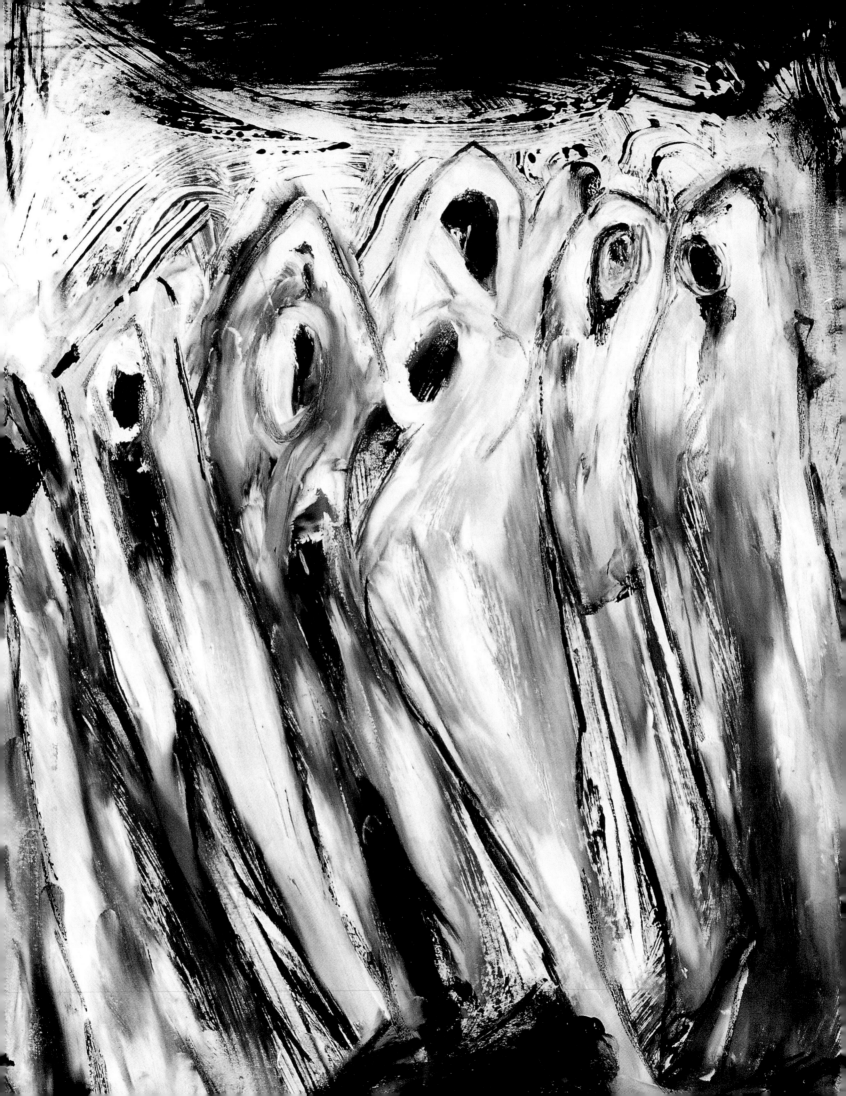

A PEACEFUL TRANSLATION

THE QUIET TOWN OF MARKET BOSWORTH IS A FAR CRY FROM THE TURBULENT WAR-STRICKEN EUROPE OF THE MID-20TH CENTURY.

Both Jürgen and Ruth Schwiening enjoyed what the Germans call, *Gnade der späten Geburt*, meaning, 'the blessing of late birth'. However, their families were not so lucky and suffered the cruel reality of war at first hand. Ruth's family who are Jewish, were forced to flee their home country and the Nazi regime after her father was imprisoned in Dachau concentration camp. Jurgen's family were evacuated to the country after the bombing of their home in Hanover. By this time his father had been captured on the Russian front as a prisoner of war.

Ruth and Jürgen met in Berlin as students in the early 1960s, and after their marriage in Hanover, decided that teaching was their vocation. They had always dreamt of running their own professional language school together, free from the constraints of ordinary school life. The steady and quiet community of Market Bosworth offered them an ideal setting, thus the twisting lanes and gentle slopes of central England finally became their home.

The Schwiening Language School is based at Beech House, Market Bosworth which is thought to have been built in 1818 by Eleanor Frances Pochin, the daughter of the 4th Baronet Dixie of Bosworth Hall. It stands at the top of Church Street beside the wrought-iron gates of St Peter's, with an outstanding view of the church through the sweeping branches of a copper beech. When Ruth and Jurgen bought the house in 1986 it was in a poor state of repair after lying empty for a year. Determined to maintain the original features and character of the building, their unusual restoration has resulted in a very interesting period dwelling. Although the house has many fascinating features, such as the old hooks and pulleys of the laundry room and a peep from the nanny's room into the nursery, the most interesting part is the cellar. A bricked-up archway to the right of the steps once led through to the cellars of the adjoining houses, where a section of bricks has been dated to the 1790s, indicating the existence of an earlier dwelling. It is rather intriguing that part of next door's staircase overlaps into Beech House at this point – known as a flying freehold.

The front garden is an exhibition in itself of Ruth's work, containing a life-sized man and woman made entirely of wire who modestly guard the gate, clothed only in ornamental flowers. A stained-glass tiger and double-headed dragon lurk in the shrubs along with a cockerel displaying the colours of its tail feathers. Ruth is currently involved in the Carlton village sign project as she is helping to create plaques depicting the past and present of the village, based on designs by the people of Carlton.

If teaching is Jürgen's first passion, the study of history and his interest in politics are a close second. He states: "Digging into history is a small contribution to facing up to the past without which there can be no better future. Looking at history is really looking at ourselves, for we have become what we are through our own collective endeavours. Our history is the present of past generations." At the moment he is researching and documenting the history of two families– both German, one Jewish and one not. On a recent visit to Austria while tracing Ruth's family, Jürgen discovered that, "in a small Austrian town a bell was rung every day at least until 1944 to commemorate, as one local historian put it, 'the happy expulsion of Jews in 1338'. When the Austrian Nazis expelled the Jews again in 1938, 600 years later, they made a point of reminding the people that they were doing nothing new. Indeed, anti-Judaism is as old as Christianity".

Students from far and wide come to stay at Beech House to become part of the community, speaking, living and breathing the language they choose to learn. The courses are tailor-made to the students' requirements and it is with these residential students that Ruth and Jürgen are best able to develop their ideas of 'good tutoring'.

The old coach house at the side of the house is built with Carlton stone, supported by a substantial 15th-century oak beam below which hang rows of slate tiles engraved with messages of thanks from the visiting pupils. The opportunity to stay in a bustling but tranquil rural town such as Market Bosworth, accompanied by the generosity and warmth of the Schwienings, encourages the growth of language through experience and achievement through living.

Left: 'Nacht and Nebel'. This painting portrays how many of the Jews simply disappeared during the Holocaust. Painting by Ruth Schwiening.

Right: Jürgen and Ruth Schwiening at home.

THE RICHARD III SOCIETY

AUGUST, 1485

And where two roses joined, the White Boar banner crimsoned with royal blood still defiant flies.

...black needle thorns hide a spiked golden crown when, with a jangling armour crash, England's Majesty, betrayed, thuds down on Bosworth Field, and rose-red swords and axes start the final act.

...the bubbling spring that early cooled those praying lips, now foams as a weary warhorse lifts its dripping head and turns for Leicester's Guild Hall, burdened with a body, stripped and naked, bloodied and bespoilt, the body of a king. With each slow step, a dangling hand drips ruby red. And then no more. An end to Richard's reign.

AN OVERCAST, SULTRY JUNE AFTERNOON, 1985

The thud of heavy mallet, and the mason leans back to squint at the last stone. Another softer tap and it's level, and loose mortar is carefully wiped away with a gnarled thumb.

He smiles at the coincidence. This small obelisk will mark the 500th anniversary of the battle on the very day that marks his 50th birthday – 22nd August 1985.

THE LOWING OF A COW ON A WARM, STILL, AUGUST EVENING

They push through the kissing gate, one by one, and walk slowly to the centre of the small field. A blemish is wiped from the plaque before they silently read the few words: 'Richard, the last Plantaganet King of England, was slain here...' No-one speaks.

The white roses look small and insignificant as they are gently placed and arranged. Turning, the three men silently retrace their steps and smile as they open the gate.

A HOT, LATE AUGUST, SUNDAY MORNING

The door creaks open and a small girl peers into the sunlit interior. She walks tentatively into the church, tightly gripping her mother's hand. They cross the aisle and as the mother lifts and places them, the flowers flash brilliant white, reflecting sunlight. Cut glass and white roses illuminate the windowsill as the mother stands back to silently admire them, but the little girl pulls her, wanting to leave.

SUNDAY AFTERNOON, 19th AUGUST 2001

Every ancient polished wooden pew inside Sutton Cheney's tiny church is full, so several people are standing quietly below the bell tower at the back.

The Rector introduces Robert Hamblin, Chairman of the Richard III Society, who will take the next reading, to be followed by King Richard's prayer.

And as each Ricardian mouths this ancient supplication, each silently honours their long-fallen King, vowing to defend him, his life and all that it meant.

Each year they'll come again... for evermore. No end to Richard's reign.

The 1877 edition of White's *Leicestershire Gazetteer* does not explain how they travelled – there was certainly no local railway in 1862 – but it does claim that 3,000 members of the British Archaeological Society visited the battle site on the 6th August of that year. A silver-gilt replica of Richard III's crown was presented to the Reverend Trollope after his talk explaining the significance of the battle, where the bloodiest action took place and how it all ended.

The Richard III Society did not then exist (it wasn't founded until 1924), and even with over 4,000 members worldwide they doubtless can never claim to have hosted such a large gathering. However, their influence over so many years has been of far greater importance in maintaining interest in the life of this former king.

Both his birth, at Fotheringhay on 2nd October 1452, and his death are marked with the annual pilgrimage to Bosworth Field, where he died. Each August, services are held at Sutton Cheney church where he prayed before the battle, and at King Dick's Well. Perhaps not 3,000 people on any one day, but each year, and every year, innumerable Ricardians do pay homage to their hero king.

Right: The King Richard III monument in Castle Park, Leicester.

THE THESPIANS

IT WAS AN IMPORTANT YEAR. PETROL RATIONING ENDED AND THE KOREAN WAR STARTED. IN THE WORLD OF THE ARTS, GEORGE BERNARD SHAW AND GEORGE ORWELL BOTH DIED. 'THE ARCHERS, A STORY OF COUNTRY FOLK' WAS FIRST BROADCAST — AND FRANK BROWN FOUNDED THE MARKET BOSWORTH DRAMA SOCIETY.

The following year, as they staged their first production, 'Double Dealings', the 1951 Festival of Britain opened, with the Skylon, the Royal Festival Hall and 'The largest dome in the world'. The coal and steel industries were nationalised and Winston Churchill won the general election. In the world of the arts (outside of Market Bosworth), Agatha Christie's 'The Mousetrap' was in rehearsal for a 1952 opening.

And what survives? The Royal Festival Hall, and 'The Archers' still telling its daily tale of country folk – but neither the Dome of Discovery nor the Skylon. 'The

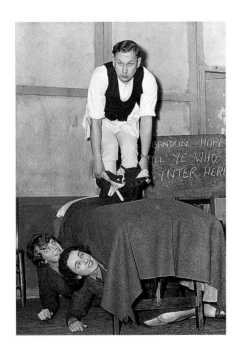

Above: Clive Dilks caught *deshabille.*

Mousetrap' often plays to full houses, as does the 50-year-old Market Bosworth Drama Society with smash-hit farces or who-dunnits – and at least one founder member, Pearl Dilks, is still involved.

"During the war, when I was about 12, my dad helped Walter Churchill to move his factory to Market Bosworth. Although the village later grew on me, I hated it on sight. I went to the Grammar School where the headmaster, Mr Ford Smith, frightened us to death. With my initials being PC, he used to call me Police Constable Morris – and I hated it! In 1950 Frank Brown asked Clive Dilks and me to join his new amateur drama society. The first production, 'Double Dealings', was in 1951. Because I had pretty frocks, I always got the part of the sweet young thing – but that doesn't say much for my acting ability.

"Other founder members included Jimmy and Doris James, the Calderwoods and Dorothy Holmes. Later, Harry Frost joined, but Clive – we married in 1954 – was always the star of the show: give the devil his due, he was very good.

"The plays have always been at St Peter's Hall. At first there was no stage, just a bare hall, so Horace Cheshire and Mr Granger built one for each production: just a simple framework on which we hung curtains – there was no set – and we just changed in the kitchen.

"The Society has produced at least two, and sometimes three, plays every year since then, never missing – a complete mixture of comedies, farces, thrillers and murder mysteries. My favourite was 'Rebecca', when I played Mrs Danvers and was told that I frightened the children – wonderful!"

Nowadays the Society has a fine stage with excellent lighting and sound systems and experts to operate them:

"We've been very lucky to have people like Terry Rowley to help, but we all muck in to build and paint the set and to move the chairs before and after each performance. We ran a Junior Drama Club at one time and in 1978 helped Stan Barrett and Stewart Glasscock stage their musical – 'The Prodigal Son'. The Society nearly folded when we lost two key members in the same year but at a meeting at the Red Lion, Nickie and Mac Clarke said, 'Come on, we can all get it going'. They've been leaders ever since – and we're still going strong. It's nice when young people join and then come back after university. Stephen and Simon Hayes have returned and Stephen says he's ready for more roles!"

Pearl eventually gave up acting, preferring to produce some of the plays, although persuading people that they were *just right for this part* was never easy. She now normally sits in the prompt corner whispering the odd forgotten line or cue – and admits that she no longer 'hates' Market Bosworth.

THE MUSIC MAKERS

Joy & John Gladman

Joy and John both came from musical families and were already enjoying singing by the time Joy first noticed John. He was playing Katherine in 'Taming of the Shrew' at their Brighton school, and romance blossomed in the local tram shelter.

Much later, in 1972, after many homes and many fondly remembered musical experiences, they settled in Market Bosworth. Both sang in St Peter's choir until 2001 but Joy is perhaps best known for her 'Joy Springs' choir, started in 1974 and still singing from their 'Purcell to Pop' repertoire.

With so many musical memories John and Joy find it impossible to name their favourite piece of music.

"There are so many. We both love all manner of music, although Beethoven's 'Pastoral' is very special. Living where we do it strikes the right chord – it's truly music of a peaceful countryside, and after the clashing thunderstorm there is a real feeling of life renewing, before it builds to a thrilling climactic ending – marvellous.

"When we lived in Manchester we were able to attend some of the Halle concerts. At that time the National Anthem was played at the start of every concert so movingly it could bring one to tears, but a favourite memory is of Sir John Barbirolli sitting on the edge of the podium and conducting his arrangement of the 'Elizabethan Suite' with just tiny finger movements."

Fred Jennings & Derrick Baker

The old St Peter's primary school in Park Street occasionally echoes to the sounds of two elderly gentlemen having fun with the 'Queen of Sheba' – or Schumann, Rachmaninov or Grieg.

Fred Jennings describes their piano duets as 'a battle', but his friend Derrick Baker, who lives at the old Park Street schoolhouse, thinks of them as 'a time to have some fun!'.

For the past two to three years Fred and Derrick have regularly settled down on Friday mornings, one at the Challen baby grand, the other at the Burling & Mansfield upright, to amuse and entertain themselves on two keyboards.

They happily attempt whatever suitable duets Derrick already has or can find at the Leicester music library, and their four-handed favourites include Grieg, Schumann and Mozart. Fred, with his large hands, can span an octave and a half, so he loves the technical challenges of Rachmaninov, but both agree with a chuckle that for certain difficult pieces, few people notice the odd note or two missed out – either by accident or design!

Above: Piano music.

HAND MADE

Paul Young

Operating from his base at Station House Pottery, Shenton, Paul produces a unique range of handmade pots and undertakes commissions for commemorative wares; he has exhibited in many UK and overseas galleries.

Paul considers that the spark that ignited his passion for pottery-making and triggered his creativity and traditionalism, can be put down to his sound education and the good fortune of having received tuition in his art school years from many of the leading potters from Britain and overseas. He classes himself as a 21st-century potter working within the framework of the English/European slipware tradition, and strongly believes that artists must continually strive to express themselves in their own individual style.

Paul produces his wares in the traditional way, his kick wheel requiring a lot of energy to operate – with his hands immersed in both water and wet clay for most of the working day, split fingers and an aching back usually constitute his typical reward at its end. Despite the hard work, however, he delights in his art and continues to push into the 21st century with what he believes to be a contemporary revival of the Arts and Crafts Movement.

Roy Thorley

In 1980, having been made redundant twice in the space of fifteen years, Roy Thorley made a decision that this situation would not happen again and so set up his own business, Bosworth Crafts. Roy first started working with leather as a hobby some 15 years previously and took stalls at many craft fairs all over the Midlands; he is totally self-taught.

Operating from the small workshop area in his shop, he has developed a range of hand-carved leather goods, many of which are unique and of his own design.

Roy's clients come from all over the country as well as from overseas, often returning to place orders for one-off pieces made to their own specification. Hand-carved rocking horse saddles and harnesses are Roy's speciality, as are three dimensional leather-framed pictures and clocks depicting British birds and wildlife. Over the years Roy has established a fine reputation for the quality of his work and has received commission work to produce facsimile church brasses for Ye Olde Red Lion Hotel and coats-of-arms for the Dixie Arms Hotel in Market Bosworth and the Red Lion in Barlestone. Roy welcomes visitors to his workshop in Main Street to see at first hand the results of the leather-worker's considerable skill.

Calley Wilkinson

By a strange coincidence Calley Wilkinson's current occupation also developed as a result of his redundancy. After virtually a lifetime's work, first as a tool-maker then in the dyeing industry, Calley was forced to take up something new. Approximately ten years ago he decided to combine his two very serious hobbies, minerals/fossil collecting and jewellery making/repairs, into one business venture; and together with his wife Reby, set up a retail sales and repair outlet, giving it the magical name – *Ore Inspired*.

The shop, which contains a small workshop at the rear, offers a wide range of unique stock not found in the typical 'High Street' jewellers. Besides displaying a large range of silver and gold jewellery, much of which is set with semi-precious and precious stones, there are displays of fine and decorative minerals and ancient fossils. Calley draws upon the hands-on experience he gained from his training in gold and silver work to add a suitable setting to the stones he collected, cut and polished during his time as an amateur lapidary.

Finding the transition from tool-maker to jeweller a fairly easy one, Calley has discovered that the major proportion of his work is taken up with repairs. Sadly unable to devote as much time as he would wish to making pieces to add to his stock, he does, however, undertake commission work, specialising in producing items of exceptional beauty from his wide range of rare gemstones. Ask to see his collection – but not perhaps on a busy day!

Above: 'Adam and Eve' by Paul Young.

Right: Calley Wilkinson.

Extracts from *New Aspect* by Keith McCarthy

BRUSHSTROKES & NEEDLEWORK

Michael Warr

Michael is a true 'Mid-lander' having been born at Meriden, near the centre of England. After studying at Coventry College of Art and a spell of teaching adults part-time, he has been painting and writing full-time since 1977.

With permanent exhibitions in Switzerland and the USA, many UK and European exhibitions, and with many art books and videos published, he is an internationally recognised artist. Having lived in Market Bosworth for fourteen years, Michael and his partner Muriel now spend part of each year at their home in France.

'Gertch'

"This is one of my favourite paintings. It is one of a series based on 'An Alpine Symphony', by the German composer Richard Strauss.

"In 1991, the painting formed part of an exhibition in Coventry Cathedral, where, on the opening evening, the Birmingham Philharmonic Orchestra played the symphony. The concert and exhibition were attended by over 800 people, including many international guests. It was truly a memorable evening... an artist's dream come true!"

Ron Cooke

At the age of nine, Ron won a *Manchester Evening News* watercolour competition, and after trying unsuccessfully to break into professional football and then spending several years with the *Daily Mail*, he decided to try to make a living in the art world.

His miniatures and paintings of local scenes will be familiar to many people, but having developed an interest in Lord Nelson, his work now includes sepia marine subjects, often researched and painted abroad.

"It was always an ambition to work and paint abroad, ideally near the sea, and several years ago I discovered the perfect spot in Corfu. Despite having to start with a painting of a giant lobster for a local restaurateur, I have been able to develop my interests in Nelson and his famous battles, as well as painting many local scenes.

"I am very lucky to be able to return there each year, but I still love painting local Bosworth scenes, and the view along Church Street to St Peter's Church is still one of my favourites."

Market Bosworth Quilters

A small group of women from Market Bosworth and the surrounding villages meet on a fortnightly basis in the comfort of each others' homes. They are the Market Bosworth Quilters who, together create beautiful pieces of art through needlecraft.

The gathering of the 'quilting bee' is mainly a social sewing occasion but is also for the exchanging of ideas, providing inspiration and ironing out technical hitches.

The team was established in 1991 by Angela Guppy and includes a further eight members, all of whom are excellent with the needle. In 1999 they won first prize for 'Best Group Quilt' in the Quilts UK exhibition. Their most recent challenge was to produce a millennium sampler quilt depicting key events throughout the year, designed by each member of the 'bee'. This project was very different from the squares and strips of a more traditional quilt displaying its theme in bright bold colours.

Above: 'Church Street' by Ron Cooke.

Left: 'Gertch' by Michael Warr.

THE WORDSMITHS

Sarah Alun-Jones

A country girl living on the edge of the small village of Carlton, Sarah Alun-Jones is surrounded by a wealth of inspiration. From an early age she entertained herself painting and creating things with cardboard and Fairy Liquid bottles. Now 12 years old she has extended her interests in the artistic field to both music and poetry, the latter being of great importance to her.

Sarah is keenly encouraged by her family, friends and teachers in terms of her literary skills and eventually hopes to study literature and art at higher levels.

The following poem is written about an old apple tree that grows in her garden, called 'The Dappled Man'. The delicate circle of bluebells and daffodils enclosing the tree in the spring is described by Sarah as smiling children in coloured robe. Since the creation of this poem she has written many others which are recorded in a small book she keeps with her at all times.

The Dappled Man

As I look up at that blossomed man
See all his fingers bloom
The wrinkles of his skin take life
A posture lost in bark lagoons

At his bare feet children stand
Clothed in coloured robe
Smiling gently by the anchors

So many years its trunk has known
Strong, sturdy like a stone.

Sarah Alun-Jones age 12 years

Above: The apple tree in Sarah's garden that inspired the poem - photograph by Erica Tomlinson.

Laura Croman

Mrs Emily Laura Croman, a born and bred Bosworthian, was Chairman of the Natural History Society for fifteen years and President of the Women's Institute for three years. On their behalf she won a competition for a Churchyard Survey in Leicestershire.

She has also won prizes for articles and pieces on local history. The following is a short extract from a prize-winning entry for a Leicestershire County Council competition entitled 'How I Remember It'.

Memories of Market Bosworth 1925 – 1931

"Did this really happen during your lifetime?" asked the bemused young lady.

I was conducting a party of Women's Institute members on a walk around Bosworth and had just pointed out where the cart for emptying the pan lavatories was stabled. Known crudely as the 'Marmalade Pot', it didn't encourage anyone to linger down the Back Lane. Further along, one of the street ash-dumps was sited, a brick-surrounded aperture where well riddled ashes were dumped to be carted away twice a year…

We lived in one of fourteen houses, which ran down Barton Lane opposite the chapel and played in street groups in the roads that were our playgrounds…

In an effort to provide colour, most of the women removed some of the front cobblestones to make a flower patch. These were carefully tended and much prized, especially by the Red Lion cow 'Bluey' who, if her minder was late, nudged open the field gate at milking time and ambled up the road nibbling these blooms until discovered by an irate gardener…

Above: Laura Croman in her teens. A pen and ink drawing by Glyn Croman.

ACKNOWLEDGEMENTS

On earlier pages our thanks were expressed to all who helped to write this book, to the artists whose work is featured and to those who helped in many other ways. We now wish to say a very sincere thank you to all of those who, either voluntarily or after just a little gentle persuasion, agreed to contribute material for the book.

In the 1700s a local resident, William King, when asked about inconsistencies in the income from some property belonging to the Dixie School, chose to remain silent. However he is attributed with the comment: "that it was best for Bosworth folk to lie still in the wagon and not speak out of turn". *

Fortunately the folk from Bosworth and the surrounding villages do not heed this advice, otherwise this book could not have been written. It is all of the people listed below, from town and village, who contributed their observations and opinions, their comments and anecdotes that show just how rich and varied village life is today.

We must, however, also apologise that so much of the fascinating material provided by these and by many others – almost enough for another book – has unfortunately had to be omitted.

Miss S Alun-Jones	Mr T Gardner	Mr G Pearson
PC G Anderson	Mrs A Gilbert	Mr T Perry
Mr S Assinder	Mr K Ginns	Reverend J Plant
Mr D Baker	Mrs A Hatton	Mr Poulson
Miss E Beard	Mr & Mrs J Gladman	Reverend A Reed
Mrs B Bhatia	Mr J Goode	Mr K Reeves
Mrs A Boston	Mr L Goodwin	Mrs F Rhodes
Mr & Mrs Brown	Mr R Gosling	Mr T Rowley
Mrs T Briggs	Mr & Mrs N Gould	Mr & Mrs W Rickard
Dr R Brittain	Mr & Mrs O Hall	Mr N Ryley
Mr F Calderwood	Mr D Hardwick	Mr E Salvador
Mr J Churchill	Miss J Harriman	Mr & Mrs J Schwiening
Mr & Mrs A Clark	Mr I Holloway	Mr M Stretton
Mr & Mrs B Claybrook	Mrs H Hough	Mr & Mrs R Symonds
Mr B Coleman	Mr R Holmes	Mr P Tebbatt
Mr J Coleman	Mr R Iliffe	Mr & Mrs L Taylor-Ryan
Mr & Mrs K Coleman	Mr A Jackson	Miss R Thompson
Mr R Cooke	Mr L James	Mr R Thorley
Nurse M Cragg	Mrs J Jamie	Mr J Thorp
Mr T Creason	Mr F Jennings	Mr A Tomlin
Mr & Mrs G Croman	Mr C Johnson	Mrs F Walker
Mr Dalby	Mr & Mrs R V Kirkpatrick	Mr S Warner
Mr & Mrs J Dawkins	Dr King	Mr M Warr
Mrs S Dawson	Mr J Knott	Mr A J Watson
Mr & Mrs P de Lisle	Mr W Lancaster	Mr R Wilford
Mrs P Dilks	Mr J Lancaster	Mr & Mrs C Wilkinson
Mr & Mrs G Earp	Mr R Lawrence	Mr R Willmott
Mr & Mrs B Eveson	Mr R Leake	Mr A Wilson
Mr S Fell	Mr J Lees	Mr B Wilson
Father T Fellows	Mr L Massarella	Mr C F Wollaston
Mr J Finney	Mr D Mellor	Mr A Wright
Mr D Fitt	Mr & Mrs J Nadin	Mr J Wykes
Mrs B Foord	Mr N Oldacre	Mr P Young

* From: A Truly Honest Man by Peter Foss and Timothy Parry.

HINCKLEY & BOSWORTH BOROUGH COUNCIL

FINANCIAL CONTRIBUTORS

We particularly wanted to make the book available at a reasonable price and our thanks are due to all of those that made this possible by their generous financial support.

The following organisations made direct grants towards the costs of the project:
- A very generous grant of £5000 from the 'Awards for All' joint scheme who provide Lottery grants to local voluntary organisations and community groups.
- The Leicestershire County Council Libraries and Information Services.
- The Hinckley & Bosworth Borough Council.
- The HSBC Bank, Market Bosworth.

A limited number of special subscription editions of the book with silver blocked cover, gilt edges and presented in an imitation leather slipcase was made available and the following people and organisations expressed their financial support by purchasing one or more copies.

Mr & Mrs D Bream
Mr & Mrs Broughton
Mr T A Clinton
Mr & Mrs K Coleman
Mr & Mrs E Davies
Mr & Mrs G Earp
Mr & Mrs J Finney
Mrs A Gilbert & Mr R Holmes

Mr R Jackson
Mr & Mrs A Knight
Mr & Mrs B Lancaster
Leicestershire County Council Libraries & Information Services
Leicester Mercury Group Ltd
Mrs J Mapp
Mrs P Marshall

Mr & Mrs K McCarthy
Mr & Mrs J Nadin
Mr & Mrs T Richardson
Mr E Salvador
Mr C Stamper
Mr & Mrs A B Wilson
Mrs J M Woodward
Mr C Wright

Aerial photograph courtesy of www.skylibrary.co.uk.
Lines from *Toads Revisited* and *Days*, from Collected Poems by Philip Larkin reproduced by kind permission of Faber and Faber.
April Rise – reprinted by permission of PFD on behalf of The Laurie Lee Estate ©: Laurie Lee 1983 – Laurie Lee Selected Poems – Published by Penguin Books.

BIBLIOGRAPHY

Cantor, Leonard – *Parish Churches of Leics. & Rutland*, Kairos Press Leicester, 2000.

Foss, Peter – *The History of Market Bosworth*, Sycamore Press, Melton Mowbray, 1983.

Foss, Peter/Parry, Timothy – *A Truly Honest Man,* The Moxon Family Research Trust, 1998.

Hall, W.T. – *A Collection for the History of Stoke Golding.*

Hamilton, Thompson, Professor – *Volume XIV of the Transactions of the Leics. Archaeological Society.*

Hoskins, W.G. – *The Heritage of Leicestershire,* 1972.

Newman, Bernard – *The Bosworth Story,* Herbert Jenkins, London, 1967.

Oakley, Glynis – *A History of Gopsall*, Barncraft Printing, Sheepy Magna, 1997.

Pakenham, Thomas – *Meetings with Remarkable Trees*, Phoenix Illustrated.

Penoyre, John/Ryan, Michael – *The Observer's Book of Architecture*, Frederick Warne & Co. Ltd, London and New York.

Pevsner, Nikolaus – *The Buildings of England (Leics. & Rutland),* Butler & Tanner Ltd, Frome.

Rowse, Dr A.L. – *Bosworth Field*, Macmillan, London, 1966.

Todd, John – *By the Foolishness of Preaching*, Barton in the Beans Baptist Church, Leicestershire, 1993.

Stafford, Alison, Editor – *Market Bosworth as I Remember It,* Leics. Libraries and Information Service, Leicester, 1993.

Tomlinson, R.R. – *The Dixie Grammar School, its refounding and its place in history.*

Lady Charlotte Cope's Diary.

Illustrated Particulars of the Bosworth Hall Estate, 1918.

White's History, *Gazetteer & Directory of the Counties of Leicester & Rutland, 1877.*

I N D E X

A Truly Honest Man (Peter Foss &
    Tim Parry) 80, 92, 149
abaci 28
abattoirs 92, 139, 148, 149
Abbans, Charlotte Comtesse d' 49
Abbot Suger's Saint-Denis Abbey 28, 30
'Adam & Eve', Paul Young *212*
Adamant (narrow boat) 147
aerial photograph *12-13*
'Affums' (jaguar) 104
agriculture *see* farming
airfields 90, 194
Alesbrook, Dave 121
Alesbrook, John 200
All Saints Church, Cadeby *108*, 109
All Saints Church, Nailstone 28
All Saints Church, Ratcliffe Culey 32
All Saints Church, Sheepy Magna 41
almshouses 166
Alpha courses 102
altar (St Peter, Market Bosworth) 40
Alun-Jones, Sarah 216
Ambion Court 8
Ambion Hill 197, *208*
ammonites *132*
Anderson, Graham 94
anemone blue *110*
Anglican churches 102, 122
Anglican United Benefice 78
angling 203
Anglo-Saxon burial ground, Stoke Golding 20
antiques 142
Appleby Magna 17, 43, 44, 87
aquatic sports 203
arboretum 152, 180, *181*, 186, 187
arcades 17, 28, 32, *33*
archaeology 14, 197
Archbishop of Canterbury 88, 124
arches
    Gothic 26
    Norman (round) 26, 28, 32, *33*, 34, 41, *72*
    Tudor 44
architecture, history of 17-18 *see also*
        specific types of architecture, e.g.
        Saxon architecture
Arnold's Crescent 92
Art Gallery 137
artists 215
Arts and Crafts
    contemporary revival 212
Ashby – Nuneaton railway 133
Ashby Sale Yard 148
Ashby Union Canal 62, 133, 146-7, *146*
Ashmolean Museum, Oxford 106
Aspect 8, 88, 189
Assinder, Steve 82
Astley family 51
Atherstone, The 130, 142
Atkinson, Jackie 157
Atkinson, Margaret 107
Awdry, Reverend Wilbert 109
Aylesbrook Cottage 166, *167*, 168

Babbage, Charles 86
Back Lane 76, 92, 217

bailey 22
Bailey, Jack 9
Bailey, John 201
Baker, Derrick 211
Bakery Cottage 175
Baldwin, Dr 90
Bamford, Ike and Lucy 138
bank 8, *99*, *119*
Baptist Chapel, Barton *150*, 151
Baptist Church 122
Bardon Hall 71
Barlestone *62*, 92, 198, 212
    cinema 198
Barnes, Patrick 203
Barrett, Stan 210
Barton Fabis 151
Barton Lane 46, 217
Barton Road 128, *156*, 175, 189
Barton in the Beans 51, 128, 139, *150*, 151,
        154, *155*
Bates, Charlie 80
Bates, Ian 201
Battle of Bosworth 120, 157, 197
    Battle of Bosworth painting 120
battlefield 8, 180, 197, 208
Battlefield Visitor Centre 197
Bayliss, Peter 157
'Bean' (John Thorp) 142, *142*
Bear Inn 118
Beard, Eunice 127
Beare Close 118
Beau Pool (now Bow Pool) 104, 162, 180,
        182-3, 186
Beaumont family 14
Beaumont, Barbara 56
Beavin, Hugh 14
Beck, William 174, 175
Beckeritt monorail system 146
Beech House, Church Street 8, 92, 123, 207
Beech House, Snarestone 55, *55*
Beeching, Dr 130
Belgrave Museum, Leicester 68
bells 30, 36
belvedere 72
Betjeman, Sir John 34
Bilstone 66, 71, 94
bird watching 202
Birmingham Bullets Basketball Team 83
Black Death 32, 132 *see also* plague
Black Horse Inn, The Square *10*, 96, 120, *120*,
        175
blacksmithing 141, 152
blind arcade 22
Blount, Sir Thomas Pope 49
Boscobel oak 67
Bose, the Saxon 14
'Boseworde' 14, 36
Bostock, Chris 121
Boston, Audrey 109
Boston, Reverend Teddy 9, 109
Bosworth and Gopsall Estates, The 10
Bosworth Antiques 142, *143*
Bosworth Battlefield 8, 180, 197
Bosworth College, Desford 100, 203
Bosworth Crafts 212

Bosworth Drama Society 137, 192, 210
Bosworth Fair 149
Bosworth Gallery 62
Bosworth Hall 10, *11*, 14, *38*, 43, *54*, 56-8, *56*,
        57, *58*, *87*, *105*, 186, 207
    bricks 45
    Dixie family crests and coat-of- arms 10,
        100, 123, 205
    ghost of Lady Anna Dixie 111
    home of the Dixie family 87, 104
    Infirmary 58, 72, 78, 92, 111, 139, 189
    Italian influence 55
    Nurse Cragg 90
    trees *see trees*
Bosworth Hall Estate 19, 72, 141, 162, 166,
        180, 189
Bosworth Hall Hotel 72, 111, *111*
Bosworth in Bloom 157, 160
Bosworth Junior Football Club 200
Bosworth Market 127
Bosworth May Fair 165
Bosworth Park 8, 162, 165, *178-79*, 186
    alligator 88
    Bosworth Show 127, 165
    deer 162
    'Inn on the Park' 87
    Owl Walk 202
Bosworth Rugby Club 201
Bosworth Sale Yard (cattle market) 165
Bosworth Show 15, 165
Bosworth showground *164*, 165
Bosworth Water Trust 194, 203, *203*
Bosworth wharf 146, 147
Bow Pool (formerly Beau Pool) 104, 162, 180,
        182-3, 186
Bowers, Canon 40
box-frame construction 43, 46
Bradshaw, John 51
Bradshaw, William 14
Braithwaite Co. 132
Brascote Lane 132
breathalyser tests 94
bricks 45
    Beech House, Church Street 20
    Beech House, Snarestone 55
    Bosworth Hall 56
    early development 44-5
    Elizabethan 46
    Georgian 62
    Osbaston Hall 49
    Shenton Hall 52, 53
brickworks 44, 45, 128
    Brickyard Farm, Stapleton 160
Briffaut, Mlle 90
Britain in Bloom competition 157
British Archaeological Society 208
British Legion 8
Brittain, Dr Richard 92
Bronze Age 14
Brookes, Joy 157
Brown, Frank 210
Brown, John 201
Brownies 157
Bruxner, Mrs 175
Bryson, Bill 68

BSE 149
Budulis, Ronnie 201
building materials *see* bricks; slates; stucco;
        thatch; wattle and daub
Bull's Head (now Dixie Arms) 70, 118
butchering 139
buttresses 28, 34
Buxton, Ben 201

Cadeby 9, *42*, 106
    Boston, Reverend Teddy 109
    Church Cottage 20, *21*, 43, 76
    giant redwood 189
    Norse settlement 14
    quarry 132, 160
    school 96
Cadeby Hall 22, *24*, 25
Cadeby Lane 201
Cadeby Manor 60, *61*
Calderwoods 210
Canaletto 67
canals 14, 52, 197
    Ashby Union Canal 133, 146-7, *146*
canoeing 203
capitals (architecture) 32
carbon-dating 25
Carlton 70, 96, 106, 189, 207, 216
    mill *129*
Castle Farm, Bilstone 66
Castle Park, Leicester 197
castles, Norman 22, 25
Catholic Church 102, 122
cattle market 15, 18, 139, 165
Cedar Drive, Market Bosworth 8, 76
census 124
Champaigne, Sir Robert 34
Chance, of Birmingham 53
chapel (Bosworth) 62
    Gopsall 67
    Barton Lane 217
Charles I 51
Charles II 36, 51
Cheshire, Horace 210
Chestnut Close 8
chevrons 22
chimney-pieces 51, 53
chimneys 43, 44, 52 *see also* fireplaces
choir, 'Joy Springs' 211
Christian life 102, 122, 151
Church Cottage (now Holy Bones) 9, *123*,
        123
Church Cottage, Cadeby 20, *21*, 43, 76
Church Hill, Twycross 136
Church of Our Lady and Saint Gregory 122
church records 205
Church Street 215, *215*
    Beech House 8, 92, *93*, 207
    Grey House 46, 70
    Holy Bones 123, *123*
    Waste, The 123
churches 102 *see also* ecclesiastical archi-
        tecture; individual churches, e.g. St
        Peter's Church
church plate 40
'Churches Together' 102

Churchill, James 135
Churchill, Walter 135, 210
Churchill's factory 128, 135
churchyard survey 217
cinemas 76, 198
Cistercian monks 26, 28
Clare family, coat-of-arms 36
Clark, Margaret *117*
Clarke, Nickie and Mac 210
Classical (architecture) 43, 55, 60, 70
clays 45
Claybrook, Brian and Sandra 160
clerestories 36, 40, 41, 106
Cliff House, Twycross 136
Clock Clubs 151
Clock shop 128
clock, church 36, 151
clockmakers 151
close-stud framing 43, 44
coal mines 146
coats-of-arms 58, 212
  Clare 36
  Dixie *19,* 36, 56, *56,* 205
  Harcourt 36, 205
  Verdon 36
  Wilson 205
cobbler 96
Cock Inn, Sibson *43*
Coleman, John 8
Coleman, Ken and Vivien 130
Colts 201
Community 10, 78
Community Centre 8
Community College and High School 78,
    100, *101*
computer games 136, *136*
computer simulation 137, *137*
Congerstone 14, 66, 68, 96, 148
Congregational Chapel, Newton Burgoland
    151
Congregational Church 122
Conker (computer game) 136
Cooke, Ron 215
Cooper, Mary 96
Copper, Mr 96
Cope family 49, 106
Coprinus atramentarius 186
Corner Cottage Antiques 142
Corner Cupboard (now Bosworth Antiques)
    142
Coton Lane *189*
Coton Priory *16,* 44, *45,* 127, *127,* 152, 176,
    177
Couchman, Henry 22
Council Offices, Station Road 8
Court Leet 118
craftsmen 212
Cragg, Nurse Mary 90, *91*
Cristy, Thomas 48
Croman, Emily Laura 30, 217, *217*
Croman, Glyn 152, 175, 217
Cromwell, Oliver 36, 198
Crown, estate 68
Crown Hill, Stoke Golding 197
crown-posts 49

crow-stepped gable 44
cruck construction 20, *21,* 43, 46
Cubs 157

Dadlington 28, 197
dairy cattle 154, 175
Dark Ages 20
Davies, Teresa 130
Davis, William Henry 192
Dawkins' abbatoir 128
Dawkins, David and John 148-9
de Lisle Mr & Mrs 49, 172
Deacon, Samuel 128, 151
Decorated Period (architecture) 17, 26, 32
deer 127
  black old English 162
  red 162
deer parks 58, 66, 180
Delius, Daphne 90
Delius, Squire 180, 186
dendro-dating 20, 43, 189
Desford 92, 100, 197
'Desford Bill' 197
Desford chock 146
Desford Pit 146
Dickenson, Anne 106
Dilks, Clive 210, *210*
Dilks, Pearl 210
Dingle Dell 159
Disraeli 192
Dissolution of the Monasteries 17, 44, 46
Dixie Arms Hotel (formerly Bull's Head) 70,
    118, 141, 201, 212
Dixie crest 123
Dixie Educational Foundation 40, 52
Dixie Estate 123, 166, 180
Dixie family 10, 36, 62, 162
Dixie Grammar School 8, 40, 78, 87, *98-9,*
    100, *100, 106, 107,* 118, 205, 210
  founded 14
  Headmasters:
    Evans, Rev'd Arthur Benoni 106
    Ford Smith, James 210
    Gosling, William Flower 40
  re-founded 87
Dixie, Caroline 87
Dixie, Eleanor 87
Dixie, Lady Anna 111
Dixie, Lady Florence 14, 87, 104
Dixie, Lady Penelope 87, 165
Dixie, Rector John 40, 205
Dixie, Sir Wolstan, 1st Baronet 14, 56, 58, 87
Dixie, Sir Beaumont, 2nd Baronet 56
Dixie, Sir Wolstan, 4th Baronet 111, 207
Dixie, Willoughby (half brother of the 5th Bar-
    onet) 205
Dixie, Sir Willoughby, 7th Baronet 118
Dixie, Sir Alexander Beaumont, 11th Baronet
    58, 87, 104, 118, 162
Dixie, Sir Wolstan, 13th baronet 87, 106, 127
Dixon, William 123
dog cemetery 25
dog-leg staircase 53
dog-tooth decoration (Norman) 26
Domesday Book 14, 17, 20, 25, 36, 49, 109

doors
  Norman 28
  Queen Anne 60
dovecotes 52
Dower House 17, *18,* 46, 76, 82, 118, 135
Drackley, Tom 9
Drama Society 137, 190, 210
Duckery (Cadeby Hall) 25
Dutch architecture 44
Dutch gable 19

Eames, Nancy 109
Early English Period (architecture) 17, 26, 28
Earp, Gordon 158
earthquakes 34
East Lodge 18, *19,* 70
ecclesiastical architecture 20, 26-41
Edestone 51
Educality Ltd 137
education 14, 82-3
  pre-school (playgroups) 8, 157
  primary 96, *97*
  secondary 100
  see also schools
Edward VII 68
effigy
  All Saints, Sheepy Magna 41
  William Humphrey (St Peter,
    Swepstone) 26
  William Roberts (St James, Sutton Cheney)
    46
elderly, accommodation for the 8, 78
Elizabethan architecture 43, 46, 51, 62
  style 205
Elohim Church 78, 122
enclosure 14, 52, 197
engineering 135
English bond 45
Entente Floral 157
evangelical revival 151
European Eagle owl *202*
Evans
  Anne 106
  Reverend Arthur Benoni 15, 106
  George 106
  Joan 106
  John 106
  Sebastian 106
Evans family 106
Eveson, Brian and Lynne 122
eyebrow windows 68, 76

Faber, Alfred 118
fairs 149, 165 *see also* markets
fairy ring 186
farming 127, 152, 154, 165, 175, 184
farriers 141
fatstock market 175
Fell, Stan 86, *86*
Fellows, Father Terry *79,* 122
Fenny Drayton 14, 22, 51, 184
Fernot, a knight 56
Ferrers, Earl Henry de 66
feudal system 43
Field Days, Sheepy 80

Finney, John 144, 198
fire-fighters 121, *121,* 166
fireplaces 44
  Bosworth Hall 58, 111
  Gopsall Hall 53, 67
  Odstone Hall 51
  Old Rectory (Rectory Lane) 205
  Shenton Hall 53
  see also chimneys
fire station 121
fishing 203
fishpond (Bosworth Manor) 56
Fitt, David 100, 203
Flemish bond 45
Fletcher, Amos 139
Flick (Rhodes) 172
flight simulators 137
Flower Club 192
flower industry 160
Fly Agaric (*Amanita muscaria*) *187*
font 26, 34, 36, 122
Foord, Biddy 203
foot and mouth disease 94, 147, 152, 165,
    175, 184-5
football 200
Forest, National 152`
Forge, The 128, *140,* 141, *141,* 152
Foss, Peter 80, 92, 149, 205
fossils 132, 212
Fotheringhay 208
Fox, George 14
frame-knitters' cottages *128*
Free Church 102, 122
French Revolution 30
Friends (Quakers) 14
Frost, Harry 9, 210
fungi 152, 186-7, *186, 187*
Furbey, Mr 127

Gadsby, Matt *201*
gallows *see* gibbet posts
garages 130
garden centre 160
gardens and gardening 152, 172
Gardner, Tony 144, 166
Garratt, Ashley 139
Gas works 133
gate, court d'honneur (Bosworth Hall) 56
gatehouses 43, 44, 53
George III 30
George and Dragon public house 92
George Inn 18, 46, 118
Georgian architecture 18, 26, 51, 62, 67, 70,
    71, 76
'Gertch', Michael Warr *214*
Gibbet Lane, Bilstone 71
gibbet post 94, 151
Gibbons, Grinling 58
Gibney, Bern 202
Gibson, Michael and Anne 118
Ginns, Kevin 121
Gladman, John 88, 211
Gladman, Joy 211
Glasscock, Stewart 210
gnomon 34

Goatham 189
Godsons Hill 76, 135, 139
Goldney, Elizabeth 106
Good Samaritan, The (St Peter, Market Bosworth) 40
Goode, Joe 146, 147
Goodwin, Les 121
Goppeshull 66
'Gopsall Circle' 67
Gopsall Estate 136, 142
Gopsall Hall 51, 53, 66, 67, 67, 68
Gopsall Park 82, 106
Gopsall Temple 10, 68, 69
Gopsall Wharf 147
Gosling, William Flower 9, 40, 106
Gothic
  architecture 26, 28, 30, 46
  doorway 100
  style 106
Gothic Revival 18, 70
Gould, Brenda and Norman 159
Grange Farm, Barton in the Beans 154
Grange, The, Barton Road, Market Bosworth 76
Granger, Mr 210
Grant of Arms 205
Great Rebuilding 46
Greek goddess 72
Greek temple 69
Greenacres 160
Grentemaisnell, Hugh de, Baron of Hinckley 25
Grewcock, Darren 201
Grewcock, Freda 127
Grewcock, Harry 139, 139
Grey House, Church Street 46, 70
Griffin, Brian 132
Grundy, John 14
Guinness family 172
Guinness, Sir Jonathan 49
gun licences 94
Guppy, Angela 215
Guttes, Albert and Grace 159

hagioscope 40
Hall Farm, Stoke Golding 20
Hall, Os and Peggy 80
Hamblin, Robert 208
Hampton, Leanne 121
Handel, George Frederick 67
Harcourt family 14, 56
  coat of arms 36
Harcourt, Sir Robert 36, 205
Harcourt, Sir Thomas 36
Hardwick, David 180
Harris, Val 120
Hatton, Avril 76, 112
Hatton's cafe 157
Hayes, Stephen and Simon 210
health care 92
Heathcote, T.B (author) 71
Helen (ice-breaker) 147
Help Out Mill 71, 71
Henry VII 197, 205
Henry VIII 17, 44

heraldry see coats-of-arms
Hercules Inn, Sutton Cheney 162
Hercules, statue of 162, 162
Hextall, Fred 122
High Decorated Period (architecture) 32
High School and Community College 8, 100, 101, 157, 201
Higham airfield 90
Higham on the Hill 22, 90
Hinckley 78
Hinckley Rugby Club 201
Hinckley Scanner Fund 165
Holden, Florence 40
Holdsworth, Edward 68
Hollies pre-prep school, The 82
Holmes, Dorothy 210
Holocaust 207
Holy Bones (formerly Church Cottage), Church Street 9, 123, 123
Home Farm 70
  Osbaston 172
Hoodmould 28
Hooker, Thomas 14, 100
Hook's covert 127
horse bones 25
horse-trading 120
hospital see Infirmary
housing developments 8, 76
Howe family 68, 106
Howe, Earl 30, 51, 68, 68, 136
Hudman, Neil, 131
hunting 130, 142, 191

industrial estate 15, 135
Industrial Revolution 70
infant school 8
Infirmary, Bosworth Hall 58, 72, 78, 92, 111, 139, 189
  Leicester 90
Inner Circle 157
inns 118-20 see also individual inns, e.g. Wheatsheaf Inn
Internet 202
iron-smelting furnace, Moira 147

Jackson, Roger (Barton) 79, 116, 154
Jackson, Roger and Alan (Cadeby) 132
Jacobean architecture 25, 43, 46, 55, 66
James, Jimmy and Doris 210
James, Les 194, 203
Jarvis, Robert 139
Jelley, Derek 132, 201
Jenkins, Phillip (Ted) 9, 88
Jennens, Charles 67, 68
Jennens, Humphrey 66
Jennings, Fred 211
Jennings, R of Atherstone 22
Jesus College, Cambridge 109
jetties (architecture) 43
jewellery 212
Jewry Wall, Leicester 22
Johnson, Keith (artist) 174
Johnson, Samuel 14, 100
Jones, Canon Edryd 9
Jones, Inigo 55

'Joy Springs' choir 211
Jubilee Terrace 120
Junior Drama Club 210

Kati's village (Cadeby) 14
Keeper's Cottage 71
keeps, Norman 22, 25
Kelly, Dr Gordon 8, 92
Kelly's garage 130
Kempe, C.E 32, 36, 40
Kenilworth Castle 51
Kenning, Phil (artist) 69
King Charles I 51
King Charles II 36, 51
King Dick's Well 197, 208
King Edward VII 68
King George III 30
King Richard III monument, Leicester 197, 209
King William IV 30
King William IV (inn) 120, 157
Kirkby Mallory 18
Kirkpatrick, Mr & Mrs 82
kitchen garden, Bosworth Hall 72
  Osbaston Hall 170-1, 172, 173
Knight, Andy and Wendy 118
Knight, W.H of Cheltenham 53
knitting frames 14, 128
Knossos Palace of, Crete 106
Knyveton, John 80

Lady Agnes Drive 152, 162
Lampard, James William (Billy) 139
Lampard, Jim 139
Lancaster, Boyton William Jellico 139
Lancaster, John 132
lancet windows 28
Larkin, Philip 192
Lawrence, Richard 184
leather-work 212
Lebanese cedar 67
Lee, Laurie 152, 190
Leicester, Castle Park 197
Leicester City Foxes 200
Leicester, Earls of 14
Leicester Tigers Rugby Club 201
Leicester Infirmary 90
Leicester Mercury 127
Leicester Museum 151
Leicestershire County Council 58, 217
Leicestershire Gazetteer 208
Leisure Time 11, 192
Lewis, Doug (artist) 20, 28, 60, 62, 64-65, 100, 102, 122, 168, 204
library, Gopsall Hall 67
Lichfield Road, old 194
Ling, Lenny 80
Local History 14
Local Industry 10, 128
lock-up, Snarestone 94, 95
longcase clocks 151
long galleries 46
long straw 166, 168
Long, Alice 189
Long's abattoir 92

Looking Glass lake 162
Lords of the manor 14
Loseby, Mr 180
Lower Farm, Coton 127
Lunchtime Technology Club (Churchill's) 135
Lycett's shop (now Corner Cottage Antiques) 142

Magic Lantern Society 198
magic lanterns 198, 198, 199
Main Street, Market Bosworth 62, 119, 201
  No.2 62
  No.3 62
  No.4 (Michaelmas House) 62
  No.5 62
  No.9 138, 142
Main Street, Carlton 70
Manor cottages, Wellsborough 43, 45
Manor Farm, Barlestone 92
Manor Farm, Barton in the Beans 154, 155
Manor Farm, Twycross 60, 60, 136
Manor House, Barlestone 62
Manor House, Cadeby 60, 61
Manor House, Snarestone 63
manor houses 43
Marina 147
Market Bosworth, passim
Market Mews 18, 76
Market Place see The Square
Market Square see The Square
markets 14, 87, 127
  cattle 18
  fatstock 175
  see also fairs
Marsden, Tommy 165
mass clock 34
Maud, Lady 36
McCarthy, Keith (author) 36, 50, 52, 56, 120, 212
Meakin, Harry 95
medical care 92
Medieval period 30, 36, 43, 44, 60, 70, 76
Memorial Garden 141
Menander 100
Messiah, Handel 67
Methodist Church 122
Middle Ages 62, 168
Midland West Coast railway 147
Millennium capsule 123
Millennium Men 102
Minoan Civilisation 106
minerals 212
mines and mining 146
mink 175
Moat House, Appleby Magna 17, 43, 44, 44
moats 5, 43, 44, 44, 56, 58
Moira 147
Mole, Matron 189
Moore, Samuel 118
Morris, William 106
Mortimer, Ralph de 49
Mother Church 102
motte 22, 25
Moxon, Joseph 14, 92, 149, 205

Muntjac deer 180
music 211

Nadin, John 79, 127, 174, 175, 175
Nadin, Pam 79, 115
Nailstone 28
 churchyard 158
Naneby 132
Naneby Hall Farm 132
Napoleonic War 204
narrowboating 147
National Forest 152, 180
National Health Service 90
Natural History Society 192, 217
Nature & Environment 10, 152
Nemean lion 162
Neo-Classical 55, 56
New Aspect 78, 88, 89, 124, 184, 192
Newbold Heath 144
Newbold Verdon 92, 198
Newton Burgoland 86, 151
Noel Wentworth family 18
Noell, William 18, 118
Norfolk reed 166, 168
Norman architecture 22, 28
Norman churches 22
Norman keeps 25
Normanton le Heath 151
Nuneaton Schools League 83

Oak Ring 162
Oakley family 141
Oakley, Brian 140
Oakley, John 14
Od's settlement (Odstone) 14
Odstone 14, 51, 86
Odstone Hall 50, 51, 62
ogee 32
old bank 98-99
'Old Beasty' 158
Old Black Horse Inn 10, 96, 120, 121, 175
Old Fox Covert 162
Old House, The, Cadeby 43
Old Park Spinney 175
Old Parks 175
Old Police House, Market Place 94
Old Rectory (Bosworth Hall) 205, 205
Old School, Carlton 70
Old School, Shenton 52
Old Weighbridge Furnishing shop 142
Oliver, Bill 201
'openhall' house 43, 76
Orchard House 8, 78
Ore Inspired 124, 212
ornithology 202
Orton, Bill and Violet 159
Osbaston Hall 48, 49, 60, 106, 111, 172, 172, 189
Osbaston House Farm 158
Osbaston kitchen garden 170-1, 172, 173
owls 202
 European Eagle 202

Palgrave Brown 76, 133

Palladio, Andrea 55, 62, 67
Parasol mushroom (Lepiota procera) 186
pargetting 58
parish chest (St Peter, Market Bosworth) 40
Parish Council, Market Bosworth 157
parish register (St Peter, Market Bosworth) 40
Park House (now Wood House) 162
Park Street 102, 201
 cruck construction 20
 forge 141
 Gothic Revival 18, 70
 primary school 96, 97, 211
 Roman Catholic meeting place 122
parks
 Bosworth Park 104, 162, 165, 178-179, 186, 189
 Bosworth Water Park 203, 203
 deer parks 58, 66, 180
 Southwood Park 162
Parnell, Terry 166, 201
Parry, Timothy 80, 92, 149, 205
Parson's Yard, Verdon 144
Pearson, Graham 113
Peckleton, St Mary Magdalene 26
Peckleton Hall 26
Peppercorn Cottage 20, 46, 139
Perpendicular Period (architecture) 26, 36, 41
Perry, Samuel Hunt 123
Perthes Leg Society 203
petrol station 120, 130
Pevsner, Nikolaus 28, 32, 52
Phillips, Clement 141, 165
Phillips, Harry 30
Phillips, Jack 136
phonographs 199
pianists 211
Pickering, Cicely 10
piers (architecture) 28, 32
pilaster 46, 55
piscina 26, 28, 36
pit ponies 146, 175
plague 32, 5, 132 see also Black Death
Plant, Rector John 102, 205
Pochin, Eleanor Frances 207
Police Station 118
policing 94
Poole, Percy 9
Post Office 86
pottery 46, 212
Power, Robert 92
Power, John 92
prehistory 14
Pre-Raphaelites 106
pre-school playgroups 8, 157
Prince Charles 197
Prince, Mr 136
Princess Diana 197
prisoners of war 53, 127, 176
Proudman, Mr 9
Public Bath House 92
Pull, Dr Robert 84, 84
Purefoy, William 51

Quakers 14
Queen Alexandra 68
Queen Anne houses 48, 49, 55, 55, 60, 60, 61, 82
Queen Anne Revival 19, 70, 72
quilters 215
'quilting bee', 215
Quincentenary 157, 197
Quod dixi dixi 15

Radio Leicester 202
Railway Trust 192
railways 14, 18, 52, 109, 130, 133, 197
Rainbow Cottage 20, 166, 168
Randall's estate 175
Rare Ltd 136
Ratcliffe Culey 32, 43, 102
Rawson, John 157
Rectory
 new (Park St) 166
 old (Cadeby) 189
 old (Rectory Lane, Bosworth) 205, 205
 old (c.1690-1848, Bosworth) 204
 old (Sutton Cheney) 70, 74-75
Rectory Lane 8, 205
Red deer 127
Red Dragon (King Henry VII of Lancaster) 197
Red Lion, Barlestone 212
Red Lion, Ye Olde (Bosworth) 46, 120, 122, 130, 142, 201, 210, 212, 217
reed, Norfolk 166, 168
Reed, Reverend Annette 102
Reeves, Ken 130, 202
Reformation 17
Regency Period (architecture) 70
religious life 102, 122, 151
Rembrandt 67
Renaissance 17, 43, 46, 55, 67
residential developments 8
Richard III 43, 197, 205
 King Richard III monument, Leicester 209
 Richard III Society 208
Richmond House 62
Ringer, Paul 201
River Anker 71
River Sence 80
Roberts, Bob and Jill 142
Robertson, Richie 201
Roberts, William 46
Robinson, Mr 71
Robinson, Neil the Venerable Archdeacon 8
Romans 43, 151, 186
 engineers 194
Roman Catholic church 78, 122
Roman villas 14
Romanesque architecture 22
rood-lofts 40
rood-screens 40
rood-stairs 40
Rotary Club 8, 192
Rotary Cottages 10, 46, 120, 166, 168
Roubiliac, Louis Francois 68
Routiers de Rouen, Les 197, 197
Rowley, Terry 137, 210

Royal Abbey, Saint-Denis 28, 30
Royal Academy 106
Royal British Legion 192
Royal College of Arms 205
rugby football 201, 201
Rural District Council 15
Ryley, Nigel & Jo 194, 203

sailing 203
Saint-Chapelle, Paris 30
Saint-Denis Abbey 30
Salmon, Finlay 165
Salvador, Eugene 126, 127, 152, 176
Sawmill, Verdon 144, 152
Saxon architecture 20
Saxon churches 20
Scentone (now Shenton) 52
schools,
 Cadeby (old school) 96
 Bosworth High 101, 101
 Carlton (old school) 70, 96
 Congerstone 96
 Bosworth College, Desford 100, 203
 Grammar see Dixie Grammar
 Hollies pre-prep, Twycross 82
 Shenton (old school) 52
 St Peter's C of E (old school), Park St 70, 96, 97, 211
 St Peter's C of E primary, Station Rd 8, 96
 Twycross House 82-83, 82-83
 Wolstan Preparatory 87
Schwiening Language School 92, 123, 207
Schwiening, Jurgen & Ruth 207, 207
Scott family, Tollemache 87, 104, 141
Scott, Lady Agnes 72, 123, 162
Scott, Sir Charles Tollemache 186
 adoption of Queen Anne style of architecture 19, 70
 Bosworth Hall Estate 15, 56, 58, 60, 72
 Lady Agnes Drive 152, 162
 renovation of Peppercorn Cottage 46
Scott, James Tollemache 60
Scouts 192
sculptures, wooden 144, 145, 166
secular architecture 43-72
sedilia 28, 36
Sence, River 52, 71, 80
sessile oak 144
Shackerstone 22, 25, 66, 86, 134, 144
Shackerstone Station 68, 71, 130, 131
Shackerstone Steam and Canal Festival 147
Shackerstone Walk 66, 66
sheep dipping 94
Sheepy Magna 41, 80, 102
 Parish Council 80
Shenton 52, 53, 159, 197, 212
Shenton Hall 46, 52-3, 52, 53
Shenton Lane 159
Shenton station 130
Shore, Andy (artist) 104, 119, 120, 146
Sibson 32, 68, 76
Signe of the Beare 118
singing 211
slates 56
slaughtering and slaughterhouses 92, 139,

148
Small, Reverend Nathaniel Pomfret 205
Smith, Evelyn & Ivy 176
Smith, Ford 210
Smith, Frank 176
Smith, Harry 136
Smith, Jackie and Alice 159
Smith, Matt 146
Smith, Oliver 201
Smith, Roland 127, 176
Smut (dog) 104
Snarestone 55, 86, 94
Snarestone Manor House *63*
Snarestone Tunnel 147
Snow Leopard 100, 123
Society of Friends 14
Softleys 62
Southwood Park 162
Sparkenhoe Hundred 14, 152
special education 100
Spencer, Alan (artist) *32, 72, 76, 141*
'Spike, The' 78
Spring Wood 162
Springman, Dr Sarah 203
Square, The 8, 10, 14, 45, 62, *64-5*, 70, 76,
    92, 94, 96, 118, 120, 137, 139, 157,
    166, 168
squint 40
St Andrew's Church, Carlton *125*
St Botolph's Church, Sibson 32
St James' Church, Dadlington 28
St James' Church, Sutton Cheney 28, *46, 196*,
    197, 208
St James' Church, Twycross 28, 30, *31,* 32, 82
St John's Church, Shenton 52, 53, *53*
St Margaret's Church, Stoke Golding 17, 28,
    32, *32, 33,* 34, *34, 35*
St Mary Magdalene's Church, Peckleton *26*
St Michael's Church, Fenny Drayton *22, 29*
St Nicholas 34
St Nicholas's Church, Leicester 22
St Peter's Church, Higham on the Hill 22, *23*
St Peter's Church, Market Bosworth *9, 17,* 32,
    36-40, *36, 38-9, 103,* 123, 141, 151,
    207, 215, *215*
    15th-century alterations 41
    financial costs 102
    gates 141
    graveyard 40, 49, 84, *85,* 106
    nave and tower 32
    sketch by Sebastian Evans 106
    west doorway 122
St Peter's Church, Swepstone 22, *27,* 32
St Peter's Hall 8, 210
St Peter's primary school 70, 96, *97,* 211
Stables End Court 137
stained glass
    All Saints Church, Ratcliffe Culey 32
    Cadeby church 109
    Perpendicular period 41
    St James' Church, Twycross 28, 30, *31,* 136
    St John's Church, Shenton 53
    St Peter's Church 106
staircases 51, 52, 53, 58, 205
Stamper, Tim and Chris 136
Station bridge, Market Bosworth 147

Station Garage 130
Station House Pottery, Shenton 212
Station Road 8, 96, 120, 121, 135, 165, 168
Statue of Religion (Gopsall) 68, *69*
steam train 130
stocking frames *see* knitting frames
stocks 120
Stoke Golding 17, 20, 28, 32, 34, 185, 197
straw, long 166, 168
stretcher bond 45
stucco 70, 118
Styche, Sue (Guide Book) 124, 137
sundial 34
sunflowers 72
surgery, Bosworth 92
surveyor's plan 123
surveys
    census 124
    churchyard 217
    Hastings' (1588) 18, 56, 118
    national (1592) 118
    see also Domesday Book
Sutton Cheney 80
    Boston, Reverend Teddy 9
    Gothic Revival 70
    Hercules Inn 162
    prisoners of war 127
    St James' Church 28, 46, *196,* 197, 208
    Old Rectory *74-75*
Sutton Cheney Hall 46, *46, 47*
Sutton Lane, Market Bosworth 46, 144, 162
    No. 9 168, *169*
Swepstone 22, 32, 71, 86
Swithland 56
Sycamore Farm, Barton in the Beans 154
Sycamore Way, Market Bosworth 76, 77
Symonds, Dick and Blanche 157

Tacherting (Bavaria) 200
Tapp, Miss 96
Tawny owl *165*
Tebbatt, Phil 94
Temple Hall, Wellsborough 51, 87
Temple, Peter 51
Ten Commandments (tablets) 40
Terrapin Triathlon 203
terrapins, red-eared 147
thatch 26, 40, 43, 46, 60, 62, 166, *167, 169*
thatching 168
Thomas the Tank Engine 109
Thompson, Rosamund 92
Thorley, Roy 212
Thorp, John ('Bean') 142, *142*
Thorpe, Grace and Marianne 142
Thorpe, James 158
Throsby, John 84
Timber Fireproofing Company 133
timber-framed buildings *42, 43, 43, 44, 44,* 49, 60,
    62, 70, 80
Time and Chance 106
Timms, Elijah 71
Tin Tin 157
tithe 80
tithe barn, Sheepy Magna *81*
tithe maps 123
Tollemache Scott family *see* Scott family,
    Tollemache

tomb
    All Saints, Sheepy Magna 41
    Purefoy, William (St Michael, Fenny Dray-
        ton) 51
    St Margaret, Stoke Golding 34
    St Mary Magdaline, Peckleton 26
Tomlin, Arthur 165
totem pole (Verdon Sawmill) 144, *145*
tourist attractions
    Bosworth in Bloom 157
    Bosworth Battlefield 197
tracery
    flowing, curvilinear 32, 34
    geometrical 32, 34, *35*
    intersecting 32
    panel *36,* 41
    plate *28*
    reticulated 32, 17, 32, *34, 35,* 41
tree surgeons 166
trees 189
    beech *163, 172*
    beech (Appleby Magna) 153
    beech, Lady Agnes Drive 163
    beech tree (Osbaston) 152, 158, 189
    copper beech (Bosworth Hall) 83, 111,
        189
    giant redwood (Cadeby) 189
    lime 59, 111, *190*
    maple 180, *181*
    oak (Carlton) *188*
    oak (Coton Lane) *189*
    see also arboretum; National Forest
Trivett family 120
Trivett, Mrs 122
Trollope, Reverend 208
Tudor architecture 43, 44, 62
    style 205
turkeys 127
turret clock 151
twitchers 202
Twycross 28, 30, 32, 66, 68, 136
Twycross House School 60, 78, 82-3, *82, 83*
Twycross Manor Farm 60, *60*

Unicorne, The 118
United Benefice of Market Bosworth and
    Sheepy 102
Upper Coton Farm 184-5
Upton 80

Van Dyck 67
Verdon family, coat of arms 36
Verdon Sawmill 144
vernacular architecture 17, 18, 43
vestry 40
veterinary practice, old *174,* 175
Victorian Period (architecture) 70
Victorian Revival movement (architecture)
    17, 18, 25, 70
virtual reality 137, *137*

walks, guided 202
Waller, Sir Wathen 30
Waring, Lord 68
Waring, Thomas 185
Warner, Mr and Mrs 25

Warr, Michael & Muriel 137, 215
War of the Roses 43, 197
Warwick Close 175
Warwick House 44, 94
Warwick Lane 120
Waste, The, Church St 123
Water Tower *15,* 18, 70, *70,* 72, *73,* 111
wattle and daub 26, 43, 44, 46, 62
weather cock 36
Webb, Mr 136
Webster, Jill (author) 34
Wellsborough 43, 45, 51, 80, 87
West, Dorian 201
Westhaven Bosworth Union House 8, 78, 139
Weston, Harry 8
Wharf Farm 135, 194
Wheatsheaf Courtyard 46, 118, 157
Wheatsheaf Inn 46, 118
Wheeler, Sir Arthur 122
White's Gazetteer & Directory of Leicester &
    Rutland 208
White Boar (King Richard III of York) 197,
    208
Whitemoors 197
Wilderness, The 58, 72, 104, 111
Wilkinson, Calley & Reby 212, *213*
Willement, Thomas 30
William IV 30
William of Normandy, Duke 22, 66
Williamson, Mrs 157
Willmott, Richard 100
Wilson, Brian 205
windows
    bow 70
    Early English 28, 102
    eyebrow 68
    Georgian 62
    lancet 28, *28*
    Norman 22, 28
    Perpendicular 41
    sash 60, 62
    Saxon *20*
    Tudor 44
    see also stained glass; tracery
windsurfing 203
Wollaston family 53
Wollaston, Fred Eustace Arbuthnot 53
Wollaston, Reverend 53
Wollaston, William 46, 52, 53
Wolstan Preparatory School 87
Women's Institute 8, 90, 192, 217
Wood House (formerly Park House) 162
Wood Lane, Cadeby *42*
Wood View 159
Woodward, Shaun and Joanne 51
workhouse 78 *see also* almshouses
Wothers family 141
Wren, Sir Christopher 60
Wright, Thomas 118
Wrightson Mundy family 49
Wyatt, Ron 139
Wykes, Joe 168

Yew Tree Farm, Barton in the Beans 154
Young, Paul 212
'Your Guide' system 86